CONTENTS

PREFACE

Few books can be written without periods of misgiving and deliberation beforehand but in the case of this particular essay the time of gestation was short. A year ago it could truthfully be said that I had no intention of writing a book on the subject which gives this work its title. At that time a general interest in medico-legal problems was given added stimulus by the cases of Gallagher and Bratty. Both cases revolved round psychiatric complexities; and from the reports of the trials it did not appear that medical attitudes to such matters as psychopathy, alcoholism and disturbances of consciousness were correctly appreciated by jurists. Whether these pages will shed any light on these difficult questions is not for me to say, and it may well be that when I appear critical of legal rulings I am most open to criticism myself. For in legal matters I write as a layman, and it would be too much to hope that in all instances I have appraised the facts of certain trials and appeals correctly.

Having no formal knowledge of law, it has been necessary to turn to authority for guidance. For me it was fortunate that the second edition of Dr. Glanville Williams's *The Criminal Law* became available shortly before I began to collect the material for this book. It will be evident to the reader that I have relied on Dr. Williams's opinions, particularly those expressed in his chapters on insanity and drunkenness in relation to criminal process. I am indeed grateful for his permission to quote the opinions he offers and can only trust that I have reported him correctly.

My other major source book has been the report of the Royal Commission on Capital Punishment which dealt exhaustively with all aspects of criminal procedure relating to homicide and mental abnormality up to the time of the presentation of the report. I assume that the Homicide Act, 1957, derives from the recommendations made by the Royal Commission. The admission of a plea of diminished responsibility in homicide trials understandably has led to an alteration of certain features of such trials with consequent modifications of the psychiatric evidence required.

The law on diminished responsibility in English Courts is still in the process of growth so that at present it is difficult for the layman to discuss, with any authority, such judgments as have been passed in the last five years. Such comments as I have made may well be obsolete following further judicial rulings, and at present it is not possible to say, for example, what ultimate view will be taken of the psychopath who murders during an alcoholic bout. Jurists have commented on the various leading cases taken under the Homicide Act, 1957, but when the law is not entirely clear

vii

it has been necessary to go to the reports and trust that my interpretation of the rulings is correct.

This book has been written by a practising psychiatrist so it will be understandable that forensic psychiatric problems will be seen through medical eyes. At the time of writing there appears to be a gap in British medical literature which, in the past, was filled by the works of the late Sir Norwood East. I hope, therefore, that this book will be of some interest and practical value to those called upon to give psychiatric evidence in court. It is also my hope that the pages devoted to current psychiatric thought will be of some help to lawyers and jurists who, understandably, are not familiar with modern developments in this subject. I think that, despite disclaimers to the contrary, the doctrine of partial insanity is still accepted by some legal writers; that the mechanism and effects of delusional beliefs are but poorly understood; and that the medical doctrines relating to psychopathy are in such an uncertain state as to make it very difficult, at times, to convince laymen of the existence of this class of psychiatric disorder. I can only hope that this book will have contributed a little to the clarification of these problems.

Without a great deal of helpful advice and encouragement from Professor Martin Roth this book would never have been written. To him I am most grateful, as I am to my friend, Mr. J. M. Reay-Smith, who has given time to discuss legal problems and generally to interpret technicalities with which I as a layman was unfamiliar.

Finally, I must thank my friends and colleagues for their willingness to engage in controversy over medico-legal problems whose solution required discussion and criticism rather than my own unaided opinion. I can only hope that they have enjoyed these debates, and at the same time learned something of the subject which has pre-occupied me over the past year.

F. A. WHITLOCK

1—Introduction

The long, uneasy flirtation between law and medicine is unlikely ever to end in harmonious matrimony with understanding and acceptance of the points of view of each side. At the very best one might foresee some *mariage de convenance* but, more likely, there will be a shotgun wedding forced on the parties concerned by a public impatient both with legal argument and psychiatric differences in open court. Certainly, at times, it has seemed that, rather than there being a happy ending to the courtship, mutual antipathy might lead to an open and irreconcilable breach. Conflicting opinions have been expressed in forthright terms to such a degree that one wonders how far it will ever be possible to bring together in a spirit of mutual toleration two forces, each bent on asserting its own views to the exclusion of the others.

To some extent this book is an examination of the attitudes and opinions of the opposing parties in the hope that by so doing it will be possible to bridge some of the differences and plain misunderstandings which from time to time have arisen over medico-legal problems on which both sides should be co-operating rather than engaging in open conflict.

Many books have been written on the subject of criminal responsibility and it could be said that there is little to add to a debate which has persisted for many decades. Yet because of certain changes brought about by legal enactments, public feeling and medical advances over the past 10 years it could be said that the time is opportune for a fresh examination of the psychiatric aspects of criminal responsibility. Both sides stand to gain by a better understanding of each others problems and it is felt that, because of advances in psychiatry and changes in the law, the differences which have kept law and medicine at arm's length from one another are no longer so absolute. In the long run it is to be hoped that both law and medicine have a greater desire to help rather than condemn, but this laudable intention can only be implemented if we understand clearly how each side has reached its present stage of development and what ultimate facts make it difficult for one side to accept wholly the wishes and aims of the other. It is, for example, futile to argue in a court of law that all forms of wrongdoing are instances of mental sickness; and in justice to psychiatry, there are few psychiatrists in Great Britain who would be willing to propound such an extreme opinion. On the other hand, it is equally useless to dismiss all medical

1

evidence which might exonerate an accused man as so much special pleading designed to avert the punishment which he richly deserves.

Between these two extreme opinions lie all grades of thinking, authoritarian or liberal, which seek to understand the ways of thought and behaviour which can and do lead to horrifying acts. To say that a man must be mad to behave in such a way may well be true, but it helps very little. What is more important is understanding the nature of the mental processes, normal or morbid, which accompany any act in the hope that, when faced by an enormity, it will be possible to preserve detachment in order to examine and comprehend. There is no room for extremes of opinion or over-riding rights in the controversy over criminal responsibility. Somehow it is essential to face the medical facts as well as the legal facts, fit them together in a proper manner so as to diagnose and, when possible, treat the offender for the benefit of the individual and society.

In attempting to bring mutual understanding to the parties concerned in the management of the mentally ill offender it is necessary to examine fundamentals, not the least of which is the language which each side uses in its everyday practice. Both psychiatry and law use a technical language which often makes for confusion over words used in a special manner differing from their normal meaning as defined in ordinary speech. Behind the use of language is a basic philosophy of ideas relating to the human personality and its place in society and the cosmos. No doubt these large issues should receive a longer and more expert consideration than has been granted to them in these pages, but without even this somewhat superficial examination of basic tenets it will be difficult for jurist and psychiatrist to begin understanding each others modes of thought. Perhaps most fundamental of all is the differing personality structure separating those who become lawyers and those who become doctors. Much could be written on this theme but it is likely that the known facts barely justify the speculations.

Undoubtedly the psychiatrist is so directly concerned with the welfare of the individual patient that, at times, the needs of society seem scarcely to be acknowledged. On the other hand, much of the lawyer's time must be taken up with balancing the respective claims of society and the individual; and at times the needs of the individual must seem of small importance besides the over-riding demands of the law of the land. The problem becomes more involved when the person under judicial examination is mentally ill. The psychiatrist must, by his training and outlook, come to see the offender as a sick man in need of treatment, whereas the judge, as the representative of society, may well only see him as a criminal requiring a long period of detention for the protection of others. Between these two extreme points of view it is necessary to

2

reach a mutual understanding so that neither society, which has a right to be protected, nor the individual, who has a right to be treated, should be wholly excluded from consideration in the interests of one side or the other. So long as exclusive claims are made then so long will the situation be strained. Happily, there is every reason to believe that the present time is favourable to a greater mutual understanding of the position of psychiatrist and jurist in the matter; with the consequence that ultimately we may see the day when it is no longer a question of deciding on the appropriate punishment for an offender, but more a matter of right disposal to the benefit of all concerned.

In order to achieve the medico-legal millenium it is necessary that both law and medicine should put their own houses into order. It is hardly possible for the author to comment with any authority on the legal side of the debate, but in the light of modern psychiatric knowledge it is understandable that medicine should feel some impatience with the retention of the M'Naghten Rules and the outmoded concept embodied in this test of mental disease as a disorder of intellect. Because of the wording of the Rules it is very clear that all manner of wholly deranged persons, quite irresponsible for their behaviour, could be found guilty. Indeed, it is certain that their rigid application would have led to the conviction and execution of such manifestly ill persons as Hadfield[1] and even M'Naghten himself.[2] If the Rules are by their very nature incapable of being interpreted to include the grossly psychotic then it is not easy to understand what purpose they serve. It is understandable, therefore, that many psychiatrists feel badly constrained when asked to give evidence within the framework of rules which, by their very wording, make nonsense of modern psychiatric techniques and theories.

To the medical mind much legal debate appears so far divorced from the clinical realities as to make one wonder whether it will ever be possible to convince jurists of the fact of mental illness and its essential basis in neurophysiology. If counsel can argue that a person suffering from arteriosclerotic dementia[3] with disturbances of consciousness is suffering from a disease of the brain and not of the mind it is understandable that such pleading may cause the observer to conclude that Cartesian metaphysics are more important to the courts than any amount of clinical knowledge.

No doubt this is an extreme example of legal dualism. Yet until such dualism, which appears to inform much legal thought, is reconciled with the essentially monist concepts employed by the psychiatrist it is not

[1] R. *v.* Hadfield (1800), 27 State Tr. 1281
[2] (1843), 10 Cl. & F. 200
[3] R. *v.* Kemp, [1957] 1 Q. B. 399

easy for the two professions, both concerned with finding a just verdict, to begin to understand each others modes of thought.

It would also be as well if judges and jurists could rid their minds of the suspicion that all psychiatrists are only waiting for the time when they can take over the function of the courts, examine the evidence, formulate a diagnosis and prescribe treatment for every offender who comes up for trial. It can be said with confidence that very few psychiatrists have the least wish to do anything of the sort, being fully aware that the correspondence of sickness with sin is a theory which has yet to be substantiated.

What seems to be of greater importance is the need for expert psychiatric evidence in those cases where such evidence seems necessary. To avoid the situation of medical evidence being given for or against the defendant—with the inevitable clash of opinion—much would be gained if such testimony could come from an independent source presenting the facts of the case to the court as impartially as possible with the right for both Crown and defence to cross-examine the witness and to call rebutting evidence should this seem desirable. It is perfectly proper for psychiatrists to ask that their evidence should be taken seriously however far-fetched some of their pronouncements may at times appear. It is not always possible to avoid technical terms in medical evidence but anyone with ordinary common sense will do his best to frame his replies in a manner understandable to the court. By so doing he may need to use words inexactly, but as such approximations are made largely to fulfil the requirements of the occasion it is only fair to ask that the evidence should be taken for what it is worth even though some of it may appear strange or fanciful to laymen.

On the other hand, it is understandable that lawyers will from time to time experience irritation at the vagueness and fluidity of some psychiatric concepts. Admittedly, psychiatry is not an exact science and it is unlikely ever to become one; nevertheless, we should make some effort to put our ideas more clearly, give some sort of definition to our terms and try to avoid the exposition of controversial theories as if they were fully established facts. What, for instance, do we mean by mental disease? In a recent case[1] a senior prison medical officer, having diagnosed hysteria in the prisoner, was asked by the trial judge whether the accused suffered from a mental illness; to receive the reply, 'Not a mental illness, a psychoneurotic condition, hysteria'. Yet on an earlier occasion[2] the accused, charged with the murder of his foster-mother, was convicted of manslaughter on the grounds of diminished respon-

[1] R. v. Bentley (1962), *The Times*, March 15
[2] R. v. Lawrence (1958), *The Times*, May 9

4

sibility. Medical evidence indicated that he was suffering from hysteria, which was accepted by the court as a disease of the mind. Faced with such confusion over a basic fact one can have some sympathy with lawyers who express scepticism over the value of psychiatric evidence.

Something has already been said about the extreme claim that all forms of wrongdoing are but symptoms of mental sickness. To define social misbehaviour as illness and then to argue that illness is often manifested by deviant actions is a tautological process which helps nobody. Depending on one's judgment of what is right and wrong it will follow that some forms of crime may appear to be signs of health in certain circumstances and societies. The corollary of this claim is the implication that all persons who find themselves on the wrong side of the law require psychiatric treatment rather than punishment, a claim which may also imply that such treatment would be more effective in producing a law-abiding society than contemporary penal measures. Whether or not this is so outside utopias of the Erewhon variety has yet to be seen but there is nothing in current therapeutics to suggest that psychiatrists have particularly effective techniques in dealing with the socially deviant, even when these methods are applied to those who have some measure of explicit mental abnormality as in the case of the psychopathic offender.

A moment of introspection would reveal how unfounded is the assertion that those who break the criminal law are mentally ill, a claim, incidentally, which would be stoutly resisted by a good many habitual offenders. Even psychiatrists have been known to do things which they know to be wrong. Few, in the author's experience, have sought advice from their colleagues or treatment for what we all know to be perfectly understandable lapses from the conventionally accepted canons of behaviour. We may be able to explain in psychiatric terms why we act as we do but this in no way exonerates us if detected in some minor breach of the law or moral waywardness. Why, then, should we apply different criteria of behaviour to others? In fact, we do not do so in the great majority of cases in which offences are perfectly explicable in terms of the pursuit of wealth in an acquisitive society. Only when circumstances of a special and peculiar nature relating to the offence are present can we begin considering whether, in fact, the man is suffering from a mental disorder of which his wrongdoing is but one manifestation. Deviant actions may well be symptoms of serious mental illness; but this is very different from the statement that deviant acts *are* mental illnesses. At times, both psychiatry and the law show evidence of confusion over this particular point.

Fortunately, there is much to indicate that both law and medicine are alive to each others special problems. In the spirit enjoined by

Sir James Stephen[1], we are beginning to learn that, 'in dealing with matters so obscure and difficult the two great professions of law and medicine ought rather to feel for each others difficulties than to speak harshly of each others shortcomings'. These words, written in 1883, still have a certain appositeness despite the passage of 80 years. Yet a number of events of social and legal significance have done much to break down the barriers which for so long have separated the problems of the mentally ill from the full understanding of the public at large. Five years of the application of the concept of diminished responsibility in cases of homicide under the provisions of the Homicide Act, 1957, must have led to a greater use of psychiatric evidence and, one hopes, an improvement not only in the presentation of such evidence but a greater understanding of its significance and limitations. The psychiatrist's role is that of expert witness to help the court, and not to act as an arbitrator of the court's decision. Provided he keeps to his special province justice will benefit from an expert opinion on matters which are the proper concern of the medical witness.

Perhaps, at times, we expect too much from judge and jury who, we sometimes feel, should have the same understanding of psychological complexities as ourselves. For, as Lord Devlin recently remarked[2], psychiatrists must not talk to the judge as if he were a fellow expert. He went on to elaborate the point saying that a High Court Judge spends only about one-quarter of his time on criminal cases and that it would be unreasonable to expect him to be an expert on all other matters which come under his jurisdiction. In any case, psychiatric evidence is required in only a small proportion of all criminal cases and it would be as ridiculous to expect a judge to be expert on psychiatric problems as to require a judge of the Probate, Divorce and Admiralty Division to be a skilled waterways' navigator.

The Report of the Royal Commission on Capital Punishment, 1949–53 (Cmd. 8932) devoted a great deal of time to consideration of the special problems of the mentally ill offender, his position under the M'Naghten Rules, the defects of these Rules in the light of modern psychiatry, other matters pertaining to court procedure, and the final disposal of those found to be insane before or at trial. The recommendations of the Royal Commission included the suggestion that when a person is found to be so severely disordered at trial as to be certifiable as insane there is a very strong presumption that the crime with which he is charged was wholly or largely caused by his insanity. Consideration was given to the special problem of the psychopath and the epileptic but although the Royal Commission did not feel able to advise the introduc-

---

[1] Stephen, J. F. (1883). *History of the Criminal Law.* London; Macmillan
[2] *Violence and the Mental Health Services,* N.A.M.H. 1962

tion into English Law of the Scottish principle of diminished responsibility there can be little doubt that the deliberations and opinions incorporated in the report did much to prepare the way for the defence of diminished responsibility in homicide cases now allowed by the Homicide Act, 1957.

A further impetus to bringing psychiatric problems before the public was provided by the Mental Health Act, 1959, based largely on the recommendations of the Royal Commission on the Law Relating to Mental Illness and Mental Deficiency, 1954–1957 (Cmd. 169). Because of the great advances made in psychiatric treatment over the past 20 years a more hopeful attitude can be taken towards the outcome of a mental illness than was the case in the past. The major consequence has been that patients are no longer locked away in county mental hospitals remote from the areas they serve, and patients are being kept in the community or returned to society after hospital treatment with much greater frequency. The fear aroused by mental illness still persists but, in general, the public is more aware of the nature of mental illness and of the possibilities and limitations of psychiatric treatment. One consequence of this change in attitude has been a more enlightened use of psychiatric help and, so far as the Magistrates' Courts are concerned, many offenders are now remanded for a medical opinion or receive treatment for offences which might in the past have been dealt with along ordinary penal lines.

In addition to many other changes, the Mental Health Act, 1959, gave formal recognition to the psychopathic personality as a person who may be helped by medical treatment. This change from the former judicial attitude to the older concept of moral insanity hardly needs to be emphasized although, because of the special difficulties of this class of offender, it is scarcely surprising if conflicting opinions are expressed concerning the nature of his offence and its relationship to mental disorder. Finally, under section 60 of the Mental Health Act, the courts are empowered to order the detention and treatment of certain classes of offenders in hospital or to place them under the guardianship of a local health authority rather than award a prison sentence. It is too early to assess the full workings of the Mental Health Act, but already section 60 of the Act has been applied in a number of cases where persons have been found guilty of manslaughter by reason of diminished responsibility.

In 1959, the case of Podola[1] raised acutely the whole problem of medical evidence and fitness to plead. Neither law nor medicine came out of this contest with much credit and, as one jurist has remarked, perhaps the less said about it the better. Despite this, as points of law as well as medical views on amnesia and its relationship to

[1] R. *v.* Podola, [1959] 3 All E. R. 418

7

criminal acts were discussed, the special problems of Podola's case as well as the general problem of fitness to plead and stand trial can hardly be omitted from a book which sets out to discuss the nature of criminal responsibility.

In 1960, Lady Wootton in her Cambridge lecture[1] attacked the idea of criminal responsibility and its present application in the courts. In so far as it is never possible to say what was happening in the mind of the defendant at the time of an alleged offence, and as it is never possible to give a firm answer to the question of how substantial was the impairment of responsibility, she suggested that it might be better to cease trying to define the undefinable, leave the courts to find whether or not the charge is proved, and then, in the light of all the facts, dispose of the offender in the manner most suited to his and society's requirements. For a number of reasons it is unlikely that these forthright opinions will commend themselves in their entirety to jurists, but as the law has now admitted the plea of diminished responsibility in homicide cases it has clearly become the duty of the courts to try to establish whether or not the plea is justified. Inevitably, the jury will be asked to examine the antecedents of the crime in order to assess the extenuating circumstances reducing the verdict from murder to manslaughter. Although courts of law take no note of the causes of mental disorder the nature of the illness is of some importance in deciding the issue and, once the principle of fitting the treatment or punishment to the criminal rather than the crime becomes accepted, it will be necessary to discuss the causation of a given case of abnormal behaviour in the hope of finding some means of treating the offender in the best and most economic way.

No doubt in trivial offences it would be a waste of time inquiring too closely into the defendant's mental state. If a person is charged with riding a bicycle without lights after dark it is enough to find the facts proven and fine him; but if he is up before the court for the twelfth time for the same trivial offence it might be advisable to seek psychiatric help as the deterrent effect of repeated fines is obviously non-existent. It might then be discovered that the offender suffers from paranoid schizophrenia, believing that should he ride his bicycle with the lights on after dark he will thereby betray his presence to hidden enemies. The more serious the charge the greater is the necessity for an examination of the prisoner's mental state. The need becomes imperative in homicide cases for there is every evidence to show, in Great Britain at least, that this is a highly abnormal crime and that its perpetrators have a high incidence of mental illness.

One thing seems fairly certain: because of the legislative and medico-social changes over the past decades there seems every reason to believe

[1] Wootton, B. (1960), 76 L. Q. R. 224

that there will be a greater use of psychiatrists and psychiatric opinions in the future. If this forecast is correct, then all the more reason why lawyer and psychiatrist should have the fullest possible understanding of each others modes of thought and the limitations imposed on them both by legal enactment as well as ignorance of all the facts concerning human behaviour, normal and abnormal.

At present the M'Naghten Rules set the framework within which the issue of insanity at the time of the alleged crime will be decided. It is no use the medical expert pleading that he cannot or will not adapt his evidence to the Rules, however outdated or misleading he feels them to be. He will still be asked whether in his opinion the accused was deprived of normal understanding of right and wrong and of the physical circumstances of his act because of mental illness. He may wish to qualify his replies but inevitably, unless he refuses to offer an opinion, he will have to return a firm answer, yes or no, to this question. Fortunately, as Lord Cooper observed[1], in all probability most juries ignore all directions concerning the M'Naghten Rules, asking themselves whether or not the accused man was insane in the ordinary sense at the time of the act with which he is charged. If they are satisfied that he was, in fact, insane, they will in all likelihood return a verdict to that effect. Nevertheless, it is a highly unsatisfactory state of affairs and one can but agree with Mr. Justice Frankfurter's opinion that the Rules are a 'sham'[2] if their proper interpretation is ignored by the jury.

Nevertheless, the law will not alter merely because medical witnesses object to its application, but lawyers should try to understand the special difficulties experienced by such witnesses when asked to give their evidence, based on facts and theories very different from those in vogue at the time when the Rules were formulated, within the conventional structure of the Rules.

Understandably, the law likes to have clear definitions with precise, conceptual formulations. Psychiatry is, by its nature, an incomplete science which may never be able to constrain all its methods within an exact scientific framework. It is experimental, ready to discard concepts which have lost their use in the light of further knowledge and new ideas. Because of the infinite variability and complexity of the human mind it is probable that understanding of its workings will at best be an approximation to the full facts. It is understandable, therefore, that psychiatric opinion will be tentative rather than dogmatic, a matter of probabilities rather than of absolute science. Lawyers may feel impatient with this unwillingness to express a firm opinion but a little consideration should surely indicate that in this respect the psychiatrist

[1] Royal Commission on Capital Punishment (1949–53), para. 322
[2] *Ibid.*, para. 247

is in no worse state than a good many other witnesses in the court. No doubt the onus of proof and the fact that the prosecution has to prove its case beyond all reasonable doubt, whereas the defence of insanity will be accepted on a balance of probabilities, makes a firm opinion more imperative when insanity is under consideration. Possibly the outcome of an adverse verdict in a murder trial prior to 1957 added urgency to the need to establish, if possible, that the accused man was, in fact, insane at the time of the killing.

None of the modern legislation relating to homicide and mental health has come into being without much anxious examination of precedents, enshrined legal opinions, and much former legislation on the same subjects. Consequently, a brief historical review of earlier enactments and pronouncements on the legal responsibility of the insane is given in Chapter 2 as an introduction to the discussion of the period following the formulation of the M'Naghten Rules in 1843. Because psychiatric and legal thinking appears, so often, to be based on wholly disparate theories of a metaphysical nature concerning the human mind it has been necessary to include a chapter which tries to examine such ancient problems as free will, determinism, and mind–body relationships.

It would require a bold man to claim that in a single chapter all these difficult matters had been clarified in such a manner as to leave to the philosophers little to ponder over, but the mere fact of trying to expose the differences and difficulties may be of value when legal antipathies are at their strongest. The fact that both law and medicine use technical terms makes it imperative, so far as possible, to clarify their meaning, yet at the same time retain the precise concepts which certain words define. It is not easy to translate a technical word such as 'schizophrenia' into non-technical speech, and, judging by the misuse of the word in popular journalism—whole nations as well as their representatives are dubbed 'schizophrenic'—the lay public have not the haziest notion of the meaning of the term, confusing the functional splitting of the schizophrenic process with the dissociative reaction of the hysteric. Consequently, although technical words have been used, it is hoped that when unexplained their meaning will be clear from the context of their use. Involved explanations would be superfluous for the medical reader; the interested jurist should have little difficulty in grasping the meaning of such psychiatric technicalities as are inevitable in a text of this nature. It should be made explicit that this is not a textbook of psychiatry which would require full accounts of psychiatric syndromes. No doubt practically any class of psychiatric disorder can accompany criminal behaviour but to list all such disorders would not necessarily help one to single out the significant symptom or syndrome having a real bearing upon the act with which the prisoner has been charged. Rather than give a long list of mental illnesses attention has been given to certain symptoms which, singly or in combination, seem most frequently to be present when mental illness is the direct cause of an offence.

Since the passage of the Homicide Act, 1957, a number of cases have gone to the Court of Criminal Appeal and it is possible to discern some general pattern of the working of the Act, although, as will be seen, not all its possibilities have been tested in the courts. Many of these cases will be discussed and criticisms expressed over the management of some offenders who have been dealt with under the Act. The law relating to drunkenness and to crimes committed while under the influence of drink or drugs requires examination. The problem of the drunken psychopath who kills has not yet been considered fully in English Law although this matter was given the fullest examination in the case of Gallagher.[1]

Interesting problems concerned with drugs, driving, and the plea of automatism have developed and, to the medical observer, it seems strange that a plea of automatism leading to acquittal if the plea is accepted should have occurred in English courts only in recent years. It is even odder that what is termed 'non-insane' automatism leads to unqualified acquittal rather than a court order requiring medical treatment for the defendant. Amnesia, genuine or feigned, mutism as a reason for being unfit to plead as well as the wider problem of whether a mentally disordered man is fit to stand trial all have a bearing on the general subject of criminal responsibility. Again, only in comparatively recent times have amnesia and mutism led to much difficulty in procedure, and it is probably too early to say in what way such cases will be taken in the future. Undoubtedly, conflicting opinions have been expressed, not only by jurists but also by counsel and judges during actual trials.

It could hardly be expected that in a book of this nature the final conclusions or recommendations will commend themselves to both jurists and psychiatrists. It is possible to foresee that at some future date the M'Naghten Rules may appear as anachronistic as the certification of psychotic patients by lay magistrates. The day may well be far off before we can with any certainty assign to any human being the precise degree of responsibility he bears for his part in a criminal act. In the meantime it might be profitable to examine some of the issues involved to see how far we can go to ensure that injustice is not done.

[1] Attorney-General for Northern Ireland *v.* Gallagher, [1961] 3 All E. R. 299

2—Criminal Responsibility of the Mentally Disordered before 1843

Little note was taken in English Law of the criminal acts of the insane until the beginning of the seventeenth century when Sir Edward Coke's observations drew attention to the subject. No doubt mental derangement needed to be severe in order to exculpate the offender of his crime, since popular notions of insanity were probably derived from observations of those unfortunates who roamed the land in various stages of destitution and derangement, as portrayed in Shakespeare's delineations of insanity. Such was the general picture of the type of behaviour which would have been recognized as insane in Tudor times.[1] In the reign of King Alfred, high treason by killing or offering to kill the king was not excused by the insanity of the offender.[2] On the other hand, infants under the age of 12 years could not be executed for theft. Athelstan raised the age to 15 years but by the time of Henry II the younger age of 12 years was generally accepted.[3] There is reason to think that infants and insane persons were excused from punishment for high treason as required by the statute of Edward III (25 Ed. III cap. 2) and in an earlier reign (Edward II) it seems that insane murderers were dealt with on much the same lines as prevail today.

'A jury, to take an actual instance, finds that one Geoffrey, "*tanquam demens et furiosus occidit predictum J. et non per feloniam*", and so he must remain in prison during the King's pleasure—"*remanet ad gratiam Regis*"'[4]. Similar rules of humanity did not prevail under Henry VIII who ordained that persons committing high treason who became insane following conviction should not be spared from execution. As Coke commented, 'It was further provided by the said Act of 33 Henry VIII, Cap 20, that if a man attainted of treason became mad, that notwithstanding he should be executed; which cruel and inhuman law lived not long, but was repealed, for in that point also it was against the common law, because by intendment of law the execution of the offender is for example, *ut poena ad paucos, metus ad omnes perveniat*, as before

[1] Ray, I. (1873). *Contributions to Mental Pathology*, p. 482. Boston; Little, Brown and Co.
[2] *Collinson on Lunacy*, London, 1812
[3] Paris, J. A. and Fonblangue, J. S. M. (1823). *Medical Jurisprudence*. London; Phillips
[4] Introduction to *Selden Society Year Book Series*, Vol. 5 (Eyre of Kent, 1313–14, Vol. 1) (1909) Vol. 24, p. lxxi. London; Bernard Quaritch

is said: but so it is not when a madman is executed, but should be a miserable spectacle, both against law, and of extreme inhumanity and cruelty, and can be no example to others.'[1] The law was repealed in the reign of Phillip and Mary (1 & 2 Ph. & M. cap. 20). It is notable that the execution of criminals who became insane after conviction was not accepted in King Alfred's time[2] for it is recorded that Cole, who convicted and executed one Ive when out of his senses, was himself hanged on that account.

Bracton commented on insanity as it affects civil law.[3] 'A peremptory exception is available to the tenant against the person of the claimant, if the claimant should be a madman not of sane mind or so that he cannot discern, or has no discretion at all. For such persons do not much differ from brutes who are without reason, nor ought that to avail which is transacted with such persons during madness, for some may enjoy lucid intervals, and some have perpetual madness.' Bracton's remarks appear also to indicate that the type of insanity would need to be severe if it did not permit the observer to distinguish the sufferer from the brutes.

In the case of Beverly[4] Coke ruled that no felony or murder can be committed without a felonious intent or purpose. If a person was so deprived of reason that he resembled a beast rather than a man he could have no felonious intent and, therefore, could not be convicted of crime. Coke recognized four kinds of persons *non compos mentis*: the idiot or fool natural; he who was of good and sound memory and by the visitation of God has lost it; *lunaticus qui gaudet lucidis intervallis*; and he rendered *non compos mentis* by his own act as a drunkard. On the basis that the person needed to resemble a wild beast rather than a man before his insanity was accepted it seems probable that only those in the first two categories of Coke's classification would be excused punishment. It is quite certain that excuse was not given to the last group. 'Lastly, although he who is drunk is for the time *non compos mentis*, yet his drunkenness does not extenuate his act or offence nor turn to his avail.' Or, as was said in an even rougher age, 'He that kylleth a man drunk, sobur schal be hangyd' (T. Starkey, *England in the Reign of Henry VIII*.[5])

Towards the end of the seventeenth century Sir Matthew Hale[6] commented on insanity and its status in criminal law. 'It is very difficult to determine the invisible line that divides perfect and partial insanity; but it must rest upon circumstances duly to be weighed and considered both by judge and jury, lest on the one side there should be a kind of

[1] *Institutes*, Part III (1797), p. 6   [2] *Collinson on Lunacy*, London, 1812
[3] Bracton, H. de (1883). *De Legibus et Consuetudinibus Angliae*, Vol. VI, p. 321. Ed. by Sir Travers Twiss.   [4] Beverly's case (1604), 4 Co. Rep. 123b
[5] Quoted by Williams, G. (1961). *The Criminal Law*, p. 560. London; Stevens
[6] Hale, M. *Pleas of the Crown*

inhumanity towards the defects in human nature; and on the other side, too great an indulgence given to great crimes. The best measure I can think is this: such a person as labouring under melancholy distempers hath yet ordinarily as great understanding as a child of fourteen years hath, is such a person as may be guilty of treason or felony.' On this last observation Stephen was to comment caustically some two centuries later that there was not much similitude between the mind of a healthy child of fourteen years and the mind of an insane person.

Hale also distinguished between partial and total insanity. Partial insanity is no excuse. '. . . and this is the condition of very many, especially melancholy persons who for the most part discover their defect in excessive fears and griefs, and yet are not wholly destitute of the use of reason; and this partial insanity seems not to excuse them in the committing of any offence . . . .'[1] By partial insanity Hale seems to mean that class of persons who give the appearance of being deluded only in respect of one subject but who appear to be sane in all other matters. Pitt-Lewis, Smith and Hawke[2] felt that 'partial' might mean 'intermittent' insanity but it seems likely that the other interpretation is the more correct. It will be noticed that Hale, like Coke, regarded insanity as a disturbance of reason and intellect, and it was clear that in order to be excused of one's offence the disturbance had to be severe.

In addition, Hale recognized that those who were insane on arraignment could not face trial, that those found to be insane at the time of the offence could not be sentenced and that those who became insane after trial could not be executed. Similar observations were made by Sir John Hawles[3] and by Blackstone[4]. Hale justified this ruling on the following grounds: 'If a man in his sound memory commits a capital offence . . . (and) after judgment he becomes of non-sane memory, his execution shall be spared; for were he of sound memory, he might allege somewhat in stay of judgment or execution.'[5] Sir John Hawles, however, felt that the reason for sparing the life of the insane criminal was to avoid doing a disservice to the soul of the culprit by despatching him into the next world before he had recovered sufficient mental capacity to make his peace with his Creator.

In the eighteenth and nineteenth centuries a number of celebrated cases focused attention on the problem of insanity and crime. In 1724, at Kingston Assizes, Arnold[6] was arraigned for attempting to murder Lord Onslow. The prisoner had shot at and wounded the peer under

[1] Pleas of the Crown, Vol. I, p. 30
[2] Pitt-Lewis, G., Smith, P. and Hawke, J. A. (1895). *The Insane and the Law*, p. 17. London; Churchill
[3] (1687), 11 State Tr. 476   [4] Blackstone's Commentaries
[5] Pleas of the Crown, Vol. I, p. 34
[6] Arnold's case (1724), 16 State Tr. 695

the influence of the delusional belief that Lord Onslow was responsible for all the disturbances which took place in the County and that he caused devils and imps to be introduced nightly into the bedroom of the accused in order to persecute and plague him. In his summing up Mr. Justice Tracey commented on the prisoner's defence of insanity in the following terms: 'it is not every kind of frantic humour or something unaccountable in a man's actions that points him out to be such a madman as is exempted from punishment: it must be a man that is *totally* deprived of his understanding and memory, and doth not know what he is doing no more than an infant, than a brute, or a wild beast. Such a one is never the object of punishment.' On this basis the jury found Arnold to be guilty and he was sentenced to death although, at Lord Onslow's personal request, his sentence was commuted to life imprisonment. The Judge's ruling follows closely that of Hale for, despite the insane nature of Arnold's beliefs, he was far from being in that state of mind which would bring him under the term of what Maudsley was to refer to as 'the wild beast form of knowledge test'.

Lord Ferrers who shot and killed his steward against whom he cherished a deep resentment[1] and William White who shot a schoolmistress who had refused his courtship[2] were less fortunate than Arnold, both being convicted and executed. Lord Ferrers was subject to bouts of towering rage during which he appeared to have no control of his behaviour, but it is doubtful whether this fact would have averted a verdict of guilty in the present century. White, on the other hand, was clearly insane and alleged to be so by three independent witnesses.

The trial of Hadfield[3] who shot at King George III at Drury Lane, London, in 1800 is notable for Erskine's defence. He was able to relate his offence to Hadfield's insane belief that he was required to sacrifice his life to save the world. As he did not wish to commit the sin of suicide it was ordained that he should carry out an act for which he would be hanged. Erskine described the head injuries sustained during the wars by the accused, his delusions and hallucinations, as well as his behaviour as observed by his friends and relatives during the day of his assault on the King. In commenting upon Coke and Hale he said: 'If total deprivation of memory was intended by these great lawyers to be taken in the literal sense of the words:—if it was meant that, to protect a man from punishment, he must be in such a state of prostrated intellect as not to know his name, nor his condition, nor his relation towards others . . . then no such madness ever existed in the world. It is idiocy alone which places a man in this helpless condition.' Erskine went

---

[1] Lord Ferrers' case, (1760) 19 State Tr. 886
[2] R. *v.* White (1795), Bridgewater Assize, cited in Collinson on Lunacy, (1812)
[3] R. *v.* Hadfield (1800), 27 State Tr. 1281

on to consider the nature of delusions. 'Their (the victims of delusional beliefs) conclusions are just and frequently profound; but the premises from which they reason, when within the range of the malady, are uniformly false:—not false from any defect of knowledge or judgment; but, because a delusive image, the inseparable companion of real insanity, is thrust upon the subjugated understanding, incapable of resistance, because unconscious of attack. Delusion, therefore, where there is no frenzy or raving madness, is the true character of insanity. . . .'

Upon the basis of this reasoning and the clear evidence of Hadfield's insanity at the time of his assault, Lord Kenyon, C. J. stopped the trial. In his direction to the jury he said: 'With regard to the law, as has been laid down there can be no doubt upon earth; to be sure, if a man is in a deranged state of mind at the time, he is not criminally answerable for his acts; but the material part of this case is whether at the very time when the act was committed, this man's mind was sane.' The jury accordingly returned their verdict. 'We find the prisoner is not guilty; he being under the influence of insanity at the time the act was committed.'

One of the more immediate consequences of Hadfield's acquittal was the introduction and passing of the Criminal Lunatics Act, 1800, regulating the disposal of persons found insane on arraignment or not guilty of the offence on the grounds of insanity. Prior to the passing of the Act insane persons acquitted because of their insanity were either cared for by their relatives or set free; with the risk that they might repeat their offence. Under section 2 of the Act the court is empowered to order such a person to be kept in strict custody until such time as Her Majesty's pleasure is known.

Compared with earlier judicial rulings the verdict in Hadfield was a great advance. Despite the fact that the accused was well aware of the nature and wrongness of his act the clear evidence of his insanity at the time and the relationship of his delusions to his attempt to shoot King George III were accepted by the court to exonerate him of the charge.

Such enlightened reasoning was not accepted in later proceedings, for Bellingham[1], who shot the Prime Minister, Mr. Spencer Perceval, in 1812 was tried, sentenced and executed within a week of his action despite the evidence of his paranoid and deluded state. Sir James Mansfield, C. J. directed the jury that, in order to establish insanity as a defence, they had to consider whether the prisoner 'had sufficient understanding to distinguish good from evil, right from wrong, and that murder was a crime not only against the law of God but against the law of his country'.

---

[1] Bellingham's case (1812). Cited by Keeton, G. W. (1961). *Guilty but Insane*. London; Macdonald

Also in 1812 Bowler,[1] an epileptic, shot at and wounded one William Burroughes. There was every evidence to indicate that the prisoner suffered from insanity arising from his epilepsy and a Commission of Lunacy had reported to that effect. Mr. Justice Le Blanc directed the jury in the following words. 'The question was whether the prisoner when he committed the act with which he stood charged was or was not incapable of distinguishing right from wrong; or whether he was at that time under the influence of any illusion in respect of the persecutor which rendered his mind at the moment insensible of the nature of the act which he was about to commit since in that case he would not be legally responsible for his conduct.' He then put the alternative argument which would render him guilty. In 1840, Baron Alderson was to comment on the verdict of 'guilty' which was returned, 'Bowler was executed, I believe, and very barbarous it was'. Pitt-Lewis and his colleagues felt that at the time of writing (1895) Bowler would in all probability have been found guilty, arguing that the Judge's summing-up was fair and the verdict reasonable. There was no evidence to indicate that Bowler was in a post-epileptic state when he shot at Burroughes and there was much to indicate that the assault was premeditated and done with malicious intent. Despite this argument it seems very likely that the epilepsy had a direct bearing on Bowler's behaviour and today, had he succeeded in killing Burroughes, a verdict of manslaughter on the grounds of diminished responsibility would probably be returned.

It is not clear why Oxford, a barman aged 18 years, discharged two pistols at Queen Victoria and the Prince Consort in 1840.[2] It seems not to have been fully established whether the pistols were loaded or not. He was arraigned for attempting to shoot the Queen and at his trial there was sufficient evidence as to his delusional insanity to convince the jury that he was deranged at the time. He was found not guilty, to live in an asylum for many years afterwards. Lord Denman, C. J. advised the jury that 'a person may commit a criminal act and not be responsible. If some contributory disease was in truth, the acting power within him which he could not resist, he would not be responsible.'

In 1843, Mr. Edward Drummond, the private secretary of Sir Robert Peel, was shot dead by Daniel M'Naghten[3] who believed himself to be persecuted by the Tory Party. In his statement to the examining magistrate he said that he believed his life was in danger on account of the persecution to which he had been subjected. He shot Edward

---

[1] Bowler's case (1812), cited by Keeton, G. W. (1961). *Guilty but Insane.* London; Macdonald

[2] R. *v.* Oxford (1840), 9 C. and P. 525

[3] R. *v.* M'Naghten (1843), 10 Cl. & F. 200

Drummond in error, believing, in fact, that he was the Prime Minister, Sir Robert Peel. In an eloquent defence Mr. A. Cockburn traced the history of the prisoner's delusional beliefs, related them to the crime and dealt with the law regarding insanity at that time. M'Naghten clearly suffered from paranoid delusions and was acquitted on the ground of his insanity. Cockburn had made much of the doctrine of 'partial insanity' as promulgated by Esquirol and Ray under the concept of 'monomania'. It was believed that it was possible for a patient to be deluded on one subject only and that this symptom was the sole evidence of his illness. Apart from this he was to be considered as a normal and sane person.

The correctness of the verdict in M'Naghten's case is not in question, but it was based on erroneous psychiatric doctrines which still appear to influence jurists to this day. It is understandable, therefore, that, following his acquittal and the general public concern over the case, the House of Lords asked the Judiciary certain specific questions relating to the law of insanity and crime. The replies to those questions came to be known as the M'Naghten Rules which have remained in effect in both civil and criminal cases ever since. Before proceeding to the examination of the Rules it may be helpful to summarize the law of the preceding centuries.

Up to the time of Hadfield's trial it is evident that deluded persons who committed felonies were likely to be convicted even though their delusional beliefs had a direct bearing on their offence. They came into Coke's third category of persons *non compos mentis*, and so long as the view prevailed that a prisoner had to be wholly deprived of his memory and reason to be excused the consequences of his actions it was likely that a number of insane persons would be convicted and executed. It is possible that popular and professional opinion concerning insanity had something to do with this ruling. As Isaac Ray wrote[1] concerning Hale's opinions, 'In the time of this ancient jurist insanity was a much less frequent disease than it is now, and the popular notions concerning it were derived from the observation of those wretched inmates of the madhouses whom chains and stripes, cold and filth, had reduced to the stupidity of the idiot or exasperated to the fury of a demon. Those nice shades of the disease in which the mind, without being wholly driven from its propriety, pertinaciously clings to some absurd delusion, were either regarded as something very different from real madness or were too far removed from the common gaze . . . to enter much into the general idea entertained of madness.'

Erskine's pleading in Hadfield's case allowed the jury to take special note of the prisoner's mind both before and at the time of the com-

[1] Ray, I (1838). *A Treatise on the Medical Jurisprudence of Insanity.*

mission of the offence. He also brought the existence of his delusions firmly into the centre of the problem, thus including Hale's 'partially insane' persons into the category of those who could claim immunity from conviction on account of their mental condition. In any case, Lord Kenyon had ruled that clear evidence of insanity at the time of the crime was sufficient to allow the jury to return a verdict of 'not guilty'. Had Bellingham received a fairer hearing it is possible that he too would have been acquitted despite the public outcry at his offence. By the time Oxford was tried it seems that the general evidence of insanity with its effect upon his conduct and power to control his impulses was sufficient to secure his acquittal. M'Naghten was clearly found 'not guilty' on grounds similar to those which secured Hadfield's discharge despite the fact that on Cockburn's showing he suffered from partial insanity. For he argued, 'I trust that I have satisfied you that the disease of partial insanity can exist, that it can lead to a partial or total aberration of the moral senses and affections, which may render the wretched patient incapable of resisting the delusion'.

This is coming near to a plea of irresistible impulse, a defence which has always been regarded with suspicion and distrust by English jurists. To clarify some of these conflicting opinions the Lords took the unusual step of asking the Judges' opinions on the law relating to crime and insanity.

3—The M'Naghten Rules

'To establish a defence on the ground of insanity it must be clearly proved that, at the time of committing the act, the party accused was labouring under such a defect of reason, from disease of the mind, as not to know the nature and quality of the act he was doing, or, if he did know it, that he did not know he was doing what was wrong.'

The foregoing paragraph is that part of the Judges' answers to the Lords usually known as the 'M'Naghten Rules,' but as the other answers still appear to affect judicial reasoning the first four questions with the answers and Mr. Justice Maule's separate answers will be given in full. The fifth question relating to the evidence of a doctor who had not examined the accused prior to seeing him in court no longer has any relevance to current practice and will not be discussed.

Question 1. What is the law respecting alleged crimes committed by persons afflicted with insane delusion in respect of one or more particular subjects or persons: as, for instance, where at the time of the commission of the alleged crime the accused knew he was acting contrary to law, but did the act complained of with a view, under the influence of insane delusion, of redressing or revenging some supposed grievance or injury, or of producing some supposed public benefit?

Answer 1. Assuming that your Lordships' inquiries are confined to those persons who labour under such partial delusions only, and are not in other respects insane, we are of opinion that, notwithstanding the party accused did the act complained of with a view, under the influence of insane delusion, of redressing or avenging some supposed grievance or injury, or of producing some public benefit, he is nevertheless punishable according to the nature of the crime committed, if he knew at the time of committing such crime that he was acting contrary to law; by which expression we understand your Lordships to mean the law of the land.

Question 2. What are the proper questions to be submitted to the jury, where a person alleged to be afflicted with insane delusion respecting one or more particular subjects or persons, is charged with the commission of a crime (murder for example) and insanity is set up as a defence?

Question 3. In what terms ought the question be left to the jury as to the prisoner's state of mind at the time when the act was committed?

Answer 2 and 3. As these two questions appear to us to be more conveniently answered together, we have to submit our opinion to be, that the jurors ought to be told in all cases that every man is to be presumed to be sane, and to possess a sufficient degree of reason to be responsible for his crimes, until the contrary be proved to their satisfaction; and that to establish a defence on the ground of insanity, it must

20

be clearly proved that, at the time of committing the act, the party accused was labouring under such a defect of reason, from disease of the mind, as not to know the nature and quality of the act he was doing or, if he did know it, that he did not know he was doing what was wrong. The mode of putting the latter part of the question to the jury on these occasions has generally been, whether the accused at the time of doing the act knew the difference between right and wrong: which mode, though rarely, if ever, leading to any mistake with the jury, is not, as we conceive, so accurate when put generally and in the abstract, as when put with reference to the party's knowledge of right and wrong in respect to the very act with which he is charged. If the question were to be put as to the knowledge of the accused solely and exclusively with reference to the law of the land, it might tend to confound the jury, by inducing them to believe that an actual knowledge of the law of the land was essential in order to lead to a conviction: whereas the law is administered upon the principle that everyone must be taken conclusively to know it, without proof that he does know it. If the accused was conscious that the act was one which he ought not to do, and if that act was at the same time contrary to the law of the land, he is punishable; and the usual course, therefore, has been to leave the question to the jury, whether the accused had a sufficient degree of reason to know that he was doing an act that was wrong: and this course we think is correct, accompanied with such observations and explanations as the circumstances of each particular case may require.

Question 4. If a person under an insane delusion as to existing facts commits an offence in consequence thereof, is he thereby excused?

Answer 4. The answer must, of course, depend on the nature of the delusion: but, making the same assumption as we did before, namely, that he labours under such partial delusion only, and is not in other respects insane, we think he must be considered in the same situation as to responsibility as if the facts with respect to which the delusion exists were real. For example, if under the influence of his delusion he supposes another man to be in the act of attempting to take away his life, and he kills that man, as he supposes, in self-defence, he would be exempt from punishment. If his delusion was that the deceased had inflicted a serious injury to his character and fortune, and he killed him in revenge for such supposed injury, he would be liable to punishment.

Mr. Justice Maule gave separate answers to these questions as set out below.

Answer 1. So far as it comprehends the question whether a person circumstanced as stated in the question, is for that reason only to be found not guilty of a crime respecting which the question of his guilt has been duly raised in a criminal proceeding, I am of the opinion that he is not. There is no law that I am aware of that makes persons in the state described in the question not responsible for their criminal acts. To render a person irresponsible should, according to the law as it has been long understood and held, be such as to render him incapable of knowing right from wrong. The terms used in the question cannot be said (with reference only to the usage of language) to be equivalent to a description of this kind and degree of unsoundness of mind.

Answer 2. If on a trial such as is suggested in the question the judge should have occasion to state what kind and degree of insanity would amount to a defence, it should be stated conformably to what I have mentioned in my answer to the first question, as being, in my opinion, the law on the subject.

Answer 3. There are no terms which the judge is by law required to use. They should not be inconsistent with the law as above stated, but should be such as, in the discretion of the judge, are proper to assist the jury in coming to the right conclusion as to the guilt of the accused.

To the fourth question, Mr. Justice Maule replied that his answer to the first question was applicable to this one.

It has often been observed that the M'Naghten Rules have no statutory basis, but despite this they have come to be regarded as the embodiment of the opinions of the judiciary on criminal responsibility in cases where insanity is raised by the defence. Undoubtedly they represented the opinion of the majority of the judges at the time and have continued to do so ever since. It can be said that Mr. Justice Maule's minority opinion which restates the views of Hale has not commended itself to jurists, although it is evident that partial delusions as defined in the questions and answers gave trouble to the judges when they came to frame their replies. Mr. Justice Maule, however, is quite firm that delusions and partial delusions are not to be accepted as exculpating the offender, asserting, as he does, that the knowledge of whether the act is right or wrong is the main consideration for the jury. Had this somewhat uncompromising opinion come to be accepted as the sole factor to be taken into account it is evident that many persons who had been and have been acquitted on the ground of insanity would, in fact, have been found guilty.

Before going on to an examination of the component parts of the Rules something must be said about the general attitudes embodied in them. It is quite evident that at the time of their formulation ideas about mental illness and the effects thereof upon the personality were far from accurate. The relationship of emotional disturbance to disordered behaviour appears not to have been known to the judges who insist throughout in their replies that 'defect of reason' is the touchstone of insanity whereby the judge and jury will be guided to a correct decision. It is also evident that delusions are regarded as the obvious manifestations of defects of reason for little attention is paid to other forms of insanity in which delusional beliefs do not figure so prominently.

Both Erskine and Cockburn had rightly concentrated on the delusional beliefs of their clients, but although Cockburn indicated that such beliefs will affect the total behaviour of the patient this fact was ignored by the judges in their deliberations over the M'Naghten Rules. In their answers to the first and fourth questions they state quite clearly that a

22

delusional belief will exculpate the offender only if that belief is of such a kind as would lead to a plea of extenuating or exculpating circumstances in the case of a sane prisoner. The accused is expected to be reasonable in considering his delusions and it was this piece of theorizing which led Maudsley to write, 'Here is an unhesitating assumption that a man having an insane delusion has the power to think and act in regard to it reasonably; that at the time of the offence he ought to have and to exercise the knowledge and self-control which a sane man would have and exercise, were the facts with respect to which the delusion exists real; that he is in fact bound to be reasonable in his unreason, sane in his insanity.'[1] Somewhat similar reasoning appears to have guided the court in a recent divorce case[2] in which a husband obtained a decree of divorce from his wife who suffered from a paranoid psychosis. Her delusional beliefs concerned her husband whom she accused of infidelity and homosexuality, leading her to assault him physically in the hope of coercing him to refrain from the activities of which, in her delusional state, she accused him. Mr. Justice Scarman in his judgment[3] commented, 'In those accusations she was wholly deluded, quite unable to appreciate that she was wrong. But save for the field covered by the delusions, she was a rational being. She knew what she was doing and was able to distinguish between right and wrong. It followed that her legal responsibility had to be determined as though her delusions were true. She must be treated as a rational person save for her delusion . . .' It is evident from this judgment that in some judicial circles it is still thought possible for psychotic persons to be reasonable and to suffer no other ill-effects from their insanity save for the delusional beliefs which are the main presenting symptoms of their illnesses. It would appear that the answers of the judges to the first and fourth questions put to them after M'Naghten's case still guide the thoughts of jurists despite the fact that partial insanity and partial delusional state have no place in psychiatric practice. It is also clear that the physical assaults of the wife did not act in her favour, presumably because they were for the purpose of 'redressing or avenging some supposed grievance or injury'. On the basis of this reasoning, had the unfortunate woman killed her husband she would have been convicted of non-capital murder despite the medical evidence of her insanity.

Undoubtedly, a deluded person is more clearly insane to the layman than one who is not so obviously affected. Consequently, it has not

[1] Maudsley, H. (1874). *Responsibility in Mental Disease*. London; Henry S. King
[2] Elphinstone *v.* Elphinstone (1962), *The Times*, May 4
[3] Since the recent decision in Williams *v.* Williams (1963) (*The Times*, June 28) insanity is no longer a useful defence against divorce proceedings brought on the grounds of cruelty. [1963] 2 All E. R. 15

always been easy to persuade jurists to accept that insanity can occur without obvious delusions just as it has been difficult to convince them that a deluded person is not sane in every other respect. In the case of Townley,[1] Baron Martin held that the accused should show evidence of delusions before he could be exculpated under the M'Naghten Rules. 'If he knew what he was doing and that it was likely to cause death and was contrary to the law of God and man . . . he was guilty of murder.' Townley was undoubtedly insane. He killed a girl who had refused to marry him stating that as she had deceived him she deserved to die.

In an earlier case[2] Baron Parke had argued that 'it was difficult to see how the defence could establish a plea of insanity where there was a total absence of delusion'. Although Mr. Justice Horridge concluded that delusions were evidence of general insanity[3] it is obvious that the concept of partial insanity has a place in judicial reasoning and that the presence of delusions is more likely to be accepted as exculpating evidence than is the evidence of psychosis unsupported by delusional symptoms.

Rivett carried out a motiveless murder of a girl with whom he had been associating and gave himself up to the police afterwards. Unchallenged medical evidence indicated that he suffered from schizophrenia and was unfit to plead. Despite this he stood trial and was convicted of murder. On appeal[4] Lord Goddard, C.J. observed, 'Let it be assumed he suffered from schizophrenia, or whatever doctors may call it; let it be assumed that he killed the girl on a sudden impulse; a jury of his country are satisfied that he was responsible, and it is not for this court to say he was not.' Had Rivett shown some delusional belief it is possible—but by no means certain in the face of such uncompromising hostility to medical evidence—that a different verdict would have been returned.

From the foregoing discussion it is clear that legal views of the nature of insanity have little to do, at times, with current psychiatric concepts. Despite Dr. Glanville Williams' statement[5] that the concept of partial insanity is now obsolete there is much to show that it still influences legal thinking. It may well be that the Judges' comments on this in the first and fourth answers in the M'Naghten Rules is the main reason for the persistence of this erroneous doctrine. For that reason it is all the more important that the Rules should be examined in their entirety rather than that the discussion should be limited to that part of the second and third answers usually quoted as the M'Naghten Rules in courts

[1] R. v. Townley (1863), F. and F. 839
[2] R. v. Barton (1848), 3 Cox C. C. 275
[3] R. v. Gilbert (1914), 11 Cr. App. Rep. 52
[4] R. v. Rivett (1950), 34 Cr. App. Rep. 87
[5] Williams, G. (1961). *The Criminal Law*, Sect. 145, 2nd ed. London; Stevens

of law when the plea of insanity is being considered. Nevertheless, it is over this particular portion of the Rules that controversy has most often occurred. The examination of the component parts of the Rules as quoted at the beginning of this chapter should help to indicate the manner in which they have been applied since their formulation.

Clearly Proved

Whereas the question of insanity on arraignment can be raised by the Judge, Crown or defence, a plea of insanity at the time of the alleged offence can only be raised by or on behalf of the accused.[1] The duty of the prosecution in this matter is limited to placing before the defence any evidence which is in their possession relating to the insanity of the accused.[2] It is not enough to prove that the accused was insane at the time of the alleged crime for it must be shown that he was insane so as not to be responsible according to law for his actions. In short, his insanity must be directly related to the offence in such a way as to satisfy the jury that the mental abnormality had a direct causative relationship to the offence, and that the offence would not have happened had the mental abnormality been absent.

It is accepted that the burden of proof on the defence when a plea of insanity is raised is less onerous than that imposed on the prosecution. In R. *v.* Carr-Briant[3] Mr. Justice Humphreys quoted an observation of Lord Hailsham, L. C.[4]: 'It is certainly plain that the burden in cases in which the accused has to prove insanity may fairly be stated as not being higher than the burden which rests upon a plaintiff or defendant in civil proceedings. That this is the law is not challenged. It is, consequently, for the jury to decide the issue on a matter of probability rather than beyond any reasonable doubt.

It has been observed that it is usual in most cases for the prosecution to prove the guilt of the accused rather than for the defence to prove his innocence.[5] However, in cases where insanity is the issue it is obvious that the absence of *mens rea* in the accused at the time of the alleged offence must be proven by the defence. To insist that the Crown must prove beyond all reasonable doubt the sanity of the prisoner who has pleaded insanity would be an impossible task which could lead to abuse. Presumably this point was in the minds of the judges when they formulated the M'Naghten Rules, although at that time it led to

---

[1] But see Lord Denning in Bratty *v.* Attorney-General for Northern Ireland, [1961] 3 All E. R. 523
[2] Royal Commission on Capital Punishment (1949–53). Cmd. 8932, para. 226
[3] (1943), 29 Cr. App. Rep. 76
[4] Sodemann *v.* R., [1936] 2 All E. R. 1133
[5] Director of Public Prosecutions *v.* Woolmington, [1935] A. C. 462

the anomalous result that the proof of 'innocence' was for the defence which, if successful, led to a verdict of 'not guilty'. It is perhaps less anomalous since the Trial of Lunatics Act, 1883, provided for the special verdict of 'guilty but insane' instead of a formal acquittal.

Defect of Reason

By the use of the words 'defect of reason' the judges clearly implied that the test whereby a man was to be acquitted or convicted on account of insanity was an intellectual one. It was necessary to show that the accused's intellectual or cognitive faculties were so deranged that his reasoning powers as to facts and actions were no longer functioning normally. It followed that a rigid adherence to the requirement of a defect of reason ruled out any consideration of crimes committed during stages of acute emotional disturbance.

No doubt the judges believed that delusions were, in fact, evidence of a defect of reason, not appreciating that delusions rest on and derive their force from underlying emotional derangement. Numerous attempts have been made to enlarge the scope of the Rules so as to allow consideration of overwhelming emotional tension to exonerate the prisoner. This has usually been regarded by the courts as a plea of irresistible impulse which has not yet been accepted by the Court of Criminal Appeal as coming within the terms of the M'Naghten Rules.[1] In all these cases a plea of irresistible or overwhelming impulse had been put forward by the defence without success at trial or on appeal. In the case of Coelho there was clear evidence of insanity and it is probable that he killed his wife under the delusional belief that she was poisoning his food. The court felt that he knew what he was doing and that his act was wrong, despite the medical evidence. In the case of Kopsch the law was stated by Lord Hewart, C.J. with uncompromising rigour. 'The law with regard to criminal insanity is that every man is presumed to be sane, and to possess a sufficient degree of reason to be responsible for his crimes, until the contrary is proved to the satisfaction of the jury.' Lord Hewart went on to quote the usual passage from the M'Naghten Rules and then continued, 'In the present case the judge... explained the law to the jury, but it is said that he misdirected the jury as he omitted to direct them that "a person charged criminally with an offence is irresponsible for his act when it is committed under an impulse which the prisoner is by mental disease in substance deprived of any power to resist." In other words, the complaint against the

[1] R. *v.* Thomas (1911), 7 Cr. App. Rep. 36; R. *v.* Alexander (1913), 9 Cr. App. Rep. 139; R. *v.* Coelho (1914), 10 Cr. App. Rep. 210; R. *v.* Holt (1920), 15 Cr. App. Rep. 50; R. *v.* Quarmby (1921), 15 Cr. App. Rep. 163; R. *v.* Kopsch (1925), 19 Cr. App. Rep. 50; R. *v.* Flavell (1926), 19 Cr. App. Rep. 1941: Sodeman *v.* R., [1936] 2 All E. R. 1133

judge is that he did not tell the jury that something was the law which was not the law. . . . It is the fantastic theory of uncontrollable impulse which, if it were to become part of our criminal law, would be merely subversive.'

Disease of the Mind

There is no generally accepted definition of disease of the mind but usually it is assumed to mean one of the major functional or organic psychoses. The Royal Commission on Capital Punishment (para. 212) took this to be the meaning of the phrase and that the neuroses and character disorders were thereby excluded. They admitted that such a classification would not be acceptable to all psychiatrists and for that reason a further discussion of this problem will be deferred until a later chapter. In the meantime it is necessary to consider what classes of mental illness have been accepted by the courts to excuse a mentally disordered person from the consequences of his actions.

As has already been indicated, at one time it seemed necessary that a person should be deluded before a plea of insanity would be accepted, and although this notion has been specifically repudiated by the Court of Criminal Appeal[1] there can be little doubt that the presence of delusional beliefs in the accused has a more convincing effect upon the lay mind than do other manifestations of insanity. Motiveless murder such as may occur on impulse in some cases of schizophrenia without evident delusions clearly had no appeal to judges in the last century, although today it is likely that such an act would be considered as evidence of insanity over and above any other evidence which would be available from other sources. Haynes[2] carried out such an action on impulse but was not acquitted. For, as Baron Bramwell said, 'if an influence be so powerful as to be termed irresistible, so much the more reason is there why we should not withdraw any of the safeguards tending to counteract it'.

Burton[3] killed a boy without apparent motive other than his expressed desire to be hanged. He gave himself up to the police and pleaded guilty. At the trial evidence of moral insanity was offered but Mr. Justice Wightman said 'It was not mere eccentricity of conduct which made a man legally irresponsible for his acts. The medical man . . . described moral insanity as a state of mind under which a man, perfectly aware that it was wrong to do so, killed another under an uncontrollable impulse. This would appear to be a most dangerous doctrine and fatal to the interests of society and security of life. The judge went on to argue that although the accused killed in order to be hanged he was

---

[1] R. v. Windle, [1952] 2 All E.R. 1   [2] R. v. Haynes (1859), 1 F. and F. 666
[3] R. v. Burton (1863), 3 F. and F. 772

not deluded, despite the evidence of a morbid state of mind. He knew what he was doing and that it was wrong.

The motiveless nature of the murder carried out by Rivett in 1950 did not exculpate him despite the unchallenged medical evidence of schizophrenia, but in 1951, Powell,[1] a schizophrenic who killed his grandmother, was found guilty but insane despite the lack of evidence of delusions and despite the motiveless nature of the killing. It was held that schizophrenia was a disease of the mind which left him no control over his emotions and, at times, of his speech or actions. The accused knew the nature and quality of his act but was incapable of knowing that what he did was wrong. 'For once', as the medico-legal correspondent remarked, 'doctors, lawyers and laymen were all in agreement about schizophrenia in relation to criminal responsibility.'

In general, it can be said that the major functional psychoses as well as the symptomatic or organic psychoses will be accepted as diseases of the mind. Severe depressive states in which the accused kills his or her children, believing that unless this is done some dreadful fate awaits them, are not uncommon. There have been two such cases in recent times and it is clear that the courts have been well aware of the pathological nature of the mental state of the accused. Similar considerations apply to the major organic syndromes but it is likely that the disorder will need to be fairly gross before it will be taken into account by the court. This point is well brought out by the Royal Commission on Capital Punishment in their discussion on epilepsy.[2] As they observe, in some cases the relation between epilepsy and the crime is close and direct. In a far greater number of cases this is not so and it is necessary to consider each case on its merits. Not all epileptics who commit crimes of violence do so in states of disturbed consciousness, and it is obvious that in some cases the crime was premeditated and done with full awareness of the consequences. The case of Bowler, already mentioned, serves to show that epilepsy as such will not excuse the prisoner despite the evidence in this particular case that Bowler had shown other symptoms of mental illness.

In the case of Treadaway[3] the prisoner had an epileptic attack during his trial. Doctors in the court testified to the genuine nature of the attack but the man was found guilty and convicted. Nevertheless, there is reason to believe that a serious crime committed by a known epileptic may have some relationship to the underlying cerebral condition. This may not amount to insanity in law but could be

[1] R. v. Powell (1951). *Brit. med. J.* **1**, 765
[2] Royal Commission on Capital Punishment (1949–53). Cmd. 8932, paras. 386–392
[3] R. v. Treadaway (1877) cited by Pitt-Lewis, G., Smith, P. and Hawke, J. A. (1895). *The Insane and the Law.* London; Churchill

regarded as diminishing the control of the accused so as to lead to a verdict of manslaughter owing to diminished responsibility.

It might be thought that serious organic disease of the brain would be clear-cut evidence of mental disease, but in the case of Kemp[1] it was argued by the defence that the accused man, suffering from arteriosclerotic dementia, was suffering from a disease of the brain and not of the mind. In a state of clouded consciousness he had seriously injured his wife, but it was suggested that the assault was due to automatism and should lead to an acquittal. Fortunately, under the guidance of Mr. Justice Devlin common sense prevailed. It was found that the accused did suffer from a disease of the mind rendering him insane within the M'Naghten Rules and he was accordingly sent to Broadmoor.

Not all cases of organic disease of the brain with resulting mental symptoms will lead to an acquittal under the M'Naghten Rules. Coelho[2] was deluded and probably had early symptoms of general paralysis of the insane. Despite this he was found guilty of murdering his wife although in this case the Rules were interpreted very narrowly. This underlines the point that the Rules are not a definition of insanity as such, but merely point to the degree of insane irresponsibility required by the courts to exculpate the offender. As Lord Reading, C.J. said in a later case[3] 'The tests in M'Naghten's case must be observed, and it is not enough for a medical expert to come to the Court and say generally that in his opinion the criminal is insane.' For similar reasons, appeal to the evidence of insanity in the accused's family carries no weight. The suggestion that a man had reverted in an 'atavistic' manner to the mental disease which had affected earlier forebears was held not to be an indication that he suffered from insanity himself.[4] Evidence of mental illness affecting relatives of the accused man appears to have been offered more frequently in the last century than it is today;[5] even then such evidence appears not to have influenced the court's decision.[6]

Although there is a general consensus of opinion that the major psychoses are diseases of the mind, it is less certain whether subnormality and severe subnormality are to be included in this category. No doubt any person so defective as to be classified as suffering from severe subnormality would be found incapable of pleading to a charge

[1] R. v. Kemp, [1957] 1 Q. B. 399
[2] R. v. Coelho (1914), 10 Cr. App. Rep. 210
[3] R. v. Holt (1920), 15 Cr. App. Rep. 10
[4] R. v. Smith (1910), 5 Cr. App. Rep. 123
[5] See Pitt-Lewis, G., Smith, P. and Hawke, J. A. (1895). *The Insane and the Law*, pp. 34 and 232. London; Churchill
[6] See R. v. Williams (1893), Exeter Assizes, cited by Pitt-Lewis *et al.* (1895)

and found insane on arraignment. Difficulties are likely to arise only when the degree of feeble-mindedness is not so great as to prevent the accused from following an occupation and leading a more or less normal life. Stephen[1] felt that the words 'defective mental power' as an exculpating plea would require legislation before they would be accepted as evidence of disease of the mind within the M'Naghten Rules. The Royal Commission on Capital Punishment also expressed doubts on whether or not mental deficiency was a disease of the mind, quoting the views of the British Medical Association who felt it was desirable to remove any doubts on the matter by providing explicitly that disease of the mind covers incomplete mental development as well as grave disturbances of mental health.[2] The Royal Commission incorporated this suggestion into their final recommendations.[3] Curiously, the question of whether or not mental subnormality is to be classed formally as a disease of the mind has never been tested in the courts but Williams[4] is of the opinion that in 1843, when the M'Naghten Rules were formulated, imbecility was included in this term although he feels that moral imbeciles—psychopathic personalities in current terminology—were excluded, not being regarded as irresponsible in law.

Although there is good reason to doubt whether or not subnormality is to be classed automatically as a disease of the mind, the Royal Commission on Capital Punishment was satisfied from the evidence presented to them that in practice the M'Naghten Rules had been interpreted as covering mental deficiency in those cases where it was shown that the requirements of the Rules were fulfilled. The evidence of subnormality does not lead automatically to a finding of 'guilty but insane', and each case has to be considered on its merits in order to reach a decision on the contribution made by the subnormality to the criminal act. Certainly, there is plenty of evidence to show that mental deficiency has not led to acquittal on all occasions in the past. Higginson,[5] a mental defective who killed his son, aged 5 years, was convicted on the grounds that he knew what he was doing and knew that it was wrong; Alexander,[6] when partially intoxicated with alcohol, murdered his cohabitee, but the evidence of mental defect which would render him more susceptible to provocation did not excuse him.

In more recent times, the case of Straffen has pointed to some of the

---

[1] Stephen, J. F. (1883). *History of the Criminal Law.* **2,** 149
[2] Royal Commission on Capital Punishment (1949–53) Cmd. 8932, para. 344
[3] Royal Commission on Capital Punishment (1949–53) Cmd. 8932, para. 790 (18)
[4] Williams, G. (1961). *The Criminal Law,* 2nd ed., Sect. 147. London; Stevens
[5] R. *v.* Higginson (1843), 1 Car. & Kir. 129
[6] R. *v.* Alexander (1913), 9 Cr. App. Rep. 139

anomalies of a plea of insanity due to mental defect[1] for whereas he was found unfit to plead when tried for his first murder he was found guilty and sentenced to death for his second, only a few months later, when he escaped from Broadmoor Mental Hospital. At the trial the Judge stressed the distinction between insanity and mental deficiency, for medical evidence had indicated that although the accused was labouring under a defect of reason, this was not due to a disease of the mind. The question of whether or not subnormality is a disease of the mind within the M'Naghten Rules remains unresolved. However, the Homicide Act, 1957, specifically includes arrested or retarded development of mind as a factor leading, or capable of leading, to substantially impaired mental responsibility. So it is presumed that a mentally subnormal person who is not so severely disordered as to be found unfit to plead, or to be found guilty but insane, will still be able to escape the full rigours of punishment on a plea of diminished responsibility.

It appears generally to be accepted that psychoneurosis and character disorder—including psychopathic personality—cannot be classed as diseases of the mind which will bring them within the terms of the M'Naghten Rules.

No doubt it is illogical to regard a severe, incapacitating illness such as hysteria or obsessional neurosis, as not being diseases of the mind, but as such illnesses rarely lead to serious criminal acts their exclusion may not be of serious importance. In any case, different opinions have been expressed in the courts, for Lawrence[2] who killed his blind foster-mother 'to put her out of her misery' was considered to be suffering from hysteria which was accepted by the Court on medical evidence as a disease of the mind. The charge was reduced to one of manslaughter owing to diminished responsibility under the Homicide Act, 1957. On the other hand, Bentley,[3] said to be suffering from hysteria for some 18 years, was said not to be suffering from a mental illness. When questioned by the Judge the prison medical officer said that it was a psychoneurotic condition and not a mental illness. Insanity as a defence is rarely offered when the charge is less than one of capital murder, and, fortunately, it is unusual for psychoneurotic persons to commit capital crimes. Should they do so it would still be necessary to show a direct connection between the neurosis and the criminal act before it became essential to consider whether or not the neurosis was a mental disease within the M'Naghten Rules.

The psychoneurotic nature of compulsive stealing, drug addiction and certain sexual offences is well recognized by the courts without

[1] R. *v.* Straffen, [1952] 2 All E. R. 657; *see also* Keeton, G. W. (1961). *Guilty but Insane*. London; Macdonald
[2] R. *v.* Lawrence (1958), *The Times*, May 9
[3] R. *v.* Bentley (1962), *The Times*, March 15

the need to invoke the concept of insanity before deciding how best to deal with the offender. It follows that although psychoneurosis might be considered as impairing the prisoner's responsibility it is unlikely that this has much relevance to those cases where a plea of insanity under the M'Naghten Rules is offered. Similar considerations apply with even greater force to the problem of psychopathic personality, which will be considered more appropriately in the chapter dealing with diminished responsibility.

Pitt-Lewis and his colleagues[1] considered the problem of moral insanity, which can be regarded in some respects as the precursor of the present-day category of psychopathic personality. They cited the cases of Burton[2] and Townley[3] as laying down the proposition that in law, moral insanity is no defence. It is held that moral insanity or psychopathic personality are abnormalities of mind not amounting to a legal concept of insanity. Hence, they cannot be included as diseases of the mind within the framework of the M'Naghten Rules.[4]

'To Know the Nature and Quality of the Act'

It has been ruled since the case of Codère[5] that the phrase 'to know the nature and quality of the act' refers to the physical quality of the act. The accused had killed a sergeant in the Canadian Army and there was disputed evidence as to his sanity. Counsel argued that the word 'nature' referred to the physical nature of the act and that 'quality' meant moral quality. On these points Lord Reading, C.J. said, 'The Court is of the opinion that in using the language "nature and quality" the judges were *only* dealing with the physical character of the act and were not intending to distinguish between the physical and moral aspects of the act.' In the same judgment it was held that 'wrong' meant wrong according to the ordinary standards adopted by reasonable men and in relation to murder means, in effect, punishable by law.[6]

Pitt-Lewis, Smith and Hawke[7] stated that the nature and quality of the act must refer to the physical facts of the act. They argued that if a confused man hits out at what he supposes to be a large animal attacking him but kills a man he cannot be said to have either knowledge of the true physical circumstances or the necessary *mens rea* for the act to be criminal. Williams[8] said that the ruling in Codère covers only

[1] Pitt-Lewis, G., Smith, P. and Hawke, J. A. (1895). *The Insane and the Law*, pp. 222–225. London; Churchill

[2] R. *v.* Burton (1863), 3 F. & F. 772   [3] R. *v.* Townley (1863), 3 F. & F. 839

[4] Archbold (1962). *Criminal Pleading*, 35th ed., p. 18. London; Sweet and Maxwell

[5] R. *v.* Codère (1916), 12 Cr. App. Rep. 21

[6] Royal Commission on Capital Punishment (1949–53) Cmd. 8932, p. 404

[7] Pitt-Lewis, G., Smith, P. and Hawke, J. A. (1895). *The Insane and the Law*. London; Churchill

[8] Williams, G. (1961). *The Criminal Law*, 2nd ed. Sect. 156. London; Stevens

two situations, that of automatism and simple ignorance such as can occur only in gross confusional states. He wrote, 'It has been determined that this phrase refers to the physical character of the act, not to its legal quality'. He went on to argue that to know the nature and quality of an act implies knowledge of consequences, saying that one so mad that he can kill another without knowing what he is doing will probably be found unfit to plead. Much appears to turn on the meaning of the word 'know' which in the strict legal view, according to Williams, means a 'phonograph theory of knowledge which disregards everything that is human'.

It was laid down in the case of Codère that 'wrong' means 'punishable by law', a ruling that was re-affirmed by Lord Goddard, C.J.[1] He ruled that if a man knows what he is doing is wrong, and by wrong is meant contrary to law, he is responsible. Earlier writers, including Pitt-Lewis and his colleagues, felt that wrong referred to a knowledge of moral as well as legal wrongness thus obviating the need to prove that the prisoner at the time of his act was aware of the precise law of the land. Norval Morris[2] also believed that at the time when the M'Naghten Rules were made the judges assumed that 'wrong' meant legal and moral wrong. He quoted Stephen who also took this to be the meaning of the word. Similarly, Baron Martin in the case of Townley referred to wrong as being contrary to the law of God and man, so it would seem that up to comparatively recent times the word has borne its common sense meaning rather than a strict legal meaning. It should be emphasized that the knowledge of the nature and quality of the act and the knowledge that the act was wrong refer to the act of which the prisoner is accused. In the case of Vaughan[3] Lord Tindal, C.J. said, 'It must be shown that the prisoner had no competent use of his understanding so as to know that he was doing a wrong thing in the particular act in question'. It follows that an abstract knowledge of right and wrong or of the legal aspects of crime in general are not required, a fact which was brought out in the judges' answers to the second and third questions in M'Naghten's case.

What is really meant by the word 'know'? If, as Williams asserts, the knowledge of an event is the mere ability to reproduce the facts as if from some mechanical recorder, then the great majority of insane persons who commit serious crimes can be said to know what they are doing and that what they do is wrong by legal standards. Unfortunately, such a theory takes no account of the emotional concomitants of knowledge; and it is surely the emotional coldness or detachment of

[1] R. *v.* Windle, [1952] 2 All E. R. 1
[2] Morris, N. (1953), M. L. R. 433
[3] R. *v.* Vaughan (1844), 1 Cox C. C. 80

the schizophrenic, who may kill without any particular feeling of horror or apparent awareness of the likely consequences to his victim or himself, which makes this interpretation of 'knowing' inadequate. Undoubtedly, we know some things in a purely mechanical way such as knowing the multiplication table; but our knowledge of emotionally significant facts must imply our ability to experience those emotions appropriate to the act, without which we cannot be said to have true knowledge. Furthermore, a strict insistence on the knowledge of legal wrongness makes no provisions for the deluded person who believes that he is above the law or immune from the consequences of his action.

Hadfield was clearly aware that if he killed King George III he would be hanged. Nevertheless, he had to attempt this crime because he believed that by incurring his own death he would be saving the world. He must have been aware of the wrongness of his actions in order to envisage the consequences to himself, but one can assume that the higher purpose for which his crime was committed made any purely legal considerations superfluous. Yet on a strict interpretation of the M'Naghten Rules Hadfield would be found guilty despite the clear evidence of his insanity. In any case, a deluded person who commits a crime to revenge a supposed wrong or for some purpose other than self-defence against a supposed attack would be considered guilty on the grounds that, despite his deluded state, he should be able to distinguish between one delusional belief and another and the consequences of acting thereon.

How far this part of the Rules is still accepted by the judges is uncertain, but Turner[1] appears to approve the judgment on a man who was convicted of obtaining money by false pretences despite his delusional belief that he was the son of a well-known prince. At present it would appear that the lack of appropriate affect, without which our knowledge of events can scarcely be said to be complete, would not be taken into account if the Rules were strictly applied. In the case of Powell, already mentioned, however, it does look as if the court accepted that the emotional disturbance of schizophrenia prevented the accused from having a proper knowledge of the nature, quality, and wrongness of his act. Such understanding of the nature of schizophrenia was, unfortunately, not forthcoming in the case of Rivett some two years earlier. The words of Henry Maudsley[2] still need to be emphasized: 'Of few insane persons who do violence can it be truly said that they have a full knowledge of the nature and quality of their acts at the time they are doing them.'

[1] Turner, J. W. C. (1962). *Kenny's Outline of the Criminal Law*, 18th ed., p. 78. Cambridge; Cambridge University Press
[2] Maudsley, H. (1874). *Responsibility in Mental Disease*, p. 96. London; Henry S. King

4—Comments and Criticisms of the M'Naghten Rules

From their inception the Rules have been subjected to constant criticism from both legal and medical commentators. Most have fastened on to the extremely narrow and incorrect conception of mental illness as a defect of reason, an intellectual derangement which takes no note of the emotional disturbance which is the basis of much mental disorder. The arguments have been summarized by the Royal Commission on Capital Punishment (para. 227) in the following passage.

'Briefly they (the medical and legal critics) have contended that the M'Naghten test is based on an entirely obsolete and misleading conception of the nature of insanity, since insanity does not only, or primarily, affect the cognitive or intellectual faculties, but affects the whole personality of the patient, including both the will and the emotions. An insane person, therefore, may often know the nature and quality of his act and that it is wrong and forbidden by law, but yet commit it as a result of the mental disease. He may, for example, be overwhelmed by a sudden irresistible impulse; or he may regard his motives as standing higher than the sanctions of the law; or it may be that in the distorted world in which he lives, normal considerations have little meaning or little value. Most medical men would take the view that in the violent acts of an insane man his insanity has been, as a general rule, an essential and predominant cause, and that therefore, he should not be judged by the same standards as normal men. The medical view was well put as long ago as 1883 by Stephen.[1]

'"A delusion of the kind suggested never, or hardly ever, stands alone, but is in all cases the result of a disease of the brain, which interferes more or less with every function of the mind, which falsifies all the emotions, alters in an unaccountable way the natural weight of motives of conduct, weakens the will, and sometimes, without giving the patient false impressions of external facts, so enfeebles every part of his mind that he sees and feels and acts with regard to real things as a sane man does with regard to what he supposes himself to see in a dream."'

It is interesting to note that Stephen referred to disease of the brain in this context and in another passage in the same work he wrote, 'Insanity means a state in which one or more of the above named mental

[1] Stephen, J. F. (1883). *History of the Criminal Law*, Vol. 2 p. 157

functions (feeling, knowing, emotion and willing) is performed in an abnormal manner or not performed at all by reason of some disease of the brain or nervous system. That the brain and nervous system are the organs by which all mental operations are conducted is now well established and generally admitted.'

Stephen has been one of the more forceful and lucid critics of the M'Naghten Rules and further attention will be given to his criticisms later in this chapter. As early as 1848, however, Lord Brougham[1] was to comment, 'We must always keep in view that which the inaccuracy of ordinary language inclines us to forget, that the mind is one and indivisible . . . We therefore cannot, in any correctness of language, speak of general or partial insanity.' Lord Brougham went on to discuss partial insanity, 'which would be better described by the phrase "insanity" or "unsoundness" always existing, though only occasionally manifest.' In arguing that insanity affects the whole mental functioning of the patient he said, 'If the being, or essence, which we term the mind, is unsound on one subject, provided that unsoundness is at all times existing upon that subject, it is quite erroneous to suppose such a mind really sound on other subjects. It is only sound in appearance.' It is evident from these observations that the concepts of partial and total insanity as embodied in the M'Naghten Rules were not acceptable to all members of the legal profession only five years after the rules had been formulated.

Lord Coleridge, C. J. was even more forthright in 1888 when he said, 'The law in the matter of insanity is not incapable of being so interpreted as to do terrible injustice.'[2] Yet only 14 years earlier Baron Bramwell had with supreme inconsistency when being questioned about the M'Naghten Rules stated, 'I think that, although the present law lays down such a definition of madness, that nobody is hardly ever really mad enough to be within it, yet it is a logical and good definition.'[3] It is to be noted that Baron Bramwell evidently regarded the Rules as a *definition* of insanity although it is generally held that this is not the case; they merely lay down the criteria which have to be observed before the man's insanity can be considered as an exculpating factor. It is for this reason that a rigid interpretation of the Rules can lead so easily to the conviction and punishment of an insane person.

Sir James Stephen[4] criticized the Rules at some length and proposed certain amendments which he attempted to embody in his Homicide Law Amendment Bill in 1874. In his book he later asserted that the law

[1] Waring *v.* Waring (1848), 6 Moo. P. C. C. 341
[2] Quoted by Robinson, E. (1947). *Just Murder.* London; Lincolns Prager
[3] Royal Commission on Capital Punishment (1949–53), p. 401
[4] Stephen, J. F. (1883). *History of the Criminal Law*, Vol. 2, Chap. 17. London; Macmillan

on insanity in England was as follows (and he quotes from his *Digest of Laws*): 'No act is a crime if the person who does it is at the time when it is done prevented (either by defective mental power or) by any disease affecting his mind (*a*) from knowing the nature and quality of his act, or (*b*) from knowing that the act is wrong, (or (*c*) from controlling his own conduct, unless the absence of the power of control has been produced by his own default).'

Stephen admitted that the passages between parentheses were doubtful and might require legislation to render this interpretation of the M'Naghten Rules more definite. However, his attempt to obtain recognition for his point of view in the matter was not accepted either in 1874 by a Select Committee of the House of Commons, nor in 1878 by the Royal Commission set up to consider his Draft Criminal Code Bill.

In the meantime medical opposition to the Rules had been expressed at a meeting of the Association of Medical Officers of Hospitals and Asylums for the Insane in 1864 when they passed a resolution stating, 'That so much of the legal test of the mental condition of the alleged criminal lunatic as renders him a responsible agent, because he knows the difference between right and wrong, is inconsistent with the fact well known to every member of this meeting, that the power of distinguishing between right and wrong exists very frequently among those who are undoubtedly insane, and is often associated with dangerous and uncontrollable delusions.'

Some of Henry Maudsley's strictures on the Rules have been quoted in the previous chapter. He was particularly critical of the concept of partial insanity and went on to discuss the replies given by the judges. On the fourth answer he wrote, 'This answer really conflicts with a former answer; it is obvious that the knowledge of right and wrong is different from the knowledge of an act being contrary to the law of the land; and it is certain that an insane person may do an act which he knows to be contrary to law because by reason of his insanity he believes it to be right because . . . he is a law unto himself and deems it a duty to do it, perhaps with a view to producing some public benefit.'

Other medical writers were no less critical of the Rules but the combined medico-legal attitude is well expressed by Pitt-Lewis and his colleagues who examined the Rules and their antecedents, indicating that compared with the judgments given in the cases of Hadfield, Oxford and M'Naghten, the Rules are, as interpreted, unduly restrictive. They were particularly concerned to demonstrate that what was termed 'moral insanity' and 'irresistible impulse' should be included under disease of mind within the framework of the Rules, but admitted that their interpretation of the Rules would not be accepted by all authorities. They wrote, 'The reader must, however, be distinctly and very plainly warned that the broad and benign cohstruction which it has been sought to place upon the Rules laid down in M'Naghten's case has, as a whole, never yet received the support of any reported decision.' It might be added that since the time when this was written the Court of Criminal Appeal has consistently refused to accept that irresistible impulse can exonerate the offender. Pitt-Lewis and his colleagues also considered the meaning of the word 'know', in the phrase 'he did not know he was doing what was wrong'. They argue that knowledge means the power to foresee consequences of an act, the ability to discriminate based on the knowledge of such consequences, and the ability to exercise free choice between alternative courses of action. They go on to say: 'In cases where it is shown that such a discriminating power was wanting, it may at least be argued that a defence is afforded which was merely moral insanity or which took the form of an irresistible impulse.'

Dr. Charles Mercier considered some of the arguments for and against the Rules, saying[1] 'It still remains the law in criminal cases that the only faculty of mind whose disorder is formally and certainly evidence of irresponsibility is the faculty of knowing or judging.' On the matter of delusions and their relationship to criminal acts he quoted Sir James Stephen with apparent approval. Stephen wrote, 'It undoubtedly is, and I think it is equally clear that it ought to be, the law, that the mere existence of an insane delusion which does not, in fact, influence particular parts of the person affected by it, has no effect upon their legal character.' This is a repetition of the doctrine of partial insanity; for however remote the delusion may appear to be from the criminal act nobody can be certain that the man's evident insanity did not play a part in the committing of the act whether or not the delusion is specifically relevant.

Between 1894–96 Dr. Mercier acted as secretary of a committee of the Medico-Psychological Association to consider the matter of criminal responsibility. In this report it is stated[2] that 'Judges of the highest eminence have greatly doubted the constitutional propriety of putting abstract questions of that kind to the Judges, and of getting such answers from them' (the committee are referring to the M'Naghten Rules). They go on to say: 'In the words of one eminent Judge: "The terms of those answers are not incapable of being so interpreted as to do terrible injustice." And in those of another eminent Judge: "The law with respect to the responsibility of criminal lunatics seemed to him in a very unsatisfactory state, and in saying this he had not spoken only his own views upon the matter, because more than one of the Judges had expressed the desire that the subject should be reviewed."' Despite

[1] Mercier, C. (1905). *Criminal Responsibility*, p. 103. Oxford; Clarendon Press
[2] Royal Commission on Capital Punishment (1949–53), p. 403

these comments from the Bench the committee felt unable to make any recommendations for amendment of the law. Not surprisingly, as Dr. Mercier wrote: 'The report met with very great opposition from members of the Association.'

From the purely psychiatric point of view the criticisms of the Rules have concentrated on the wording and meaning of that part of the Rules usually quoted in courts of law. Less is heard about the doctrine of partial insanity than was the case in the last century mainly, one presumes, because most psychiatrists have never heard of it, or, if they have, pay no attention to it as it has no place in current psychiatric theory. As was indicated in the last chapter, there is reason to believe that legal thinking still accepts this doctrine. In the twenty-first edition of *Stephen's Commentaries* one reads the following passage.[1]

'The prisoner may be partially insane. He may retain his sanity as a general condition, but suffer from some particular delusion as to the surrounding facts, which prevents his apprehension of the true nature of his act. In such circumstances his liability will depend upon the character of the delusion. He is to be considered in the same situation as to responsibility as if the facts with respect to which the delusion exists were real. If, for example, under its influence he supposes another man to be attempting his life and he kills that man, as he imagines in self-defence, he is exempt from liability; but if his delusion is that the deceased has injured his character, and he kills him in revenge for the supposed injury, he will be liable.' This passage, in short, accepts without question the fourth answer in the M'Naghten case and, presumably, is approved by the editor of the 1950 edition of the book.

Dr. Glanville Williams argued[2] against the existence of partial insanity. The legal fiction that a man—insane and deluded—must be wholly so to be held irresponsible does not square with knowledge and experience. In any case, how can one know for certain what goes on in the mind of an insane person at the time of the offence? As Lady Wootton said, it is a metaphysical question without answer.[3] Dr. Williams clearly agrees with Maudsley and Ray that madmen reason madly and concludes that 'partial delusions' do not exist.

Despite Dr. Williams' reasoning, which is consistent with modern psychiatric thought, there can be little doubt that the passage quoted from *Stephen's Commentaries* more frequently guides judicial thinking when cases of insanity are before the court. One recent divorce case[4] has

---

[1] (1950), Vol. IV, pp. 17, 18 (edited by W. H. D. Windsor). London; Butterworths
[2] Williams, G. (1961). *The Criminal Law*, Sect. 161 London; Stevens
[3] Wootton, B. (1960), L. Q. R., 76, 224
[4] Elphinstone *v.* Elphinstone (1962), *The Times*, May 4

already been discussed. A further case[1] shows how the Court of Appeal refused to reverse a decision of the lower court which had not granted a wife a decree of divorce against her husband who was said to be of incurably unsound mind and had been under treatment for 5 years. Prior to the proceedings the husband had discharged himself from hospital, had returned to his home but lived separately from his wife, and was earning his living. On appeal Lord Justice Willmer remarked, 'A feature of the case which was completely novel was that the husband gave evidence himself. He emerged with credit from a searching cross-examination and his evidence was accepted by the commissioner as that of a truthful and credible witness.' The learned judge made this remark despite both the wife's evidence as to his delusional beliefs concerning her fidelity and the observations of Lord Justice Donovan: 'To make a touchstone out of demeanour in a case where a witness had a long history of mental unsoundness behind him would be a dangerous proceeding. On the same day that the husband had given evidence he had told the medical superintendent in the corridor outside the court that the wife's counsel might be having immoral relationships with the wife. The doctor's evidence was unchallenged. His Lordship respectfully dissented from the conclusion of the commissioner that there was no acceptable evidence of unsoundness of mind.' Despite this, Lord Justice Donovan went on to concur with Lord Justice Willmer on the point that 'it could not be said to have been proved that he (the husband) could not now lead a normal married life.' Clearly, the learned judges were more impressed by the reasoning of Lord Cockburn, C. J. in the case of Banks v. Goodfellow[2] than by that of Lord Brougham in Waring v. Waring 22 years earlier. But it will be recalled that Lord Cockburn had secured the discharge of M'Naghten by his advocacy of the concept of partial delusion, whereas Lord Brougham had insisted that no such symptom of mental illness existed. It could certainly be argued today that until this doctrine is firmly eradicated from legal thinking cases of injustice will persist.

Some consideration has already been given to the words 'defect of reason from disease of the mind'. It should no longer be necessary to labour the point that psychosis is not to be equated with defect of intelligence, judgment and discrimination, which symptoms are more usual in cases of dementia, subnormality, or, in some instances, toxic-confusional states due to organic disorder of the brain, whether transient or permanent. It is perfectly clear that a person suffering from a paranoid psychosis is able to reason correctly on many matters, as Lord Justice Willmer discovered in the case just quoted. It is not a

[1] Webb v. Webb (1962), *The Times*, May 21   [2] (1870), 5 Q. B. 549

new discovery; for it is related that Erskine[1] recounted an anecdote told to him by Lord Mansfield concerning a patient called Wood who brought Dr. Munro to court for wrongful detention in an asylum. All efforts of the defendant's counsel to expose the plaintiff's insanity were of no avail until Dr. Battye who happened to be in court asked Wood what had become of the princess with whom he had corresponded in cherry-juice. Whereupon Wood complained that being deprived of ordinary writing materials he was compelled to write with this substance, that he threw the message into the river surrounding a high tower in which he was imprisoned and that the princess received the letters in her boat. Needless to say, there existed neither princess, cherry-juice, tower nor river and the case was dismissed despite the previous demonstration by the plaintiff of apparent normality.

It follows that, unless the offender is in an acute confusional state, demented or in a state of automatism, he can and does know the quality of his act, by which, as has been shown, is meant the physical quality of the act. It is possible for a severely subnormal person to inflict a severe injury on another person without appreciating the likely consequences, and it could be argued that lack of knowledge of the results of such an injury cannot be equated with a full knowledge of the physical facts.

The great majority of offenders in the cases so far quoted clearly knew the nature and quality of their act. Hadfield shot at the King in order to kill him so that he himself might be hanged, and M'Naghten shot Mr. Drummond to put a stop to the persecutions to which he felt he was subjected by the Tory party. Did they know that it was wrong? In the sense that they knew that murder in general was wrong there can be little doubt again that both these men were fully aware of this fact. This, of course, made little difference to their feelings about the criminal act itself, and it has been ruled that a knowledge of the law in abstract is of no concern to the court. What matters is whether or not the accused believed the offence for which they were being tried was wrong. It cannot be said too often that knowledge must imply a full appreciation of the consequences of an action, the ability to choose between alternative courses of action, and the capacity to feel the appropriate emotion when considering whether or not to commit a criminal offence.

The loss of this appropriate feeling being one of the chief features of many schizophrenic illnesses, it follows that a person so affected might well carry out a brutal or murderous act without any apparent show of feelings whatsoever. It is very hard to believe that a person like Rivett,[2] a diagnosed schizophrenic who strangled a girl for no

---

[1] Lord Erskine in R. *v.* Hadfield (1800), 27 State Tr. 1281
[2] R. *v.* Rivett (1960), 34 Cr. App. Rep. 87

obvious reason and then gave himself up to the police, had the feelings which would enable him to appreciate properly the enormity of his act. Despite this he was found guilty and sentenced to death, a verdict which was upheld by the Court of Criminal Appeal.

The M'Naghten Rules with their insistence, it would appear, on what Dr. Glanville Williams refers to as a phonograph theory of knowledge, make no allowance for this well-known psychiatric symptom. It seems that knowing an act to be wrong is one type of experience to a normal person but a very different matter to those who are mentally ill. For not only may the appropriate affective component of knowledge be absent but, as Maudsley indicated, such a person may well feel himself to be above the law, or that his act was justified solely on the grounds that he was redressing an injury which his psychosis had induced him to believe had occurred. In such a person it is highly unlikely that, at the time of the offence, he was swayed by the ordinary considerations of morality or legal right and wrong which would influence a more normal man. Questioned later he may admit that his act was wrong, but then go on to justify it. In any case he may well have an inappropriate affective response to the act which should make it clear to the investigator that he really has no true knowledge of the wrongness of his offence. Perhaps the jurist should say the last word on the matter.

Professor Hart writes,[1] 'Another factor making for concentration on cognitive elements in responsibility is the survival of the belief, in spite of psychological doctrines to the contrary, that if a man knows what he is doing, it must be true that he has a capacity to adjust his behaviour to the requirements of the law.' More will be said about this legal belief in the next chapter for there is abundant evidence to show that it is incorrect largely because the mentally ill do not apply the ordinary processes of reason to facts involved in mental disturbance.

The insistence by the Rules that the accused should be suffering from a disease of the mind has also led to difficulty. As Mr. Justice Blackburn said in 1874,[2] there is an insuperable difficulty in devising a satisfactory definition of insanity. The Royal Commission on Capital Punishment equated disease of the mind with the major organic and functional psychoses but admitted that not all psychiatrists would accept this. Certainly it excludes all the neuroses, addictions and character disorders which must, on occasion, have a very real bearing upon the conduct of a criminal offender, lessening his self-control just as is the case with the mentally subnormal who also appear to be excluded from the ranks of those suffering from a disease of the mind. One of the difficulties

---

[1] Hart, H. L. A. (1961). *Punishment and the Elimination of Responsibility*, p. 22. London; Athlone Press
[2] Royal Commission on Capital Punishment (1949–53), p. 401

about this term is the possibility of an indefinite period of detention in Broadmoor Hospital for those found guilty but insane due to disease of the mind; and nobody wishes to send hysterical persons or psychopathic persons to a hospital for the insane criminal, even though it could well be argued that such persons are suffering from diseases of the mind. It is possible that the opening of the special hospital for certain classes of mentally disordered persons at Grendon Underwood will, to some extent, resolve this difficulty in the future.

Finally, the M'Naghten Rules make no provision for those who carry out criminal acts under the influence of an irresistible impulse. It is one of the curiosities of the law—to the layman, at least—that although the Rules have no statutory backing, and although there are a number of precedents which would admit irresistible impulse as an exculpating factor, including Oxford's case,[1] ever since the Rules were formulated the courts have refused to accept the plea. There can be little doubt that some serious crimes do occur because of overwhelming and irresistible impulses arising in the minds of the insane. Granted that it is not always easy to distinguish between such an irresistible impulse and one which is not resisted, it would appear that the interpretation of the Rules which refuses to consider the matter cannot make for sound justice.

If Sir James Stephen—not a man given to excess tenderness of feeling towards offenders—could find a place in his Homicide Law Amendment Bill for a plea that a man rendered incapable by disease of the mind from controlling his own conduct should be excused, then one might expect that, as psychiatric knowledge has grown in the past 100 years, such a plea would have become more acceptable and understood. Admittedly Stephen thought that the Rules could be interpreted to include this condition; but subsequent events and rulings have shown him to be wrong.

Two enactments, the Trial of Lunatics Act, 1883, and the Criminal Lunatics Act, 1884, both have some bearing on the management and disposal of those whose criminal acts have been considered within the framework of the M'Naghten Rules. In 1882 an insane man named Roderick Maclean fired a pistol at Queen Victoria at Windsor railway station. He was found not guilty on the grounds of his insanity and sent to Broadmoor. Her Majesty was most indignant at the verdict. 'Insane he may have been', she is reported to have said, 'but not guilty he most certainly was not as I saw him fire the pistol myself.' Mr. Gladstone bowed to the storm. Hence the special verdict under the Act of 1883.[2] The Act repealed section 1 of the Criminal Lunatics Act, 1800, which

---

[1] *See* Archbold's *Criminal Pleading*, 35th ed., pp. 17, 18. London; Sweet and Maxwell

[2] Partridge, R. (1953). *Broadmoor*. London; Chatto and Windus

had required the jury to return a verdict of not guilty on the grounds of insanity, substituting instead that 'the jury shall return a special verdict to the effect that the accused was guilty of the act or omission charged against him, but was insane as aforesaid at the time when he did the act or made the omission.' Section 2 (2) of the Act provides 'Where such special verdict is found, the Court shall order the accused to be kept in custody as a criminal lunatic—(the last four words have been repealed by the Mental Health Act, 1959)—in such place and in such manner as the Court shall direct till Her Majesty's pleasure shall be known; and it shall be lawful for Her Majesty, thereupon, and from time to time, to give such order for the safe custody of the said person during pleasure, in such place and in such manner as to Her Majesty may seem fit'.

It has been held that there can be no appeal against this verdict for in the case of Felstead v. R[1] the House of Lords refused to entertain an appeal against the finding of insanity. It was argued by the defence that the accused had been found guilty but had been excused on the ground of his insanity. Lord Reading stated that the special verdict under the Statute was one and indivisible and in fact amounted to an acquital. There could, therefore, be no appeal because the appellant was not a 'convicted person'. This ruling was re-affirmed in 1961[2] and in 1962[3].

The Criminal Lunatics Act, 1884, section 2 (4) provided[4] that 'In the case of a prisoner under sentence of death, if it appears to a Secretary of State, either by means of a certificate signed by two members of the visiting committee of the prison in which such prisoner is confined or by any other means, that there is reason to believe such prisoner to be insane, the Secretary of State shall appoint two or more legally qualified medical practitioners, and the said medical practitioners shall forthwith examine such prisoner and inquire as to his insanity, and after such examination and inquiry, such practitioners shall make a report in writing to the Secretary of State as to the sanity of the prisoner, and they, or the majority of them, may certify in writing that he is insane.'

According to the Royal Commission on Capital Punishment,[5] between the years 1900–1949, 192 such inquiries have been held, resulting in the issue of certificates of insanity in 48 cases and reprieve, wholly or partly on the grounds of the mental condition of the prisoner, in a further 37 cases.

There can be no doubt that if there is reason to question the sanity

[1] Felstead v. R., [1914] A. C. 534
[2] R. v. Duke, [1961] All E. R. 737
[3] R. v. Grant (1962). *The Times*, April 19
[4] Now repealed by the Mental Health Act, 1959; see p. 144, *post*.
[5] Royal Commission on Capital Punishment (1949–53), para. 360

of the prisoner the Secretary of State has a statutory obligation to inquire into the matter. The Royal Commission on Capital Punishment (para. 362) were told that it is now the practice to hold an inquiry whenever there is anything to suggest that the prisoner may have been insane or mentally abnormal at the time of the crime, or may have become insane since his conviction, and in particular, that if a plea of insanity is raised at the trial and rejected by the jury an inquiry is almost invariably held. Informal, non-statutory inquiries are also held whenever there are grounds for suspecting mental abnormality not amounting to insanity. In such cases a panel of medical practitioners, the majority of whom are serving in the Prison Medical Service, is convened with full access to all relevant documents in the case. They are not bound by any criterion of legal responsibility or by the M'Naghten Rules, and they can report to the Home Secretary giving their opinion whether any mental abnormality discovered has a bearing upon the crime. The Royal Commission felt that the consequence of these statutory and non-statutory inquiries was to ensure that no person who was definitely insane would now be executed.

There can be little doubt that the Act of 1884 influenced the recommendation of the Committee on Criminal Responsibility of the Medico-Psychological Association and to some extent it could be argued that the additional safeguards described above make revision or abrogation of the M'Naghten Rules superfluous. However, as was pointed out in forceful terms by Lord Goddard, C. J., the absence of formal rules binding the medical panel who examine the prisoner appears to mean that a verdict found in open court by a judge and jury bound by the M'Naghten Rules and the formal rules of evidence can be reversed on the opinion of two or more doctors who find the prisoner to be insane. Lord Goddard argued that, 'If there has passed a verdict which amounts to a finding that the prisoner was both sane at the time of the crime and at the time of the trial, unless there is a change in his mental condition after conviction, a finding by a medical Commission that he is insane, meaning that he was insane at the time of the commission of the crime, is a flat reversal of the verdict of the jury. . . . The use to which this sub-section appears now to be put is to substitute for the verdict returned in open Court after trial and argument and direction by the Judge the opinion of two or more doctors, arrived at after a private inquiry without any of the publicity which is the life-blood of justice and when it would be possible for them to apply any preconceived standards of their own, which might be contrary not only to the law of the land but also to the opinions of other members of their profession.'[1]

[1] Royal Commission on Capital Punishment (1949–53), para. 365

Lord Goddard seemed to have been under a misapprehension for, as the Royal Commission pointed out, statutory medical inquiries are concerned with the state of mind of the prisoner at the time of examination, and although they may express opinions about the possible state of mind of the prisoner at the time of the crime it is clear that their duty is to discover whether or not he is sane or insane, by medical criteria, at the time of examination after conviction. It follows that insane persons who have been convicted because their insanity did not fulfil the legal requirements under the M'Naghten Rules will have their sentence commuted because it is contrary to common law to execute an insane person. The fact that legal and medical requirements for evidence of insanity are not identical will surprise nobody who has studied the arguments between the two professions over the M'Naghten Rules.

Following the case of True,[1] which caused a great deal of public concern, the Lord Chancellor appointed a committee under the chairmanship of Lord Atkin to consider the law relating to insanity and crime and the working of the Criminal Lunatics Act, 1884. The committee took evidence from the British Medical Association and from the Royal Medico-Psychological Association, finally reporting in 1923.[2] In their evidence the latter Association made the following comments.

(1) The legal criteria of responsibility expressed in the rules in M'Naghten's case should be abrogated and the responsibility of a prisoner should be left as a question of fact to be determined by the jury on the merits of a particular case.

(2) In every trial in which the prisoner's mental condition is an issue the judge should direct the jury to answer the following questions: (*a*) Did the prisoner commit the act alleged? (*b*) If he did, was he at the time insane? (*c*) If he was insane, has it nevertheless been proved to the satisfaction of the jury that the crime was unrelated to the mental disorder?

The Royal Medico-Psychological Association also commented on the question of fitness to plead, pointing out that in rare instances an insane man, innocent of the crime with which he is charged, is debarred from proving his innocence which might avoid his being sent to Broadmoor for an indefinite period. They suggested that if found unfit to plead a formal plea of 'not guilty' should be entered, and that the trial should proceed with or without the presence of the prisoner. The Association went on to suggest that the special verdict under the Trial of Lunatics Act, 1883 should rank as a conviction with right to appeal to the Court of Criminal Appeal. They also suggested that a panel of medical assessors should be appointed to the courts with the duty of examining prisoners and reporting to the courts on their mental state.

[1] R. *v.* True (1922), 16 Cr. App. Rep. 164
[2] Committee on Insanity and Crime (1923), Cmd. 2005

46

They did not make any recommendations concerning the 1884 Act, but they gave full reasons for their objections to the M'Naghten Rules as follows. 'We take particular exception to the precise tests of responsibility laid down in the following words:' They go on to quote the M'Naghten Rules and continue. 'These rules are not wrong in holding that irresponsibility is only an inference that may or may not be drawn from insanity; where they err is in attempting to define precisely the conditions under which the inference is legitimate. They identify responsibility with knowing and reasoning. . . . Unsoundness of mind is no longer regarded as, in essence, a disorder of the intellectual faculties. The modern view is that it is something much more profoundly related to the whole organism—a morbid change in the emotional and instinctive activities with or without intellectual derangement.' The memorandum also re-affirmed their belief that all insane delusions were indicative and symptomatic of general unsoundness of mind, clearly implying that they had no use for the theory of partial insanity.

The British Medical Association submitted a memorandum in which, among other recommendations, they advised that, 'No act is a crime if the person who does it is, at the time it is done, prevented either by defective mental power or by any disease affecting the mind: (1) from either knowing or appreciating the nature or quality of his act or the circumstances in which it is done; or (2) from either knowing or appreciating that the act is wrong; or (3) from controlling his own conduct unless the absence of the power is the direct and immediate consequence of his own default.'

By 'wrong' the Association meant either morally or legally wrong. It will be observed that the British Medical Association recommendations follow closely those of Sir James Stephen as set out in his *History of the Criminal Law* and later proposed in his Homicide Law Amendment Bill. Both Stephen and the British Medical Association wished to include the concept of irresistible impulse as a mitigating plea while the Royal Medico-Psychological Association wished to go further by abrogating the Rules completely, leaving it to the jury to find whether the prisoner was insane at the time of the alleged crime and whether his insanity had any bearing upon the criminal act in question.

After studying the memoranda the Atkin Committee recommended the following.

(1) It should be recognized that a person charged criminally with an offence is irresponsible for his act when the act is committed under an impulse which the prisoner was by mental disease in substance deprived of any power to resist. It may require legislation to bring this rule into effect.

47

(2) Save as above the Rules in M'Naghten's case should be maintained.

(3) When a person is found to be irresponsible on the ground of insanity the verdict should be that the accused did the act charged but is not guilty on the ground that he was insane so as not to be responsible at the time.

The Committee also recommended that accused persons should not be found on arraignment unfit to plead except on the evidence of at least two doctors save in very clear cases. They did not agree with the Royal Medico-Psychological Association over the question of appeal. A special verdict or a finding of insanity on arraignment or after trial should be the end of the case. They felt that an accused person should be examined under departmental regulations at the request of the defence, the prosecution or the committing magistrate, but they did not feel that there was any need for a special panel of medical experts to advise the courts.

On the M'Naghten Rules they commented, 'The Royal Medico-Psychological Association appear to assume that the Rules contain a definition of insanity and that the legal definition thus obtained is contrasted with the medical conception of insanity'. They went on to indicate that opinions on insanity had changed since 1843 but felt that the judges did not intend to frame a definition of 'disease of the mind' but only to define what degree of disease of the mind negatived criminality; in short, was *mens rea* present?

It is worth noting that the Atkin Committee was composed of distinguished lawyers and civil servants. Despite this, and the known aversion on the part of the judges to the recognition of irresistible impulse, they recommended that this plea should be incorporated into the M'Naghten Rules, for in their review of this subject they were satisfied that uncontrollable impulse exists as a manifestation of insanity.

No action was taken by the Government after the presentation of the report, but in 1924 Lord Darling introduced his Criminal Responsibility (Trials) Bill into the House of Lords whereby he sought to implement the recommendations of the Atkin Committee. In the debate he said, 'My reason for bringing in this Bill is that there has long been a contest between the medical specialists and the law. These medical specialists have contended, and still contend, that directly they say that a person is insane in their sense he shall be absolutely unpunishable, no matter what crime he may have committed. Some of them call themselves determinists; some of them contend that we are merely automatic creatures who act with no control whatever over our motives or our actions. The law of England never recognized that and I hope never will.'[1]

[1] Quoted by Robinson, E. (1947). *Just Murder*. London; Lincolns Prager

Despite this disavowal of determinism and the more extreme views of some psychiatrists, Lord Darling's Bill met with no success. The old arguments as to whether an impulse is irresistible or merely not resisted were once again put forward. It was feared that to accept medical evidence on the matter would transfer the decision as to the guilt of the accused from the jury to the doctors who gave the evidence of overwhelming impulse at the time of the crime. The Lord Chief Justice, Lord Hewart, said that he had consulted twelve to fifteen judges of the King's Bench Division and that ten of them had agreed with him that they emphatically opposed the Bill. Despite much evidence to the contrary it was contended that the Rules were sufficiently flexible to allow a verdict of 'guilty but insane' to be found in those cases of irresistible impulse where this was justified. The Lords appeared to be satisfied that when the court had returned a verdict of guilty the Home Secretary would, as empowered by the 1884 Act, correct any errors which such a verdict entailed when an insane man was sentenced to death. This may well be so but it is strange reasoning which permits a miscarriage of justice at the trial rather than accept an amendment to the law which would make such errors less likely. Perhaps the general tenor of the debate can be epitomized in the words of the Lord Chancellor, Lord Haldane. 'I do not speak as an authority on these matters but I have given some attention to the subject of psychology. Any more vague science in which vague terms can so readily be made to do duty for clear conceptions I do not know. It is a most dangerous science to apply to practical affairs.'[1]

A Select Committee on Capital Punishment in 1931[2] made a conditional recommendation that the M'Naghten Rules on the subject of insanity should be revised so as to give fuller scope to general medical considerations, and to extend the area of criminal irresponsibility in the case of the mentally defective and of those who labour under some distinct form of insanity. They had noted in their report that to exonerate the epileptic it had been necessary to show that he was suffering from an epileptic seizure at the time when he committed murder. They also indicated that the courts under the Mental Deficiency Acts can order detention in hospital except in capital cases. The Home Secretary had answered in the House that there had been no case of reprieve solely on the grounds of being mentally defective, although other factors beyond this could be taken into account.

As with the Atkin Committee Report no action was taken by the Government and there the matter rested until the Royal Commission

---

[1] Quoted by Robinson, E. (1947). *Just Murder*. London; Lincolns Prager
[2] Select Committee on Capital Punishment (1931), pp. 275–6

on Capital Punishment, 1949–53, raised the matter once more in a manner so authoritative as to make further inaction scarcely possible.

There can be little doubt that the Committee's report with its comprehensive review of all matters relating to the law of criminal insanity makes earlier writings and reports appear superficial by comparison. The whole history of the controversy concerning the M'Naghten Rules is traced from their formulation to present times. The evidence presented in their favour and against them is thoroughly examined in a manner so compelling as to make it difficult to disagree with the majority recommendation that the Rules should be abrogated. The main conclusions relating to criminal responsibility are summarized as follows.

(1) It has been recognized for centuries that if a person, at the time of committing an unlawful act, was mentally so disordered that it would be unreasonable to impute guilt to him, he ought not to be held liable to conviction and punishment under the criminal law. We assume the continuation of this ancient and humane principle.

(2) Any test of criminal responsibility must take account of the fact that, where a grave crime is committed by a person who is so grossly disordered mentally that he could properly be certified as insane, the presumption that the crime was wholly or largely caused by the insanity is, in ordinary circumstances, overwhelmingly strong, and there is an equally strong presumption in the case of the grosser forms of mental deficiency and of certain epileptic conditions.

(3) We consider (with one dissentient) that the test of responsibility laid down in England by the M'Naghten Rules is so defective that the law on the subject ought to be changed.

(4) If an alteration were to be made by extending the scope of the Rules, we suggest that a formula on the following lines should be adopted. The jury must be satisfied that at the time of committing the act, the accused, as a result of disease of the mind or mental deficiency, did not know the nature and quality of the act, did not know that it was wrong, or was incapable of preventing himself from committing it. Although this formula might not prove wholly satisfactory, we consider (with one dissentient) that it would be better to amend the Rules in this way than to leave them as they are.

We consider (with three dissentients) that a preferable amendment of the law would be to abrogate the M'Naghten Rules and leave the jury to determine whether at the time of the act the accused was suffering from disease of the mind or mental deficiency to such a degree that he ought not to be held responsible. (The three dissenting members felt that it would be preferable to maintain the Rules with the amendment given in the preceding paragraph.)

The Royal Commission made further recommendations on the law in Scotland, on the tests of insanity on arraignment and on diminished responsibility. Some of these matters will be discussed in later chapters. During the debates that have proceeded over the meaning and interpretation of the M'Naghten Rules a number of conflicting attitudes on the part of the protagonists have become apparent. Broadly speaking, it would probably be correct to say that whereas the judiciary are content to preserve the Rules and interpret them as they think fit, few medical men concerned with psychiatric evidence in court, or with mental medicine generally, have been able to see much good in the Rules. To them they are wholly out of touch with modern psychiatric thought and practice.

By now it should be clear to both sides that the Rules do not set out to define insanity as such but attempt to set limits to the type of behaviour which can properly be regarded as exonerating the offender on the grounds of his mental state. Unfortunately, at the time when the Rules were drawn up, the judges appear to have believed in the doctrine of partial insanity, and that insane delusions were purely a symptom of intellectual derangement. Consequently, the wording of the Rules was based on an incorrect understanding of mental illness and only by stretching the meaning of the words can they be made to fit into current psychiatric concepts. In such circumstances there is a possibility that injustice will be done and, even if it is correct that this has rarely occurred, the words of Mr. Justice Frankfurter on the subject are worth repeating.[1]

'The M'Naghten Rules were rules which the Judges, in response to questions by the House of Lords, formulated in the light of the then existing psychological knowledge. . . . I do not see why the rules of law should be arrested at the state of psychological knowledge of the time when they were formulated. . . . If you find rules that are, broadly speaking, discredited by those who have to administer them, which is, I think, the real situation, certainly with us—they are honoured in the breach and not in the observance—then I think the law serves its best interests by trying to be more honest about it. . . . I think that to have rules which cannot rationally be justified except by a process of interpretation which distorts and often practically nullifies them, and to say the corrective process comes by having the Governor of a State charged with the responsibility of deciding when the consequences of the rule should not be enforced, is not a desirable system. . . . I am a great believer in being as candid as possible about my institutions. They are in large measure abandoned in practice, and therefore I think the M'Naghten Rules are in large measure shams. That is a strong

[1] Royal Commission on Capital Punishment (1949–53), para. 290

51

word, but I think the M'Naghten Rules are very difficult for conscientious persons and not difficult enough for people who say "We'll just juggle them". . . . I dare to believe that we ought not to rest content with the difficulty of finding an improvement in the M'Naghten Rules.'

If, as seems clear, the intellectual basis of the Rules is discredited then the recognition that emotional disturbances lie in many instances behind a given criminal offence, should be acknowledged in law. This means that the plea of irresistible impulse will have to be accepted, and it is plain from the controversy over the past 120 years that the judges are still far from willing to allow this plea in serious charges. So far, the recommendation that the Rules should be amended along the lines suggested by Stephen, the Atkin Committee and the Royal Commission on Capital Punishment has not been acted upon. Although this recommendation may not be ideal it is likely that it would be more acceptable to most jurists as well as doctors than the alternative suggestion that the Rules should be abolished, leaving it to the jury to decide whether the accused was insane at the time of the alleged offence and whether his insanity was the whole or partial cause of his act.

It is often said that to leave such a decision to the jury would be to lay upon them a responsibility which it would be unreasonable to ask them to bear. Hence, it is better that there should be rigid rules to guide their deliberations. It would seem that these fears underestimate the corporate responsibility and robustness of juries. In any case, it is probable that the Rules only act as a guide in those cases where there is considerable doubt about the correct decision. For, as Lord Cooper said, when asked whether it was not desirable to have some yardstick to guide the jury; 'I do not think so, for this reason . . . . However much you charge a jury as to the M'Naghten Rules or any other test, the question they would put to themselves when they retire is—Is the man mad or is he not?' The Royal Commission on Capital Punishment had little doubt that most English juries do the same.[1]

In Hadfield's case[2] it has been noted that the evidence of insanity at the time of his offence was sufficient to cause Lord Kenyon to stop the trial and direct the jury as to the law and the proper verdict in such cases. The Royal Commission on Capital Punishment felt that evidence of certifiable insanity, severe mental defect and certain types of epilepsy should lead to a very strong presumption that the crime was wholly or largely due to these factors. No doubt in many cases this is so, but a case such as Rivett's hardly leads one to place too much reliance on the exonerating quality of unchallenged medical evidence of insanity at the time when the crime was committed. It will readily be agreed that

[1] Royal Commission on Capital Punishment (1949–53), para. 322
[2] (1800), 27 State Tr. 1281

there is great difficulty in trying to discover what is going on in the mind of a man when he commits a serious crime. Judges and juries are faced every day with equally complex problems which makes it scarcely justifiable to argue that they are incapable of resolving this particular difficulty when it confronts them.

There appears to be little doubt that responsible medical opinion is in favour of leaving the matter of insanity to be determined by a jury, but if there have to be rigid rules it would be as well that they should be given statutory expression. At the same time they should be framed in such a manner as to give the fullest possible recognition to generally accepted psychiatric principles and knowledge. And if such knowledge is to be applied properly it is essential that the court should be empowered to obtain the maximum of information about the prisoner's mental state both at the time of the offence and subsequently. This means that any reports made to the court should be tested by questioning in open court and that the medical witness should be permitted to give a full and understandable account of his reasons for the evidence he has submitted. By doing this it is likely that the court will derive a fairer impression of the nature of the prisoner's mental condition while, at the same time, it will do away with the yes–no type of question and answer which makes a mockery of expert evidence leading, at the best, to partial truth.

5—Mens Rea, Determinism, Free Will and Responsibility

It would be beyond the scope of this essay and the competence of its author to attempt to resolve the ancient controversies which have persisted for some two thousand years over such subjects as determinism, free will, the mind–body problem and their relationship to responsibility in law and ethics. Many acute and subtle minds have devoted their time to the fullest possible discussion of these matters without satisfactory conclusions being reached.

No doubt in some cases the difficulties are more apparent than real, difficulties brought about by the misuse of language or the posing of the wrong questions. Be that as it may, there can be no possibility of a settlement of the difficulties in this essay; for to do so would require another and larger book; and in any case, for the purposes of this thesis, it is hardly necessary to make the attempt.

What is of greater importance is the examination of some of the metaphysical foundations of law and psychiatry in the hope that, by so doing, it will be possible to focus on the very real differences between them in order to understand how two professions who set out to reach conclusions about a piece of human behaviour can, in many instances, achieve diametrically opposite results. It may well be that some of these differences are not so desperate as might at first appear; for few doctors spend much time examining the basic tenets of their practice; and, with all respect, it is doubtful whether lawyers and jurists have any greater enthusiasm for metaphysics than have doctors. It follows that both professions might well be at cross-purposes on occasions, partly because they have failed to appreciate the logical position of the other side, partly because they have failed to clarify their own standpoint. It is the purpose of this chapter to try to examine some of the legal and psychiatric doctrines which appear to cause so much controversy. For unless these doctrines are made more explicit to both parties it is improbable that any agreement will be reached on how to deal with the practical problems presented every day in the courts: how best to treat the mentally ill offender.

Mens Rea

In English Law it is assumed that all persons are of sound mind and responsible for their actions unless it can be shown that there is sufficient mental abnormality to exonerate them from responsibility.

Should he commit acts or omissions contrary to the law he is liable to punishment or to make restitution unless it can be shown that certain special circumstances were operative at the time of the offence which either exonerate him completely or diminish the degree of responsibility. As Professor Hart wrote:[1] 'For some centuries, English law, like most civilized legal systems, has made liability to punishment for serious crime depend, not only on the accused doing the outward acts which the law forbids, but on his having done them in certain conditions which may broadly be termed mental. These mental conditions of responsibility are commonly, though rather misleadingly, referred to by lawyers as *mens rea.*' Professor Hart sets out these special conditions under the headings of mistake, accident, provocation, duress and insanity.

It follows that if a crime is committed, evidence to show that it was committed unintentionally, in error, through provocation or compulsion on the part of another, or while the offender was insane so as not to know the nature or wrongness of his act, he will be excused wholly or in part the legal consequences of his act. It is held that before a person can be adjudged guilty he must have shown some degree of moral turpitude and criminal intent. He must have foreseen and intended the consequences of his act; it must have been carried out wilfully and maliciously in the full knowledge that it was both legally and morally wrong. Whatever the precise meaning of the term *mens rea* may be it would seem to embrace these mental qualities in the alleged offender. It is also held that had he chosen to do so he could have refrained from carrying out the criminal act. It is an argument that presumes the freedom of moral choice and that our actions are not governed by an iron determinism from which we cannot escape.

Jurists may well cavil at this somewhat brief and, possibly, inaccurate treatment of the concept of *mens rea* but it appears to include the main propositions from which follows the presumption that all normal persons are responsible for their actions unless they can show good reason why this is untrue for the particular act of which they are accused. It also follows that in a given situation any person is able to exercise a free choice governing his actions which will enable him to conform with the usual legal and social requirements of behaviour. This may well sound reasonable enough to most persons, but closer examination of the propositions indicates that much can depend on the meaning to be attached to the concepts of free will and responsibility; for they are concepts which appear to have one sort of meaning to the psychologist and another sort of meaning to the jurist or to the layman.

[1] Hart, H. L. A. (1961). *Punishment and the Elimination of Responsibility,* p. 20. London; Athlone Press

Free Will and Responsibility

Psychology and psychiatry like to regard themselves as branches of the biological sciences. It is natural, therefore, that they should seek laws governing behaviour enabling a practitioner to deduce causes and to predict events based on observations of the individual's actions and utterances. As the psychiatrist is concerned with the problem of mental illness he wishes to be able to discover causes of symptoms so that he can institute measures which will lead to their cure or amelioration. To the best of his ability he will use scientific methods in his examination and analysis of the phenomena with which he is presented. Given certain circumstances he will assume that certain previously observed events will recur in a manner which will lead him to say that the preceding events caused the breakdown; and that the breakdown would not have happened had those preceding circumstances been different. It will be agreed that in many cases it is not possible to know all the factors leading to mental illness, but the search for all the facts will be pushed as far as possible in the spirit of a scientific determinism which presupposes that a full knowledge of the facts in a given case will enable accurate predictions to be made and appropriate remedies applied. In the words of Dr. Eliot Slater, 'No theory of mental medicine could develop without the working hypothesis of determinism. . . . The free will on which law and religion are based proves an heuristically sterile idea.'[1]

Not all psychiatrists will adhere so firmly to the determinist hypothesis as Dr. Slater but we undoubtedly look for causes of abnormal behaviour, feeling that there must be some explanation which a thorough search will reveal. An explanation does not, of course, give an exact and final cause of the piece of behaviour in question, for none of the biological sciences is sufficiently complete to do more than make tentative guesses to explain complex biological phenomena. We tend to fill in the gaps in our knowledge with current psychological theories admitting, if we are wise, that such theories are in no way absolute truths and that they may be displaced by other and more complete explanations as knowledge grows. It is worth bearing in mind that, so far, the argument has been considering abnormal behaviour with which the psychiatrist, in his role of physician, is primarily concerned. It is the assumption that deterministic mechanisms causing abnormal mental processes can equally well explain the behaviour of the sane and healthy person which can lead to much confusion of thought.

Let the argument be pressed a little more strongly; we can then put forward a case for the hypothesis that all our actions are governed by an absolute determinism which we are powerless to alter. Psycho-

[1] Slater, E. (1945). *Brit. med. J.* **2,** 713

analytic theory will point to the unconscious drives behind conscious actions. We have no knowledge of these impulses until we learn of them during treatment on the analyst's couch. We are what we are and we behave in the manner observed because of the early childhood experiences we have encountered and the inborn physical and mental constitution with which we have been endowed. It follows that even the most apparently rational of our actions occurs only because of the unconscious bias and drive which cause us to act as we do and to make us believe that we act freely. The point has been well put by Professor John Hospers.[1] 'The poor victim (the criminal) is not conscious of the inner forces that exact from him this ghastly toll; he battles, he schemes, he revels in pseudo-agression, he is miserable but he does not know what works within him to produce these catastrophic acts of crime. His aggressive actions are the wriggling of a worm on a fisherman's hook. And if this is so, it seems difficult to say any longer, "He is responsible". Rather, we shall put him behind bars for the protection of society, but we shall no longer flatter our feeling of moral superiority by calling him personally responsible for what he did.'

If these arguments are accepted it has to be admitted that our actions and utterances are due solely to our characters which have been formed, without much say in the matter on our part, during the early years of our development. If we have good moral characters this is due to our fortunate circumstances of careful upbringing, understanding parents with sound views on right and wrong, and the physical accidents of birth and social background. If we have criminal propensities, then again this is due to our characters having been warped and damaged by early childhood experiences, feckless or unloving parents and the deplorable social circumstances of our upbringing. These, perhaps, are extreme examples of two wholly disparate sets of conditions; most persons have experienced some degree of misfortune and mishandling during childhood without any obvious ill-effects. But assuming that the criminal has experienced a severe degree of frustration and unhappiness in childhood which has been mercifully absent from the life of the law-abiding citizen it is clearly as unreasonable to blame and punish the wrongdoer as it is to praise the moral rectitude of the man who obeys the law. The latter individual has merely been luckier than the former. No doubt the apportionment of blame and punishment has less urgency about it today than was the case in former times. As Professor Hart wrote,[2] 'One major reason then for querying the

---

[1] Hospers, J. (1958). 'What Means this Freedom?' In *Determinism and Freedom*, p. 20. New York; University Press

[2] Hart, H. L. A. (1961). *Punishment and the Elimination of Responsibility*, p. 23. London; Athlone Press

importance of the principle of responsibility is the belief that it only has a place if punishment is backward-looking and retributive in aim.' Society still does, through the courts and by private judgment, express condemnation in a manner which implies that to most persons the individual who is convicted and punished, is in some sense worthy of such treatment. It is no use arguing that the criminal act was solely the result of pre-ordained circumstances which the offender could not control. Determinism and fatalism have no place in courts of law nor, for that matter, in everyday assessments of behaviour. It would seem that whether it is right or wrong, the doctrine of psychological determinism is out of step with common-sense opinion which holds obstinately to the view that we are, in fact, free to make decisions in a manner which separates us from the automaton or the animal responding by reflex action to a conditioned stimulus.

Responsibility

For obvious reasons the arguments that have been advanced so far have little appeal to jurists. We are held to be capable of controlling our behaviour, to be able to perceive the differences between right and wrong, and to act in accordance with law and social obligations. In short, we are responsible persons able to exercise a free choice in ordinary circumstances when we are tempted to commit an offence. What, therefore, do we mean when we talk of responsibility and freedom? For it is clear that these two terms stand in opposition to the concept of determinism that has already been described.

Stephen wrote that the law uses the term 'responsible' to mean that a person is liable by law to be punished for the act which he has done.[1] The Royal Commission on Capital Punishment (para. 212) comment that doctors and laymen use the term in a somewhat different sense implying that it means a person ought to be punished whatever the existing law may be. Lady Wooton[2] gave three meanings, the first of which equates irresponsibility with bad social or criminal behaviour, implying that social deviants are irresponsible whereas social conformists are responsible. Her second definition means that to be responsible is to be responsive to the normal stimuli of reward and punishment, while the third definition equates irresponsibility with diminished power to resist temptation, which is more or less the same as saying that the affected person is exposed to the force of an irresistible impulse. She goes on to examine this proposition which she regards as a philosophical rather than a scientific statement. She quotes Henderson as saying that the psychopath in certain conditions can no more control his

[1] Stephen, J. F. (1883). *History of the Criminal Law*, Vol. 2, p. 127. London; Macmillan
[2] Wootton, B. (1960). 76 L. Q. R. 224

actions than a paranoiac can control his delusional beliefs but observes that such a proposition is incapable of proof. She continues, 'It may be that we are all fully responsible, at least within the limits of M'Naghten madness: it may be that none of us can help anything that he does; or it may be that responsibility varies from person to person and from time to time in the same person. But on these issues neither logic nor common sense, neither science nor philosophy, can give firm answers. Behaviour is observable: culpability, I submit, is not—unless, by God.' Perhaps this is what was meant by Prevezer[1] when he wrote, 'Responsibility is not a quality inherent in the accused but rather an attribute that is ascribed to him.'

Essential to the legal definition of responsibility is the idea that if you do something, knowing it to be wrong, you will also know that one of the consequences will be punishment. Punishment or the threat thereof is held to be one reason why persons keep within the law, but even if such a proposition was the whole truth—which it is not—it is surely a very narrow concept of human reasoning and behaviour. When we say that we are responsible for a given act we usually imply that we will accept the consequences if something goes wrong, but we also feel that the action and any possible results flowing from it are in a way our personal concern indicating some sort of moral relationship which imposes a sense of obligation. This is very far from the concept of psychological determinism which would absolve us all from any responsibility for our actions no matter how long they were premeditated. For, it is claimed, any action is merely the end-product of certain forces and instinctual urges within us which produce their effect whether or not we really wish them to do so. In short, psychological determinism requires a psychological dualism which is no less objectionable than the Cartesian dualism of mind and body. The psychologist is saying that we are not responsible because some part of our mind influences, in a manner unknown to us, another part of our mind to perform certain actions. If we do not know why we do what we do—the reasons we offer are held to have little bearing on the real reasons which are in any case beyond conscious awareness—then conscious processes are no more in control of our decisions than is the car in control of the direction which has been selected by its driver.

Lawyers, on the other hand, are no less adherents to dualism of the Cartesian kind which postulates an irreconcilable split between mind and body, but that, regardless of bodily function or dysfunction, the mind controls the body's behaviour, and somewhere above mind is a kind of special observer who decides whether or not a given act is

[1] Prevezer, S. (1961). *Current Legal Problems*, **14,** 16

legal or illegal, right or wrong, to which the mind, as it were, appeals or should appeal when decisions on these points are hard to settle. No doubt this is putting the two attitudes in a somewhat crude fashion; but just as lawyers appear to be convinced dualists of the Cartesian kind—it would need a lawyer to argue that a man suffering from arteriosclerotic dementia is suffering from a disease of the brain and not of the mind[1]—so psychologists are in some cases inferring a psychological dualism which would seek to excuse the offender of his actions on the ground that one part of his mind was under the influence of another part of which he was unaware. If this concept applies to all forms of human behaviour it is clear that none of us is in any way responsible for what we do, a conclusion which flies in the face of everyday experience and is repugnant to legal practice.

Mind–Body Relationships

Before proceeding further with this argument it might be as well to examine these dualistic concepts which clearly underlie much legal and psychiatric thinking. To the psychiatrist the human being is a psychosomatic entity and we have no need to invoke a doctrine of psycho-physical parallelism to guide our speculations about normal and abnormal mental processes. There is no essential and unbridgeable gap between the experience of a desire and the action that fulfils it. We know all too well that disturbance of brain function, whether by physical injury, the toxins of infections or drugs, or through acute emotional distress can cause profound changes in the individual's capacity for intellectual appreciation, emotional control and directed effort. We still describe mental phenomena under the classical categories of cognition, conation and affect. Yet we do not believe that the mind can really be divided up into separate compartments, each with differing functions; the mind and body are one continuum in which each part influences and is influenced by the whole; and just as we regard the three classical functions of mind as being differing aspects of a unity so we should regard any unconscious processes as also being a part of that unity and not in some way separate and different.

Because an unconscious mental process can only be inferred from the observation of conscious behaviour there is no necessity for such processes to be thought utterly distinct from conscious reasoning and action. It is certainly unlikely that conscious activity is ever wholly free from unconscious mechanisms relating to it, for introspection over our thought processes will often reveal aspects to our reasoning of which we were previously unaware. Such revelations may well make us cautious before accepting the reasons we give for our behaviour in a

[1] R. *v.* Kemp [1957], 1 Q. B. 399

given set of circumstances without some qualification. After all, it is one of the functions of psycho-analysis so to uncover the unconscious roots of action as to give us greater knowledge and control of such actions in the future. Yet in our introspective moments we do not conclude that what we learn about our motives is in some inexplicable manner wholly distinct from the ordinary thought processes of everyday life. Conscious and unconscious are in fact a continuum just as mind and body are a continuum which should leave no place for dualism of any kind.

Psychological unity rather than dualism might be easier to accept than the postulate of mind-body unity. Followers of Professor Gilbert Ryle[1] may have little difficulty in assenting to this proposition but most of us will agree that whatever is affirmed in the matter is not so persuasive as the conviction that what we think and what we do appear to belong to two different categories of experience. Possibly consideration of the processes of speech and writing will help us appreciate that thought and its expression in words are not separate processes. From this it can be inferred that thought or desire and actions which give expression to such desires are only different aspects of a unified process.

It is obvious that much of what we write and say is done after reflective thought. Nevertheless, as we write or speak there is no real gap between the thought and its expression. Both speaking and writing are essentially mechanical acts carried out by certain muscles behaving in a complex but co-ordinated manner. Yet the very acts of writing and speaking not only mirror the thoughts they express but in some way compel the form they take so that it becomes impossible to decide where, if it exists, the line between a thought and its expression should be drawn. The two phenomena are so closely interlinked that to separate them will only do violence to the essential unity of psycho-somatic phenomena which are typified by writing and speaking. The more fluent our writing and speech become, the more warmly we feel for the subject under discussion, the more difficult does it become to postulate two separate but interacting processes at work. Counsel for our defence, we hope, will spend time and care in the study of his brief. Yet when he comes to address the jury or to cross-examine a witness the warmth of his feelings for his client's case should lend wings to his words in a manner which may have been far from his thoughts in the quiet moments of reflection before the case is tried; and, indeed, it would be a poor advocate who needed to ponder between each thought and its utterance. I think it can be concluded that thought

[1] Ryle, G. (1949). *The Concept of Mind.* London; Hutchinson's Universal Library

and its expression are essentially one process which requires no psycho-somatic duality to explain it.

It follows that any psychological event must be accompanied by, but not caused by, some underlying neurophysiological event; equally psychological events can influence or disturb neurophysiological events. Neither of these phenomena are strangers to psychiatric practice for we have all seen acute psychosis caused by brain disease, and we have also seen—and experienced ourselves—the physical concomitants of fear and anxiety.

This somewhat dogmatic assertion that a psychological event must imply some electrochemical activity in the brain may not be accepted by all psychiatrists on the grounds that it is too mechanistic. In any case, no psychiatrist can state precisely what sort of neurophysiological changes are occurring, whether the psychological event is normal or apparently caused by disturbed cerebral metabolism. Not even in those cases where known physical changes in the brain are associated with mental illness can we say why the changes observed are the cause of the mental state of the patient. We infer that this is so but should acknowledge that although correction of a disturbance of metabolism or fever will lead to recovery, very considerable gaps in our knowledge concerning this process exist which at present we are in no position to fill in. In the functional psychoses and neuroses it is not possible, with present techniques, to delineate a physical or chemical change in the brain which correlates with the overt behavioural disturbances. Nevertheless, there is nothing inconsistent between the known facts and the inference that neurophysiological changes do occur in these mental disorders, however subtle and obscure these may be.

We use physical methods to bring about recovery and we also use psychological techniques such as persuasion and psychotherapy. That both psychological and physical methods of treatment appear to help the patient is precisely what we would expect if we postulate that mental functioning is based firmly on the neurophysiological activity of the central nervous system which is open to influence both by psychologically experienced events as well as by purely physical and chemical processes.

This digression into the subject of mind–body relationships has been necessary in order to try to demonstrate that human beings function as a unity. We can only infer what is going on in the mind of another person by observing his behaviour and noting his utterances. We correlate these observations with our own experiences and perceptions of our inner workings. Normally when we do something we say we do it because we want to, or because we hope to achieve some particular objective which is important to us. We do not say that we behave in a certain manner because our unconscious minds make us act as we do, and we do not explain an action by saying that our minds cause our bodies to carry out the action. We treat ourselves as units which admit no subdivisions when we come to talk about our own actions, thoughts and desires. It seems only reasonable to infer that others do likewise; and we certainly have no reason which can be deduced from our observations of others to suppose that, in fact, they do experience this split between conscious and unconscious sources of motive and between physical and mental causes of behaviour. It is not argued that that technical postulate, the unconscious mind, does not exist. Indeed, there is plenty of evidence to show that it does. What is being argued is that in normal states of health and in full consciousness we make deliberate choices. That unconscious factors enter into our decision is probably correct but the fully conscious man is aware of the differences between his impulses and his duty, and is capable of allowing for this fact when he decides whether to act as he believes he ought, or whether the instinctual needs of the moment should over-ride other claims.

We may well rationalize our giving way to an instinctual impulse by saying that in the circumstances we acted as we thought best, but if we are honest we all know perfectly well when an act is right or wrong by normal social and legal standards; that our emotional needs conflict with these standards is a commonplace of which we are all too well aware. It still remains a fact that in normal states of health and consciousness we can and do make deliberate choices which we have no particular wish to disown on the grounds that they were chosen for us by some unconscious *deus ex machina* over whom we have no control. We can conclude, therefore, that the legal presumption that all persons are of sound mind and fully responsible for their actions is a correct one, but it does apply only to adult persons, in sound mental and physical health; it needs to be shown how far the presumption is correct in the case of the mentally ill, using this term in the broadest possible sense and not in the narrow sense which equates mental illness or disease with insanity.

Emotion and Free Will

The emphasis placed on freedom of choice is important to this argument. If free will means anything beyond a metaphysical technicality it surely means that we have the power to deliberate freely over alternative courses of action in a manner which allows us, in the ordinary usage of language, to say that *we* chose to act as we did and that we were not the subjects of internal or external compulsion which over-rode all other considerations when it came to making up our minds. It follows that determinism implies that such decisions are not free in the manner just described but that we are subject to some inner compulsion which we are unable to alter or avoid.

It has been suggested that so far as the sane, healthy adult is concerned, although some of our actions might well be determined in this way, we can and do make free decisions, the freedom of which is likely to vary with the degree of emotional tension attendant upon the correctness of the decision. Whether free will and determinism mean more than this is immaterial to this discussion for it is evident that the disputes between lawyers and psychiatrists centre very largely on whether or not a given offender was free to choose his particular act which has brought him into court or whether he could not help it owing to some peculiarity of mental circumstance beforehand. The extreme opinions on this matter do not help us. It is argued that all mentally ill persons are incapable of making free choices because of their unconscious and neurotic impulses, and if all criminal behaviour is equated with mental illness, it follows that an offender is sick and not responsible for his actions. Naturally enough, this proposition has no more appeal to jurists than has to psychiatrists their more extreme claim that we are all fully responsible unless wholly deprived of our faculties. Such an assertion would mean that only total dementia or severe confusional states with disturbances of consciousness would absolve us, and it is clear that this is too limited a view of mental illness and responsibility. Perhaps a consideration of mental development and the effects of emotion upon intellectual processes might help resolve this difference.

It is one of the peculiarities of metaphysical debate that philosophers —chess-players to a man—appear to regard the world as composed of adults engaged in this most intellectual of pastimes. They appear to forget that the adult was once a child whose highest aim, possibly, was success at simpler games. They certainly ignore—what no psychiatrist can afford to do—the fact that minds develop from fairly simple origins and that the child's processes of thought and behaviour are not just those of an adult cut down to smaller proportions but are in many respects wholly different from adult mental mechanisms.

What is very evident to an observer of young children is the part played by impulse and emotion in determining their behaviour. To a considerable extent the child is very much at the mercy of the momentary impulse which may compel him to act in a particular way without thought of consequences. The ability to postpone immediate gratification of an instinctual need varies with the age of the child and the degree of self-restraint imposed by training and discipline. It would appear to be one of the aims of careful upbringing to teach the child self-control so as to free him from the tyranny of his emotional needs.

By so doing we hope that the child will be able to exercise his freedom of choice which, when small, he is incapable of doing. These facts are recognized by the law which holds that no child under the age of 8 years[1] is capable of a criminal act presumably because he has not the mental capacity to form the necessary intent or that degree of control which would enable a court to rule that the child was responsible for its actions. It is clear that the more an action is done on impulse or because of uncontrolled instinctual and emotional tensions the less are we able to say that the individual concerned was acting freely. The impulse or the overwhelming emotional drive compelled the action in a manner which made it quite impossible to resist. The greater the emotional involvement the less will be the capacity to reason freely about it; for emotionally determined actions certainly imply that dispassionate reasoning and choice were at a minimum before the act was carried out. Here then, the doctrine of determinism seems a reasonable one although it would be dangerous to apply it in a wholesale manner to all situations which involve making a decision.

It is one of the paradoxes of this problem that before making a deliberate choice we feel most strongly that we are acting freely. Once the decision has been made and acted on then we can give reasons for our choice which erroneously are sometimes regarded as the cause of our choice. Again, the ordinary usage of language should prevent us making this mistake. Although we give the reasons which decided us to act one way rather than another we do not imply that these reasons are to be equated with compulsions which overcome all other inclinations.

If it is agreed that the child's actions and decisions are strongly influenced by emotional pressures to such an extent that we can say with reason that the child's behaviour is more definitely determined than free, it can also be argued that these considerations apply with greater force to the behaviour of the mentally ill person. The man suffering from an obsessional neurosis which compels him repeatedly, however much he realizes the absurdity of the act, to carry out some ritual piece of behaviour is the classic example of an illness in which emotional tension makes all purely intellectual reasoning ineffectual. The patient knows that to wash his hands for the twentieth time within an hour is by normal standards unnecessary, yet if he struggles against the compulsion he will experience intolerable anxiety which will be unassuaged until, wearily, he gives in for the twenty-first time in the vain hope that this will at last appease the tormenting emotional conflict within him. Here is an example of behaviour against which the patient fights, knowing full well that his ritual is absurd. If he were

[1] By a Bill now before Parliament it is proposed to increase this age to 10 years

free to choose he would desist, but as the emotion of anxiety determines otherwise he has no option but to submit and carry out the ritual.

Sufferers from obsessional illnesses rarely commit criminal acts on account of their illness. However, it is arguable that certain classes of repetitive offence come into this category of disorder, notably certain sexual offences, repetitive stealing and the condition classed as klepto-mania, a condition, incidentally, which is very much rarer than the occasions on which the plea is offered.

It has already been shown that delusional beliefs are not defects of intellect, for many persons suffering from such symptoms show no impairment of their intellectual functions. It is obvious that under-lying the delusion is a profound disturbance of the affective life of the patient which makes all attempts to demonstrate the wrongness of his beliefs a pure waste of time. Try to convince by rational argument a man who believes that all his actions are being observed through instruments wired into the wall of his room; try to analyse the falsity of his notion that he is being persecuted by a religious or political body; try to persuade the severely depressed man that he and his family are not to suffer some dreadful fate because of his own alleged past misdeeds; it is just possible that temporary assent will be given to your arguments but it is extremely improbable that they will have any permanent effect until the patient has been treated by drugs and physical methods which will resolve the underlying emotional disorder. Again, it can hardly be insisted that a deluded man who acts criminally because of his delusions is a free agent. It is the emotional disturbance which drives him on in a manner which makes any appeal to rational consideration wholly irrelevant. He cannot act otherwise because his act is determined remorselessly by underlying unconscious mechanisms which are gravely disturbed.

Similar considerations apply in the case of the subnormal and severely subnormal. In some cases their intellectual and emotional development is equated with that of a child of such and such an age. Assuming that this is so it would be reasonable to regard them as being in the same legal category as children of that age and treat them ac-cordingly. Because the prisoner is an adult physically it is difficult not to feel that he must in some respects have an adult mind; but, to quote the words of the judge who first tried Straffen,[1] finding him unfit to plead: 'One might as well try a babe in arms.'

It will be argued that to admit that, because of mental illness, a person is incapable of exercising the same degree of emotional control as a healthy man is tantamount to a plea of irresistible impulse. If the emotional tensions lying behind and determining the criminal act are

[1] R. *v.* Straffen, [1952] 2 All E. R. 657

so strong as to be irresistible then all the more reason why sanctions should be available and widely publicized in order to help the would-be offender learn self-control. This is a perfectly sound proposal when applied to the healthy man but as every psychiatrist who deals with any class of mentally ill offender knows, reasoning along these lines is usually far from the patient's consideration. What might deter a normal person has little effect on the insane or compulsively neurotic. If they do consider the possible legal consequences of an act the processes of rationalization will enable them to be ignored. It cannot be said too often that mentally ill persons do not reason normally, that their freedom to choose and act dispassionately is seriously impaired, and that doctrines which presuppose this capacity although applicable to the sane and healthy person have little or no place in explaining the mental mechanisms of the mentally ill. These facts were surely implied in the observation of the Royal Commission on Capital Punishment that responsibility would be gravely impaired in those who commit a serious crime but are insane, severely subnormal or suffering from certain forms of epilepsy. It is clear that they also felt that all mentally defective and epileptic patients would have some impairment of responsibility, a consideration which should be taken into account when dealing with the psychopathic personality.

In this debate over determinism and free will it is evident that the jurist will side with what Mr. John Wilson refers to as the moralists, whereas the psychiatrist is likely to support the factualists.[1] The jurist expects all men to be reasonable and to behave accordingly, while the psychiatrist knows full well that even the most healthy of us do not act in this way all the time. The jurist assumes that men have the ability to choose freely between alternative courses of action and to choose the right rather than the wrong. Yet when he comes to applying penal principles he is apt to switch from free will to determinist principles. No doubt there are other aims of punishment besides pure retribution and deterrence, yet it is evident that both these factors are relevant to punishment and its effect on the offender. It could certainly be argued that punishment or the fear of punishment is a full-blooded application of deterministic doctrines which makes use of the emotion of fear to guide the future decisions of the offender or to deter one who is contemplating a criminal act.

Few of us, of course, are consistent when it comes to applying fundamental principles to daily actions, and in this matter psychiatry is in no better position than the law. Within limits we certainly support the doctrine of determinism as propounded by Dr. Slater. Yet when

[1] Wilson, J. (1961). *Reason and Morals*. London; Cambridge University Press

it comes to treatment by psychological techniques, in the words of Jaspers,[1] we appeal to the patient to exercise his freedom of choice. No doubt we also apply scientific and deterministic principles in our treatments, but if we are wise we will be cautious before we assume that improvement or cure is due to the remedies we have administered.

In psychotherapy the effects of chance and accident which have little to do with the therapeutic discussions play a major part in the patient's progress. Yet, knowing that we are dealing with a disorder of the patient's emotional life, we try to get them to see what causes their anxiety and then encourage them to face up to those situations in which anxiety is liable to occur. We appeal to them as human beings to disregard the unpleasant feeling they experience, so that they may rise above the limiting control of emotional conflict to take their place in society as freely acting, responsible adults. It is obvious that we wish to prevent emotional factors deciding the actions of the individual patient so that they can then achieve full stature as human beings. As Sir Walter Moberly wrote:[2] 'The desire to excuse people who labour under handicaps, however kindly in intention may be a cruel kindness, for in the long run it must impair their status in the community. . . . Men whose case is wholly pathological are disqualified from freedom. No man can contract out of his social obligations on the plea of moral incapacity without thereby abdicating his right to the direction of his own life.'

It would be appropriate here to say a word about psycho-analysis which in some minds is equated with psychiatry and psychotherapy. It would be correct, I think, so say that psycho-analysis as a theory of mental structure and function is determinist in character. It claims to be scientific and objective in its methods yet, despite this, few practising psychiatrists in Great Britain will have had a full training in the psycho-analytic technique, and few would accept the full rigours of the doctrine as expounded. To the outsider much of psycho-analytic teaching smacks of indoctrination. Whether the teaching is wholly correct or only partial truth is difficult to ascertain as only those who have had the necessary training are said to be in a position to judge the full implications of a psycho-analytic formulation. To act as witness and judge in one's own cause does not seem to be a particularly objective method of assessing the value of a proposition, but accepting for a moment that psycho-analytic statements about the function and structure of the unconscious mind are true, does this help us in assessing responsibility?

---

[1] Jaspers, K. (1962) 'General Psychopathology' Trans: J. Hoenig & M. W. Hamilton. Manchester University Press
[2] Moberly, W. (1951). *Responsibility*, Riddell Memorial Lecture, p. 20

Because of the determinist nature of psycho-analytic theory it is held that our characters and ways of behaving are laid down as a result of experience in early childhood; and that we are unable, without assistance, to alter the end-products of these experiences. It follows that everyone is in the same position as regards their character unless they have submitted to a period of psycho-analysis which should enable them to learn the full emotional force of their early training and its effects, for good or ill, upon them. If this is the case we each behave in the way we do, not because of any inherent goodness or badness in ourselves, but merely because we are made that way. Now it could be argued that nobody submits to the expense, tedium and inconvenience of a long-drawn-out psycho-analysis unless they are ill or are aware of obscure emotional forces within them which make living a problem. No doubt we could all live more happily and more efficiently than we do; and psycho-analysis might conceivably help us to achieve this objective. The majority of us do undoubtedly react neurotically to certain situations, but only the minority react in this fashion all the time.

It has been the purpose here to put forward the opinion that neurotic behaviour differs qualitatively from normal rational behaviour largely because of the strong emotional concomitants which compel the neurotic person to act in the way he does. So far as the present author knows there is not the slightest reason to suppose that a normal person, reflecting over possible courses of action, is compelled by his deliberations to choose one course rather than another. If this were the case why should we be able to distinguish the free from the compulsory act? If what has been said about psycho-analysis is correct it follows that the doctrines which this technique embodies are based upon the study of neurotic reactions. To extrapolate from the findings made during the analysis of neurotic patients to the workings of healthy minds is surely an unjustifiable procedure. It can only lead to the proposition that all behavioural events are determined in a mechanistic manner which should satisfy the most ardent supporter of the fatalist position.

No doubt it is salutary to be reminded that not all our actions are as free as we supposed; and that the emotional disturbance in the mind of the offender may well have a very real bearing upon his subsequent behaviour: but unless one is going to equate all forms of socially unacceptable behaviour with mental illness it will continue to be necessary to determine, as far as possible, just how ill the offender is before he can be regarded as irresponsible. This may well be a difficult task but no harder than many other decisions with which juries have to struggle. The fact that it is never possible to know with complete certainty what goes on in the mind of another person does not prevent us from coming to reasonably sound conclusions on the matter. Such uncertainty is, in all probability, no greater in determining responsibility than it is when trying to reconcile conflicting evidence about what are, in theory at least, objectively observable events.

Certainly there is no obvious justification for Lady Wootton's plea that we should abolish the quest to determine responsibility in law.[1] As Professor Hart has argued, there is still a place in law for this particular concept so long as the law regards punishment as the just deserts of the offender. So long as punishment is retributive there will be a place for the determination of responsibility. If punishment becomes wholly directed to reform and deterrence the need for assessing responsibility will become less urgent. Treatment, in short, will take the place of retribution even though such treatment necessitates penal sanctions. Professor Hart,[2] when considering Lady Wootton's plea, wrote: 'It is impossible not to sympathize with her conclusion that for the most part in these cases of mental abnormality all that we can do is to use the evidence to diagnose those whose mental abnormalities are likely to result in harmful conduct, and to predict what treatment will best prevent their repeating it. The moral that she draws is that the sooner we get down to this piece of honest toil instead of claiming to discover the undiscoverable the better.' This may well be true when the offender shows clear evidence of mental illness. It has little application in the treatment of those who are not so afflicted or in those whose abnormalities are slight. Psychiatrists spend much of their working life trying with varying success to discover what is going on in the minds of their patients. Our treatment is based on what we discover and nobody has yet suggested that the whole business is a waste of time on the ground that we can never have exact knowledge of events in the mind of another person. We accordingly make judgments about our patient's behaviour which enable us to assert whether or not he was able to control his behaviour or whether a particular piece of violence was due to some abnormal mental process which caused it.

The arguments of the foregoing pages can briefly be summarized. Despite much controversy over the problem it is held that we can and do exercise freedom of choice and that this freedom is likely to be curtailed the more our decision is influenced by emotional conflict and tension. It follows that small children and those suffering from serious mental illness are likely to be more limited in their range of choice than is the case with normal healthy adults. To a certain extent the law embodies these conclusions in its present attitudes towards responsibility of young children and insane persons, although it still fails to

[1] Wootton, B. (1960). 'Diminished Responsibility.' 76 L. Q. R. 224
[2] Hart, H. L. A. (1961). *Punishment and the Elimination of Responsibility*, p. 26. London; Athlone Press

give recognition to the emotional states of those who appear to yield to an irresistible impulse largely determined by the mental pathology of the offender. Psychiatrists are probably correct when they argue that mentally ill persons are precluded from the exercise of free will and choice by the peculiar conditions imposed upon them by inner disturbances which determine their outward behaviour. There is still a place for attempting to discover the degree of responsibility of any given offender even though it is never possible to ascertain all the facts which would permit an absolute and just conclusion. Both law and medicine are united in their wish to treat the offender as a fully responsible adult unless the contrary can be proved.

It is, perhaps in the realm of penology that the law is most apt to fall back on determinist principles whereas the psychiatrist, with his concern for the individual, is most likely to try by his own special methods to get the offender to accept the responsibilities of the adult. No doubt the psychiatrist is often unrealistic in his aims and, in any case, the interests of society may well preclude him from his therapeutic endeavours.

Purely from the point of view of diagnosis it is surely essential to reach as accurate an estimate as possible concerning the mental state of the accused. For the application of deterministic principles of punishment to a person who by mental illness is incapable of responding to them is likely not only to be unjust but to be a waste of time and money. The harsh treatment of mentally ill persons was never a notable success and the reforms of Pinel and Tuke need still to be extended outside the walls of the mental hospital rather than be confined within them.

It is unlikely that these conclusions will be acceptable to all philosophers, jurists and physicians, but as was made clear at the beginning of this chapter, it was never the intention of the writer to attempt a settlement of the age-long controversy between those who assert that all human action is determined and those who insist that we are all able to exercise free will. The somewhat banal conclusion that the truth probably lies somewhere between these two extremes may not be contested too hotly, but it is as well to point out that however free the decisions of the healthy adult may appear to be there is no reason to believe that his mental processes are qualitatively the same as those of the mentally ill person; and that the deterministic properties of the sick man's disordered affect is something which will be alien to the experience and thought processes of the healthy.

6—Mental Symptoms and Criminal Behaviour

Psychiatric estimates of the degree of responsibility of offenders for their acts seem to vary with the position and theoretical outlook of the psychiatrist. To those who are most impressed with psycho-dynamic explanations of behaviour the dividing line between crime and sickness is so thin as scarcely to exist. Prison medical officers, on the other hand, appear to have less difficulty in making this differentiation and the incidence of mental illness in a prison population is found to be considerably lower than might be expected. East, for example,[1] quoting from the report of the Prison Commissioners in 1950 stated that out of 48,500 prison and Borstal receptions, medical reports were asked for in 5,007 cases. Of these 266 were found to be insane and 266 were certified under the Mental Deficiency Acts. Of those convicted, 150 were found to be insane and 63 mentally defective. No figures for epilepsy were available in that year but in the previous year there were 286 definite cases of epilepsy and a further 226 who were possibly epileptic. Precise figures for subnormal, psychopathic and psychoneurotic offenders were not available but East estimated them at about 5–15 per cent of the prison population.

The Report of the Prison Commissioners for 1960 gives figures for the first 10 months of that year up to the time of the coming into force of the Mental Health Act, 1959, which are remarkably similar to those quoted by East for a period 10 years earlier. It could be concluded that the criteria whereby mental illness is diagnosed in prison are fairly constant, and that an estimate of the numbers of mentally abnormal persons in prison will work out at about 12 per cent of the prison population.

Estimates of the incidence of mental illness in the general population are difficult to assess, and the Royal Commission on Mental Illness and Mental Deficiency[2] gave figures from general practice studies which varied from 2 to 70 per cent of patients who attended. As Kessel and Shepherd pointed out,[3] much depends on the attitude of the general practitioner who makes the estimate. 'Practitioners with an "organic" viewpoint rarely give a figure above 10 per cent when estimating psychiatric morbidity. Physicians with a special interest in the

---

[1] East, W. N. (1954). *Roots of Crime*. London; Butterworths
[2] Royal Commission on Mental Illness and Mental Deficiency (1954–57), Cmd. 169
[3] Kessel, N. and Shepherd, M. (1962). 'Neurosis in Hospital and General Practice.' *J. ment. Sci.* **108,** 159

fashionable, but loosely defined, stress disorders and psychosomatic illnesses report results of about 20 per cent, while figures of 40 per cent or more have been cited by psycho-analytically oriented practitioners.' However, assuming an incidence of psychoneuroses as being about 10 per cent, if one excludes psychosomatic illness, and the overall figure of 2 per cent for the major psychoses, one is left with an unknown number of psychopathic personalities who probably do not come to their general practitioners unless they develop what Professor Sir Aubrey Lewis referred to as 'disturbances of part-functions'.[1]

From these, admittedly, speculative figures it does not appear that the overall incidence of mental illness in a prison population will differ very greatly from that in the general community. The *distribution* of illness will differ as the prison community will certainly have a larger number of psychopathic personalities as well as epileptics, about 1·25 per cent compared with a general incidence of about 0·5 per cent for epilepsy. It would be difficult on these estimates to support the notion that crime is due to mental disorder or is to be equated with illness unless one is going to postulate that the criminal act itself is a symptom of illness.

In any case, as East has shown,[2] if crime is to be regarded as a disease one will have to explain the high incidence of this form of mental disorder among young men, an incidence which decreases with each successive age period. Although men are convicted of crimes eight times more frequently than women there is certainly nothing to indicate that men are so much more often the victims of mental illness. Among first offenders over the age of 16 years convicted of serious offences, 70 per cent of the younger men and 90 per cent of the older as well as 90 per cent of all female offenders did not appear on a further charge in the next 5 years. It would be an odd form of mental illness which responded so gratifyingly to ordinary punitive measures. No doubt many of these first offenders showed signs of immaturity and emotional imbalance. Such symptoms could be regarded as indications of mental disorder in the broadest sense of the term, but it implies that any deviation from the most rock-like equanimity should be assessed in this way, a conclusion which hardly squares with common sense.

When we come to examine the figures for homicide a very different picture is presented. According to the Royal Commission on Capital Punishment, between the years 1940–49, 390 persons suspected of murder committed suicide. Of 680 committed for trial 86 were acquitted or not tried, 144 were found insane on arraignment and 164 were found to be guilty but insane. Of 262 persons convicted and sentenced

---

[1] Lewis, A. (1953). 'Health as a Social Concept.' *Brit. J. Sociol.* **4,** 109
[2] East, W. N. (1944). *Recent Progress in Psychiatry*, Vol. 2. London; Churchill

to death, 18 were certified as insane before execution and removed to Broadmoor, and a further 21 were respited partially on the grounds of their mental condition. Thus, out of a total of 1,070 persons suspected of murder, some 737 were shown to be suffering from mental illness, assuming that all those who committed suicide were mentally ill. The incidence of mental disorder among those suspected of murder is close on 70 per cent, which is very different from the estimated figure of 12 per cent for those who commit less serious crimes. These figures lend support to the belief that murder is an abnormal crime committed by abnormal persons for, comparatively, it is a rare crime, occurring about 150 times per annum in England and Wales with an incidence of about 3·4 per million of the population. As the question of responsibility is most often raised in cases of alleged murder it is obvious that the psychiatric examination of all those suspected of murder is of crucial importance.

Some attention must be given to the meaning of such terms as mental disease, mental illness and mental disorder. These terms are often used synonymously, but precise definitions are hard to come by. Once one gets away from the clear-cut clinical syndromes of psychosis there is a tendency for the argument to get bogged down in a fruitless search for definitions of mental health and disease, none of which will satisfy all the protagonists. As has already been mentioned, the Royal Commission on Capital Punishment equated disease of the mind with the major functional and organic psychoses, and although this definition is a sensible one it means that those who suffer from psychoneuroses, mental defect and character disorders are excluded. Some cases of epilepsy would be included but others might not; and as the M'Naghten Rules specifically use the term 'disease of the mind' it is obvious that the omission of seriously ill persons who are not psychotic, but are in many respects quite as severely handicapped, could lead to injustice.

The Mental Health Act, 1959, states that 'mental disorder' means mental illness, arrested or incomplete development of mind, psychopathic disorder and any other disorder or disability of mind. It goes on to subdivide and define the categories of subnormality, severe subnormality and psychopathic disorder, but is careful to exclude those whose behaviour is undesirable and anti-social. Section 4 (5) of the Act states: 'Nothing in this section shall be construed as implying that a person may be dealt with under this Act as suffering from mental disorder, or from any form of mental disorder described in this section, by reason only of promiscuity or other immoral conduct.' One assumes that the term 'immoral conduct' includes legal offences as well as the ordinary notions of wrongdoing. In any case, the Act makes a differentiation between such persons and those suffering from psychopathic disorder which it defines as a persistent disorder or disability of mind (whether or not including subnormality of intelligence) which results in abnormally aggressive or seriously irresponsible conduct on the part of the patient, and requires or is susceptible to medical treatment. Opinions differ over the validity of the last eight words in the definition, and the Act does not give any guidance as to how the differentiation should be made between those suffering from psychopathic disorder and those who merely manifest immoral conduct.

It is unlikely that any serious difference of opinion will occur over the suitability of the term 'mental disease' when applied to those who suffer from a psychotic illness. It would probably be agreed that those who are severely subnormal could also be included in this category, for the majority of such persons are defective owing to serious congenital or acquired defects of brain structure. We have no difficulty in talking of congenital disease of the heart, and a serious malformation of the brain, present before or at birth, could certainly be classed as a congenital disease of the brain manifested by the psychological features of severe subnormality. It is when we come to classify the lesser degrees of subnormality, of neurosis and of character disorder that we encounter difficulties. For just as some degrees of subnormality are merely one extreme of the range of intellectual ability as measured by psychological testing of the general population, so can we regard some neurotic reactions, such as depression and anxiety, as excessive degrees of psychological experiences which are common to everyone. In short, if intellectual dullness, anxiety and depression are, when examined medically, merely extreme variants of the norm, it is difficult to assert that such symptoms should be considered to be disease processes. Rather should they be classed as malfunctions or maladaptations no different from certain degrees of obesity or the dyspnoea attendant upon exertion in a rarified atmosphere. This seems to be the point made by Jaspers when he made a distinction between development of personality and disease process. According to Jaspers neurosis and psychopathy can be understood in terms of the personality and development of the patient. He exhibits symptoms which can, in certain circumstances, be regarded as normal, but are only abnormal in the particular patient either because of the circumstances of their manifestation or because their intensity is not in keeping with the situation in which they occur. It is normal to display fear if a bomb drops near us; it is not normal to react with terror at the prospect of an ordinary train journey. It is expected that we should show overtly aggressive behaviour when commanded to take part in a war-time assault; it is not considered normal behaviour to react with extreme anger and physical violence when an inspector asks to see our railway ticket. Yet, given a knowledge of the personality of the patients who show anxiety or aggression in inappropriate circumstances, we might predict the abnormal behaviour from our knowledge of their development. By contrast, those suffering from a mental disease show totally new forms of behaviour which not only appear strange to the observer but are largely alien to the pre-morbid personality of the patient. A disease process is wholly different from a developmental one and it would be incorrect to classify those suffering from neurosis and character disorder as diseased.

This argument has had considerable influence on European psychiatry but breaks down when applied to individual cases. There can be no doubt, for instance, that many schizophrenics have shown certain personality traits classed as schizoid before frank symptoms of schizophrenia appear. It could be argued that the abnormal personality traits are, in fact, the earliest manifestations of the disease, schizophrenia, but as a good many persons show these particular traits without ever becoming psychotic, and as many schizophrenics appear to have had normal personalities prior to their illness, it is clear that schizophrenia as a disease process as distinct from a developmental process is not so clear-cut as might be imagined from Jaspers' writings. In contrast, although many cases of hysteria, anxiety, and obsessional neurosis have shown lesser degrees of these symptoms before they became ill, in a fair number of patients this is not so; severe, enduring symptoms of anxiety with specific phobias can and do occur in persons who, prior to some acute emotional upheaval which precipitated the illness, had shown no evidence of undue neuroticism. Greater difficulty is encountered when having to classify those psychoneurotic reactions which occur in an organic setting.

Is an obsessional illness to be regarded as a disease if it follows a cerebral infection such as encephalitis lethargica, but not a disease if it arises without any known physical cause? Are severe behaviour disturbances in childhood due to organic brain disorder to be labelled diseases in such instances but to be termed psychopathic disorder when organic pathology is absent? These are difficult questions to which there is no satisfactory answer, but they certainly undermine the position of Jaspers as well as emphasizing the impossibility of reaching a satisfactory definition of mental disease. In the circumstances it might be better to avoid the term 'disease of the mind' which for all purposes applies only to the severe psychoses, and adopt the term 'mental disorder' as used in the Mental Health Act, 1959, to cover all aspects of abnormal or disturbed mental function. Should this suggestion be accepted the difficulty then arises over the inclusion of the lesser degrees of subnormality and of psychopathic personality.

The problem of subnormality is fairly simply disposed of. Those who in the older terminology were called feeble-minded persons or borderline defectives were largely recruited from persons at the lowest end of the intelligence quotient scale. Once this fact was established their degree of responsibility could be measured in terms of their intellectual capacity and cultural background. This would indicate, with reasonable clarity, the lack of emotional control or absence of proper knowledge which, had they been present, would have sufficed to prevent their committing an offence against the law. There is a clear difference between the subnormal and the severely subnormal which is not entirely a matter of degree of intellectual defect. By analogy one could point to the difference between the schizoid personality and the fully-developed schizophrenic illness which exhibits a quantitative as well as a qualitative difference from the former state.

Although subnormality merges by imperceptible stages with normal intelligence it is possible to assess the severity of defect in any given case, just as a teacher will be able to single out the children who are dull and make due allowance for this handicap. If the backwardness of children is so severe as to render them unteachable they can be separated from the rest of the school and given special educational training applicable to those with abnormal mental development. It is usually possible, with reasonable certainty, to assess the degree of subnormality and decide whether a person is to be regarded as a variant from the statistical average or is suffering from some pathological process permitting the term 'mental disorder' to describe him.

The difficulties to be overcome when considering the precise status of the psychopathic personality who is also a legal offender are far greater. The problem has been discussed in detail by Lady Wootton[1] but certain features of the condition require further emphasis.

There is no adequate definition of the psychopath, partly because the aetiology is obscure and partly because the clinical description of the patient can only be rendered, for the most part, in terms of deviant social behaviour. One then has to ask in what way the criminal offences of the psychopath differ from those of the professional criminal; leaving one to fall back on the famous observation of the Prison Medical Officers: 'A thug is a thug because he wants to be a thug. A psychopath cannot help it.'[2]

It is usually said that the concept of psychopathy stems from Prichard's description of what he termed 'moral insanity' although few of the cases he described had much in common with the modern

[1] Wootton, B. (1959). *Social Science and Social Pathology*, Chap. 8. London; Allen and Unwin
[2] Royal Commission on Capital Punishment (1949–53). Cmd. 3932, para. 398

notion of psychopathy apart from their disorderly conduct. In one of his books[1] he quoted three examples of this condition: the first appears to have been a classic example of hypomania; the second a seven-year old child with a behaviour disorder following, in all probability, an attack of encephalitis; and the third a probable case of manic-depressive psychosis complicated by excess alcohol intake during the manic phase of the disease. He also cited a number of patients who developed 'moral insanity' after cerebrovascular accidents and head injuries. From the descriptions none of these cases would be accepted as psychopaths today but it is evident that Prichard was struck by the marked change in social behaviour in his patients; and it is the disturbance of social behaviour which is the main feature of the psychopathic personality.

Curran and Mallinson reviewed the literature on the subject[2] saying: 'It must be confessed that no very clear or unitary conception of what constitutes the psychopathic personality springs to life from these definitions; yet many of them share in common an emphasis on episodic and impulsive behaviour which is socially undesirable, this episodic and impulsive behaviour being recurrent and, in the present state of knowledge, unmodifiable. The salient feature of the psychopathic personality is stressed as essentially consisting in persistent or repeated disorder of conduct of an anti-social type.' Later, they wrote, after outlining the opinions of four authorities: 'Although it will have become evident that no general agreement has been reached on this point (the criteria by which psychopathy is diagnosed) . . . these four authors . . . agree in outlining an unreliable type of individual of defective judgment, liable to impulsive acts which are often both imprudent and inconsiderate, and who is, moreover, unable to profit by experience.'

In the somewhat stronger language of the Royal Medico-Psychological Association,[3] 'Psychopaths are mentally abnormal patients whose daily behaviour shows a want of social responsibility and of consideration for others, of prudence and foresight and of ability to act in their own best interests. Their persistent anti-social mode of conduct may include inefficiency and lack of interest in any form of occupation; pathological lying; swindling and slandering; alcoholism and drug addiction, sexual offences and violent actions with little motivation and an entire absence of self-restraint, which may go as far as homicide. Punishment or the threat of punishment influences their behaviour

[1] Prichard, J. C. (1842). *Forms of Insanity*. London; Hippolyte Balliere
[2] Curran, D. and Mallinson, P. (1944). 'Psychopathic Personality.' In *Recent Progress in Psychiatry*, p. 266. London; Churchill
[3] Royal Commission on Mental Illness and Mental Deficiency (1954–57), Cmd. 169, p. 53

only momentarily, and its more lasting effect is to intensify their vindictiveness and anti-social attitude.'

Henderson,[1] whose classification of psychopaths is probably the one most widely used in British psychiatry, differentiates the predominantly aggressive, the predominantly inadequate and the predominantly creative. The description given by the Royal Medico-Psychological Association appears more appropriate for the aggressive category of offenders although the type of person described under the heading of 'unstable drifter' by Mayer-Gross, Slater and Roth[2] would approximate more closely to the unstable or inadequate psychopath. What needs to be emphasized is that although many psychopaths may show features of low intelligence this is by no means essential for the condition to develop. Many psychopaths have average or above average intelligence and an ease and charm of manner which can deceive the most experienced. Were it not for the anti-social features listed above many of them would pass as normal citizens; and it may be that, until they develop more definite symptoms of anxiety or depression which may lead them to make suicidal gestures, they will not come under psychiatric care.

It is the explosive and unstable quality of the aggressive psychopath which is so important. Often there is a history of surliness and moodiness which ends in some act of violence, triggered off by some trifling frustration. The ability to refrain from immediate instinctual gratification is minimal; they appear to have a total inability to profit from experience, for over and over again they will repeat the same offence or immoral act which has led them into trouble in the past. This fact underlines East's findings that the great majority of first offenders do not repeat their offence, or if they do within the 5 year period of follow-up, they are not detected. Hence, his conclusion that psychopaths form only a small part of the prison population and Dr. Peter Scott's statement that he does not differentiate between psychopaths and chronic recidivists.[3]

Dr. Scott's classification of psychopaths has the advantage of being based, in part, on aetiological considerations. Having excluded all those suffering from organic cerebral disease, epilepsy and recognizable psychiatric illness he goes on to consider four categories of psychopathic behaviour. The first group comprises persons whose early childhood and upbringing in adverse surroundings has trained them to accept anti-social standards. They behave as they have been taught to behave and have never had much opportunity to learn better. In the second group he places those whose offences are in some way compensating for

[1] Henderson, D. K. (1939). *Psychopathic States*. New York; Norton
[2] Mayer-Gross, W., Slater, E. and Roth, M. (1954). *Clinical Psychiatry*. London; Cassell
[3] Scott, P. (1960). *Brit. med. J.* **1**, 1642

79

underlying feelings of anxiety, inadequacy, and unconscious but unacceptable instinctual drives. The third group is composed of untrained offenders who, through weak or inconsistent handling in childhood, have never learned to resist instinctual drives or wishes; while the fourth group consists of those whose early experiences have been so overwhelmingly frustrating that they have never been able to overcome a maladapted pattern of response. Dr. Scott observes that there is a risk that unsympathetic handling of his third category of psychopathic offenders may precipitate them into the fourth group which is certainly the hardest to treat; and that, whereas penal sanctions may be of help in treating the first two groups, punishment is likely to make the last two worse.

Whatever one might feel about treatment it is obvious from the above descriptions that the psychopathic personality has very little control over his behaviour, and that it would be absurd to claim that he is fully responsible for his actions. This still does not help to solve the problem of differentiating the psychopath from the normal offender unless recidivism is to be taken as the sole criterion. The problem has not altered very much since it was posed by Maudsley nearly 100 years ago; for, after describing moral insanity according to the writings of Prichard and Esquirol, he wrote: 'It may be said that this description is simply the description of a very wicked person, and that to accept it as a description of insanity would be to confound all distinctions between vice and crime and madness. No doubt, so far as symptoms are concerned, they are much the same whether they are the result of vice or of disease; but there is a considerable difference when we go on to inquire into the person's previous history . . . The vicious act or crime is not itself proof of insanity: it must . . . be traced from disease through a proper train of symptoms . . . and the evidence of disease will be found in the entire history of the case.'[1]

Consideration of the full life history of the offender will often decide whether or not the offence is a symptom of psychopathic disorder. Often the history will comprise a bad work record with frequent changes of job for no good reason, unstable relationships with others, a tendency to take drink or drugs in excess, explosive or shiftless behaviour of a repetitive kind, and a sequence of offences of varying degrees of seriousness, many of them of a pointless nature which ordinary forethought would have avoided. It is the neurotic and impulsive quality of the psychopath's offences which often help one to differentiate them from carefully considered crimes committed for personal gain. Admittedly, this leads to the conclusion that the worse the record of the prisoner the more likely is the diagnosis that of psychopathy; but as the majority of first offenders do not repeat their

[1] Maudsley, H. (1874). *Responsibility in Mental Disease*, p. 170. London; King

offence it is probable that only with chronic recidivists does the question of psychopathy arise. By then, of course, it may be too late to prevent a serious or dangerous crime.

The foregoing account of psychopathic disorder is necessarily brief, failing to include all those forms of character disturbance which can be classed with the psychopathic states. A good many persons show disturbances of behaviour which may be socially undesirable without bringing them into conflict with the law. As this essay is concerned with the legal responsibility of the mentally ill it would be superfluous to extend the section on psychopathy to include all manifestations of this disorder. There can be no doubt that this class of disorder exists but whether those who suffer from it should be dealt with by medical or legal methods or a combination of both has yet to be decided. Ideally, psychological techniques should be the treatment of choice, but they often fail and society needs to be protected. In these circumstances, whatever the views about the responsibility of the psychopath, there is a clear need for some form of control while treatment is being given. That the ordinary mental hospital fails to provide the proper facilities is a fact which is all too obvious today.

Consideration of all those categories of mental disorder which can lead to delinquent behaviour is beyond the scope of this work. What is of greater importance is the description of those symptoms or groups of symptoms observed when mental disorder is associated with serious crime. It is extremely difficult to convince the lay mind, for example, that the emotional flatness or incongruity of the schizophrenic is not just a sign of indifference or surliness, which, if manifested in relation to a shocking crime, appears to add to the enormity of the act. Undoubtedly, this is a technical matter which must be left to the experts. Unfortunately, when medical evidence is conflicting, it is all too easy for a jury to take a common-sense view of a prisoner's behaviour; with the result that psychiatric accounts of symptoms are dismissed as so much special pleading and sophistry. The following symptoms need to be considered in some detail, largely because, when slight, they may be overlooked and their peculiar qualities unappreciated: (1) disturbances of conscious awareness; (2) disturbances of emotional congruity and control; (3) delusional beliefs; and (4) disturbances of intellectual capacity.

Disturbances of Conscious Awareness

Some of the problems, legal and medical, which arise when there is an abnormality of consciousness will be discussed in the section on automatism. Clinically, various degrees of disturbance can occur ranging from slight amounts of clouding, through delirium, to coma. In the last state the problem of criminal activity does not arise, but it is not infrequent for a plea of impaired conscious awareness to be offered when a serious charge is being tried. The extent to which such a defence will be accepted will depend not only on the past medical history of the prisoner but also on the degree of impairment witnessed at the time of the alleged offence.

Clouding of consciousness can be defined as a state of reduced wakefulness or a disturbance of awareness. It is by no means an uncommon condition which is not necessarily associated with psychiatric illness or serious organic disease of the brain. In its mildest forms it is characterized by a slight degree of swimminess in the head, a difficulty in grasping the meaning of actions or words, and a failure to concentrate or to fix attention on one's own activities or the activities of others. It is commonly experienced in states of fatigue, and many persons engaged in long motor journeys will have appreciated that not only have they failed to take note of details of the road and traffic for many miles, but have found it difficult to fix their minds on the problems of driving; so much so that accidents have occurred or been narrowly averted. However, it is usual that the sudden emergency will arouse the driver sufficiently to take avoiding action, but a good many accidents occur when the monotony of the journey, fatigue and heat, cause a definite lowering of conscious activity leading, at times, to states of sleep. These minor degrees of clouding are rarely sufficient to permit an alleged offender to deny all knowledge of his actions and only when the degree of clouding is severe can one argue that such a person would not be responsible for his acts.

Severe degrees of clouding with associated delirium occur in many acute and chronic organic disorders of the brain. The acute infections, cerebral injuries and intoxications, as well as the progressive dementias of old age are often characterized by short-lived or prolonged periods of disturbed consciousness. In particular, the epilepsies are manifested by brief episodes when conscious control is wholly absent; and on occasions these periods are prolonged for hours or days following which the patient will have very little memory of events. Head injuries with minor degrees of concussion will sometimes be followed by periods of complex, apparently purposive, behaviour of which the patient will have only a confused memory. It is during such periods of disturbed consciousness that violent acts can occur of which the patient may have no knowledge.

The principal features of these states are a disturbance of orientation in time and place, a feeling of bewilderment often associated with intense fear, excitement, restlessness and irritability, and impulsive behaviour which can be dangerous to the patient or to bystanders. Much of the behaviour can be explained on the basis of misinterpretations of surroundings, possible delusions and hallucinatory experiences and, above all, the fearful affect which causes him to strike out, believing that he is about to be attacked and must make every effort to defend his life. Following some desperate act the patient may pass into a deep sleep from which he will awake with total amnesia for recent events; or, at best, his memory will be so confused that while he may have some knowledge of his actions he will be totally incapable of giving any satisfactory explanation to account for them.

The problem of epilepsy and its relation to serious crime was considered by the Royal Commission on Capital Punishment[1] which distinguished between states of post-epileptic automatism, epileptic equivalents, epileptic insanity and disturbances of personality associated with chronic epilepsy. In all these states it is possible for serious violence to occur although, so far as automatism and insanity are concerned, it is rare for such conditions to be the cause of homicidal assaults. Should they occur undoubtedly the accused would be wholly irresponsible for his act and the Royal Commission felt that when any serious crime was committed by a known epileptic the possibility that the epilepsy was irrelevant to the commission of the offence could not be ruled out. A number of authors have commented upon the association of epilepsy with serious crime.

Hill and Pond[2] reported on 100 capital cases submitted to electro-encephalographic (EEG) examination. In 27 of these the plea of epileptic automatism at the time of the alleged crime was under consideration. Nine of these cases showed specific epileptic EEG abnormalities, 9 had no specific epileptic EEG abnormalities but had a clear history of epilepsy in the past, while the remaining 9 had an unproven history of epilepsy without specific EEG features. They go on to write: 'The evidence, therefore, for some relationship existing between murder and epilepsy in some murderers is undoubted but this is not to say that such murders are committed in an epileptic seizure or a post-epileptic automatism. In those cases we have had the opportunity to follow-up in the courts . . . we have not observed a case in which we were not in the end satisfied that the chance of an epileptic seizure preceding the murder was extremely remote.' The authors go on to give reasons for saying that violent and dangerous behaviour is rarely seen during epileptic attacks or in states of post-epileptic automatism in patients, quoting a number of authorities in support of this observation. As they

---

[1] Royal Commission on Capital Punishment (1949–53), Cmd. 8932, paras. 386–392

[2] Hill, D. and Pond, D. A. (1952). *J. ment. Sci.* **98**, 23

point out, in automatic states, when consciousness is clouded, the patient is rarely sufficiently co-ordinated to permit complex aggressive acts.

In another paper, Professor Hill[1] stated, 'The commonly-asked clinical question whether episodes of psychopathic violence are often the direct result of epilepsy receives a definite answer in the negative from this material'—referring to the cases of aggressive psychopathy submitted to EEG studies and reported on in the paper. This statement of course, does not contradict the well-established fact that aggressive psychopathic behaviour is often associated with marked EEG abnormalities, but such abnormalities are not necessarily evidence of epilepsy, neither is there evidence of clouded consciousness in many cases of psychopathic homicide.[2] Only in certain classes of epilepsy can one be reasonably certain that a violent assault occurred during the ictal or post-ictal phase of the attack, such cases requiring evidence of disturbance of consciousness or recurrent, inexplicable episodes of abnormal behaviour. To demonstrate this one would need as clear a history as possible of earlier epileptic symptoms in the life of the accused with confirmatory clinical evidence of the disorder. The offence with which he is charged is likely to show qualities of impulsiveness and lack of motive, and a clearly motivated and planned murder would make a defence of epileptic automatism hard to accept. No doubt savage and unexpected assaults do occur during the ictal and post-ictal phases of the epileptic seizure, but Lennox observed[3] that in psychomotor epilepsy the patient may be too dazed and helpless to do more than lie stupidly in bed, or he may perform complicated acts with apparent intelligence and skill. Nevertheless, in his experience of 5,000 cases of epilepsy, few have acted belligerently and none has committed murder.

Similarly, Liddell[4] remarked that although many patients, following a major seizure, are mostly violent and destructive, their automatic actions are vague, poorly sustained and not at all elaborate. This rather primitive, disorganized, aggressive behaviour is also commented on by Levin[5] saying that, although many of his patients were aggressive or combative, they were usually not considered very dangerous to others since their mental faculties were generally so disorganized that they were unable to carry out an integrated and well-planned aggression. Such reactions can be understood in the light of the predominant affect of extreme fear during psychomotor attacks described by Williams.[6]

[1] Hill, D. (1952). 'EEG.' *Clin. Neurophys.* **4,** 419
[2] Hill, D. and Watterson, D. (1942). *J. Neurol. Psychiat.* **5,** 47; and Stafford-Clarke, D. and Taylor, F. H. (1949). *J. Neurol. Psychiat.* **12,** 325
[3] Lennox, W. G. (1943). *Amer. J. Psych.* **99,** 732
[4] Liddell, D. W. (1953). *J. ment. Sci.* **99,** 732
[5] Levin, S. (1952). *J. nerv. ment. Dis.* **116,** 215
[6] Williams, D. (1956). *Brain* **79,** 29

Such states of fear were often described in the older psychiatric writings, many patients saying that they were afraid not only that something terrible was about to happen to themselves but that they might commit a murderous assault on a relative or bystander. When such assaults do occur not infrequently they are a continuation of some harmless activity in which the patient was engaged before the epileptic seizure. A recent patient known to the author, suffering from psychomotor epilepsy, recounted how she was slicing bread before an attack. When she recovered she learned that she had stabbed her husband with the bread-knife, fortunately without serious consequences. A number of well-known cases showing similar episodes leading to homicide are quoted in the literature on the subject.

It can be concluded, therefore, that although murders can and do occur in association with epileptic disturbances of consciousness such cases are comparatively rare and not so frequent as might be supposed from the number of occasions when the defence of epileptic automatism is offered. In the absence of a history of previous epileptic attacks, and when the murder shows signs of foresight and motive, one would be cautious before concluding that epilepsy serves as an adequate explanation of the offence. No doubt some epileptic attacks do occur for the first time when the homicidal assault is made. Biochemical factors such as hypoglycaemia or hydration may need to be excluded as provocative agents to an epileptic attack in a person suspected of this disorder; but when all the facts surrounding the given case are taken into account it is usually possible to point to some peculiarity of circumstances which would lead one to suspect that the offence took place during a disturbed state of consciousness in the accused.

Organic factors are the commonest causes of impairment of consciousness, and twilight states occurring in the pre-delirious phase of a toxic-confusional psychosis are particularly associated with fear and paranoid attitudes leading to dangerous assaults. Such states may develop as part of an acute illness or during some progressive brain disease.[1] How far clouding is present in certain acute emotional states is not entirely certain but there is evidence to suggest that this can occur and that serious offences are committed during such clouded states.

Gould[2] described what he terms the autonomous affective crisis of adolescence. He regarded this as a specific mental state featuring tension, clouding of consciousness, and a reversal of the dominance of the rational over the non-rational factors relating to anxiety with an abrupt end to the condition following a violent crime. Lambo[3]

[1] R. v. Kemp, [1957] 1 Q. B. 399; and R. v. Charlson, [1959] 1 All E. R. 859
[2] Gould, J. (1959). *Recent Progress in Psychiatry*, Vol. 3. London; Churchill
[3] Lambo, T. A. (1962). *J. ment. Sci.* **108,** 256

described a somewhat similar clinical picture in Africans which he discussed under the title of malignant anxiety. The states of 'amok' in S.E. Asia as well as the acute battle neuroses with evident disturbance of conscious awareness appear to have similar clinical features and aetiology. Fear will play a major part in their production, and Professor Roth (personal communication) has described such a case in which an acutely anxious man had an attack of 'amok' during a clouded state induced by acute fear. In somewhat rare instances the functional psychoses with an acute onset occur in a setting of clouded consciousness. In the writer's experience violent behaviour may well occur during these phases of a schizophrenic illness but rarely are such outbursts of aggression dangerous. The qualities of impulsiveness and incoordination are often present to such a degree as to preclude any serious risk to the nursing attendants.

Disturbances of Affect

Many mental illnesses will show marked emotional changes but not all such illnesses are necessarily associated with or causative of criminal acts. It would be usual to discover other symptoms besides the affective change in a person who is suffering from a definite mental disorder, and any of the following remarks imply that any emotional changes observed arise in a setting of mental illness characterized by other symptoms supporting the diagnosis.

One of the cardinal symptoms of schizophrenia is the disturbance of affect which is usually described as being incongruous or flat. By this is meant that the patient's emotional reaction is inappropriate to the subject under discussion. He may be describing horrifying thoughts or deeds without showing the slightest distress or, even, he may smile or laugh; and he may recount the persecutions and threats to which he has been subjected yet not show any of the normal responses of anger or anxiety which would be expected. Not all cases of schizophrenia display this disturbance of mood but careful examination will often reveal some impairment of emotional response which may lead one to consider the diagnosis of schizophrenia in patients who show only minimal signs of the disease.

It is far from easy to convince a layman that the inappropriate or absent emotion is, in fact, evidence of illness, yet many cases are on record of persons who have committed shocking crimes in a setting of schizophrenic, affective incongruity. Some patients complain of being unable to experience the normal emotions of healthy persons, and one explanation of some of their more reckless, immoral, or criminal acts is the absence of the appropriate mood which would restrain a normal subject. Other patients appear to indulge in immoral escapades in the hope that, by so doing, they will be able to recapture the emotional response which was the normal accompaniment of their actions before they became ill.

It is in the setting of flatness or incongruity of mood that a schizophrenic patient can be overcome by an irresistible impulse to kill. The absence of the normal affect of horror at such an impulse will be one reason why there is no obvious restraint upon his action. If the killing of a person has no more meaning than, say, the purchase of a packet of cigarettes, it is hardly surprising that the normal moral and legal considerations have little or no restraining effect. Indeed, it is not unusual for such a crime to be followed by the minimum of attempt to cover up its traces, or the murderer may even go to the police to confess.

On this class of illness East writes:[1] 'In dementia praecox murder may be associated with mental elation or depression and with the emotional incongruity so frequently observed in this disease. After the murder the emotional reaction is often markedly apathetic and the homicide sometimes relates the method of his killing in detail in a calm and detached manner.'

To the layman such behaviour might give an impression of cold-bloodedness and callousness which only adds to the enormity of the act. It is easier to understand a person who kills because he is firmly convinced that his victim is the agent responsible for the alleged persecutions to which he has been subjected; to enter into the world of one who kills for no apparent motive without showing the least upset over the offence is not easy even for the trained observer; only with the knowledge of the disease process and its effects upon the mental life of the patient can one begin to understand how such a crime came to be committed and why the prisoner remains so unmoved.

The affective loss of the schizophrenic is to be distinguished from the dissociative reaction, the 'belle indifference' of the hysteric. Admittedly, it is unusual for the hysteric to commit brutal or shocking crimes and when these occur in a setting of mental illness one would be cautious before diagnosing hysteria as a cause. No doubt the coolness and indifference of the hysteric to personal difficulties and misfortunes is at times hard to distinguish from a schizophrenic flatness of mood. Nevertheless, not only will other symptoms of schizophrenia be absent but it is common for the hysteric to display a lability of emotion very different from the sustained apathy or incongruity of schizophrenia. An hysterical patient displayed a marked indifference to the effects of her behaviour and stay in hospital upon her husband and family. A few minutes later she wept profusely when relating her fears lest her

[1] East, W. N. (1936). *Medical Aspects of Crime*. London; Churchill

absence might cause her pet dog to pine for her. Hysterical behaviour is more commonly seen as a consequence rather than a cause of criminal behaviour, and such symptoms as amnesia, dissociation, and apparent unconcern can give rise to great difficulties.[1]

Severe states of depression in which the patient comes to feel that as a result of past misdeeds, real or imaginary, he and his family are to suffer some dreadful fate are sometimes associated with homicide and attempted suicide on the part of the patient. He may come to feel that, rather than allow his family to face the consequences which he believes to be impending, it would be better if he killed them all and then took his own life. In such cases the psychotic nature of the accused's illness is usually clear and a verdict of guilty but insane will be returned. Batt has described 20 such cases, 19 of which occurred in women, the victims usually being their children.[2] Mania, in which the patient comes to feel immense surges of energy, well-being and elation are, according to Macniven[3] rarely associated with homicide. He argued that the distractibility of the patient and the poor co-ordination of his movements, should he make a violent assault, rarely permit a determined attempt at murder. Nevertheless, East[4] stated that out of 300 persons committed to Broadmoor for homicide, 28 were diagnosed as mania compared with 62 suffering from melancholia. It would appear that the affective psychoses can lead to homicide in a fair number of cases whether the illness is characterized by depression or manic excitement. In such cases the symptoms will usually be obvious and the diagnosis clear. It can happen, however, that a severely depressed patient shows some lightening of his symptoms after a suicidal attempt, in which case it may not be so easy to say how serious was the depression at the time. On the other hand, states of mania seem not to remit suddenly, and such a patient who had been arrested following a homicidal attack would show many of the symptoms of his illness until treatment had been instituted.

Motiveless outbursts of rage occur not only in the schizophrenic but also in epilepsy and psychopathy. How far such outbursts in epilepsy are formes frustes of major attacks is not easy to say, but undoubtedly some epileptics do experience sudden mood changes during which irritability and violence can occur. The association between epilepsy and psychopathy is, in any case, a close one, and it may be that the so-called epileptic equivalent is, in fact, an example of the psychopath's explosive irritability occurring in a person who has epilepsy in addition.

---

[1] *See* Podola's case, p. 126, *post*
[2] Batt, J. C. (1948). *J. ment. Sci.* **94,** 782
[3] Macniven, A. (1944). In *Mental Abnormality and Crime*. London; Macmillan
[4] East, W. N. (1936). *Medical Aspects of Crime*, p. 378. London; Churchill

The EEG abnormalities in states of aggressive psychopathy have already been mentioned, and although such abnormalities are in no way specific for epilepsy it is difficult to rule out completely the possibility that *some* outbursts of aggressive rage in psychopathic personalities are related to the abnormal cerebral discharges shown in the EEG recording. When, of course, there is some suggestion that the conscious state of the accused was impaired at the time of his offence the EEG evidence becomes even more important.

Delusions

To the layman delusional beliefs and hallucinatory experiences are the very essence of insanity. Certainly their presence, if proved, has always impressed courts of law for, as Cockburn said during his defence of M'Naghten, delusions are the hallmark of insanity. Nevertheless, it is as well to point out that severe psychotic states can occur without either symptom just as they can arise during the course of less serious complaints.

The subject of partial delusion has already been discussed. It is enough to say that no such state exists, and that any legal reasoning based on this particular notion is likely to be erroneous. The term was used to indicate a class of illness in which, except for certain subjects about which the patient had delusional beliefs, the patient appeared to be wholly rational. The old term of monomania was used to describe this clinical picture which could vary from a mere eccentricity of conduct and belief to a fully developed state of paranoia. Whatever the surface appearance of the patient may be, there can be no doubt that such a system of delusional beliefs indicates a profound disturbance of the patient's affective life which would not be limited to one feature of his existence. Hence, in many cases, the total lack of judgment and control which characterizes their behaviour when the particular matter on which they are deluded is being considered.

Delusions are generally defined as being false beliefs which are unshaken by rational argument and which are inappropriate to the social and cultural context of the individual who holds them. They are classified as primary or secondary depending on whether or not they arise, fully developed, in response to some trivial or apparently irrelevant episode, or occur in response to hallucinatory experiences or feelings of bodily or mental change ascribed to some alien force acting upon him. Whereas primary delusions develop almost entirely in a setting of schizophrenia, secondary delusions are not specific to any particular form of mental illness.

An example of the first class of delusion is a young woman who, during a storm, came to believe that the thunder-claps were the voice of God telling her that she was a saint. At the same time the entire population of the country in which she was living was informed of this fact through the medium of the storm. The whole experience was attended by marked emotional tension which added to the conviction of the reality of the belief. Rational argument failed entirely to alter the delusion which was maintained without any reason being given for its retention.

As an example of a secondary delusion one would cite the case of an aurally hallucinated man who believed that the voices he heard were those of some people sitting in a cafe where he was having a meal. Feeling that they were accusing him of homosexual practices, without further thought he picked up a chair to attack one of the other customers. Fortunately, he did no serious injury and was brought into hospital for treatment.

Because of the absence of reason and forethought laymen sometimes feel that delusions are due to disturbance of the intellectual or rational faculties. Nevertheless, formal testing will fail to reveal any serious impairment of intellectual capacity unless such a symptom was present before the onset of the psychosis. The fact that reason makes little impression on a delusional belief adds force to the argument that such beliefs are sustained by emotional tensions and disturbances appearing in the guise of delusional and hallucinatory symptoms.

Because of the weakened state of will and self-control attendant upon the delusion many patients find themselves without the capacity to control undesirable impulses. In such circumstances impulsive and apparently unprovoked assaults occur which may be rationalized afterwards in the light of the delusion which caused the patient to feel that an alien force guided his actions or that, because of his supposed status, he was no longer bound by the ordinary conventions of law and society. Despite the clinical evidence of the overwhelming force of such impulses it is hard to convince a court of their existence or that they may be the sole explanation of the conduct of which the prisoner stands accused.

The majority of patients suffering from delusions show no impairment of consciousness or intellect. In states of delirium or in the course of chronic organic psychoses many patients manifest paranoid ideas, usually of a poorly sustained or unsystematized character, on account of which they may act by committing violent assaults upon relatives or other persons in their vicinity. No doubt the impaired conscious state of the patient contributes to the delusional beliefs, but when such episodes are short-lived it may not be easy to say with any certainty what was the state of mind of the patient when he made his assault. The existence of other symptoms of organic brain disease may allow one to infer episodes of clouded consciousness to account for impulsive, deviant behaviour. The clearer and more systematized the delusions, the more likely it is that they arise in a setting of psychosis uncomplicated by conscious impairment. Even so, many cases of progressive dementia do manifest definite paranoid beliefs leading to homicidal attacks without any obvious change in conscious awareness. Previous abnormalities of personality such as suspiciousness and undue sensitivity to slights, real or imagined, coupled with evidence of physical disease will help one to come to a proper conclusion regarding the nature of the illness.

Disturbances of Intellectual Capacity

Impaired intellectual function will show itself either in the primary amentias manifest from early childhood, or as a symptom of the progressive organic dementias due to physical disease of the brain. The older term of mental deficiency covered all those forms of primary intellectual defect now classified as subnormality and severe subnormality. The severely subnormal rarely present any special problem largely because they will be under care. Should they commit an offence which brings them into court it is almost certain that their mental state will be recognized and that they will be found unfit to plead. In any case, persons so severely handicapped could not possibly be held responsible for their actions. No doubt these facts explain why few severely subnormal persons are to be found in prison. According to East[1] only 0·42 per cent of a prison population was derived from those who had been certified as mental defectives. This is almost certainly a low estimate of the frequency of association of subnormality with crime, and some observers put the association as high as 10 per cent, the proportion being greater in the case of chronic recidivists.[2]

Those of subnormal intelligence—feeble-minded persons in the older terminology—may, according to Lewis,[3] be charged with crimes usually associated with impulsive behaviour and social inefficiency. Theft, sex offences and vagrancy are very much commoner than crimes of violence or housebreaking. He goes on to write: 'From the medical and scientific standpoint, the mentally defective adult is simply a person of adult age with the mind of a child; and it is possible to give a fairly accurate estimate of a child's age.'

One would comment particularly on the impulsive nature of criminal offences committed by subnormal persons, and also on the inadequate

[1] East, W. N. (1938). *J. ment. Sci.* **84,** 203
[2] Mayer-Gross, W., Slater, E. and Roth, M. (1954). *Clinical Psychiatry.* London; Cassell
[3] Lewis, E. O. (1944). In *Mental Abnormality and Crime*, p. 99. London; Macmillan

steps taken to conceal offences. A sudden assault may occur because of some trifling frustration which would not trouble a normal adult. Their capacity to withstand the effects of alcohol is very limited and it is while under the influence of this drug that many feeble-minded persons lose the remnants of their self-control and commit violent, sexual crimes. The degree of responsibility that can be imputed to such a person will vary with the severity of his intellectual impairment. The more this is evident the less can the patient be said to be fully responsible. Furthermore, a good many subnormal persons suffer short-lived, atypical, psychotic illnesses during which their behaviour may become disturbed, with the possibility that some impulsive act may lead to their detention. By the time they come under observation much of the psychotic reaction will have disappeared leaving one to infer the state of mind of the offender at the time of his act. The older term 'moral defective' is no longer used. Such persons did not necessarily show any intellectual deficiency although they often manifested 'strongly vicious or criminal propensities'. The term 'psychopathic personality' is now applied to this category of mental disorder which presents many problems different from those of subnormal intelligence.

The dementias of old age are characterized by loss of emotional control, disturbances of memory and orientation, failure of grasp and concentration, transient disturbances of consciousness and, particularly in arteriosclerotic disease of the brain, short-lived paranoid reactions during which violent assaults on members of the patient's family may occur. Of much greater frequency, however, is the incidence of sexual crime among such persons due to the general disinhibition and loss of awareness of social convention. It is generally observed that along with the intellectual decline is an equally severe loss of emotional control. In such circumstances a patient may inadvertently commit some fraudulent act through sheer lack of inability to manage his affairs yet, at the same time, show a rather feeble façade of respectability behind which lies a general impoverishment of all aspects of mental function.

These four groups of symptoms, namely, impairment of conscious awareness, disturbance of affect, delusional beliefs and intellectual defect rarely exist alone but are likely to be accompanied by one or more of the others. Organic dementia, for example, will characteristically show intellectual deficiencies but may also show short periods when the conscious state is clouded, fleeting paranoid delusions and a minimum of emotional control leading to severely disturbed behaviour. Any of the organic brain syndromes can also show a similar grouping of symptoms which, taken together, adequately explain the basis of the patient's misconduct. The functional psychoses are less often typified by disturbances of consciousness or intellectual defect but in these the existence of sustained delusional beliefs with accompanying emotional disorganization are usually obvious and paramount.

Naturally, these four groups of symptoms do not exhaust the repertoire of psychological disturbance but should none of them be present it may well be very difficult to account for a criminal act in terms of psychiatric illness. It is possible that sexual offences comprise the largest group—apart from psychopathy—in which the criminal act itself is the sole evidence of psychiatric illness. On occasions acts of indecent exposure occur in a setting of excitement and a sense of compulsion which cannot be resisted, but the majority of sexual offences appear to take place without any obvious disturbance of mental function. Unless one is going to say that sexual deviation is something outside the control and volition of the individual—a fact which may be correct—one will have to admit that the majority of such offenders are fully aware of the implication of their acts and are responsible for them.

Once one moves away to consider the crimes of violence and homicide the likelihood of discovering major psychiatric abnormalities becomes greater. In the case of murder it would be very difficult to convince a jury that the prisoner was not fully responsible for his act if it occurred in a setting of clear consciousness, was premeditated and not impulsive, did not happen because of an acute emotional crisis, and if the prisoner showed no evidence of intellectual impairment or delusional symptoms. The fact that so many murders do take place in a setting of mental disorder seems to indicate that the symptoms discussed in this chapter will be features of the offender's mental state at the time he committed his crime. In the face of clear evidence of the existence of such symptoms it will be for the jury to decide whether or not the accused was responsible for his act.

7—Diminished Responsibility

The Homicide Act, 1957, section 2 (1) states that, where a person kills or is a party to the killing of another, he shall not be convicted of murder if he was suffering from such abnormality of mind (whether arising from a condition of arrested or retarded development of mind or any inherent causes or induced by disease or injury) as substantially impaired his mental responsibility for his acts and omissions in doing or being a party to the killing. In section 2 (2) it is stated that on a charge of murder, it shall be for the defence to prove that the person charged is by virtue of this section not liable to be convicted of murder. The degree of proof of diminished responsibility required from the defence is that it should be shown as a matter of probability rather than beyond all reasonable doubt that the accused was so affected. By this Act the concept of diminished responsibility taken from Scottish law was introduced into English courts; and it must be emphasized that it is a concept which applies only to cases where murder is charged and has no place in other criminal charges or in civil cases.

The Royal Commission on Capital Punishment (Cmd. 8932, p. 392) gives a useful summary of the development of the plea of diminished responsibility leading to a verdict of culpable homicide in Scotland. The doctrine appears to have originated in the case of Dingwall,[1] an epileptic accused of murder. In his instructions to the jury Lord Deas indicated that it was within their province to return a verdict of culpable homicide if murder seemed inappropriate. He felt that the prisoner's mental state would be adequate justification for the lesser verdict. Since this case the doctrine has been applied on a number of occasions and, between the years 1900–1949, of 494 persons proceeded against for murder, 54 were convicted of culpable homicide after the defence had been one of insanity or diminished responsibility. The evidence given to the Royal Commission on Capital Punishment indicated that the system worked well, covering as it did, epileptics, mental defectives, alcoholics and persons suffering from conditions 'bordering on insanity'.[2]

Various attempts have been made to define the state of mind which would justify a plea of diminished responsibility, the best known being

[1] H.M. Advocate v. Dingwall (1867), Irv. 466
[2] Royal Commission on Capital Punishment (1949–53), Cmd. 8932, para. 382

94

that of Lord Alness in the case of Savage.[1] 'It is very difficult to put it in a phrase', he said, 'but it has been put in this way: that there must be aberrations or weakness of mind; that these must be some form of mental unsoundness; that there must be a state of mind which is bordering on, though not amounting to, insanity; that there must be a mind so affected that responsibility is diminished from full responsibility to partial responsibility—in other words, the prisoner in question must be only partially accountable for his actions. And I think one can see running through the cases that there is implied . . . that there must be some form of mental disease.' In the same direction to the jury Lord Alness made it quite clear that a person who committed a crime while intoxicated with alcohol would not be covered by the plea of diminished responsibility. 'To say that a man, who takes drink and while under its influence commits a crime is to be excused from the penalty of the crime merely because he made himself drunk would, of course, be a most perilous doctrine. And it is not the law of Scotland. The man himself is responsible for getting drunk, and the mere fact that he has taken drink . . . is not sufficient to excuse him from the consequences of his crime.'

In the case of Kirkwood,[2] Lord Normand indicated that the plea of diminished responsibility would rest upon medical evidence in the case and that mental weakness or weakness of responsibility would be regarded in Scottish Law as extenuating circumstances. Lord Cooper, in Braithwaite's case,[3] reviewed a number of cases in which diminished responsibility had been pleaded, summarizing them by saying: 'You will see . . . the stress that has been laid in all these formulations upon weakness of intellect, aberration of mind, mental unsoundness, partial insanity, great peculiarity of mind and the like. . . . With those passages in your mind, I can only say to you that that is the sort of thing you have got to look for in the evidence led in support of this defence. If you can find enough to justify such a conclusion, your verdict should be one of culpable homicide only.'

It seems generally to be agreed that evidence of psychopathic personality is not sufficient to warrant a verdict of diminished responsibility. In the case of Carraher,[4] Lord Normand considered the situation of the psychopath in such cases, indicating that this is a clinical condition in which are included persons who from childhood or early youth show gross abnormality in their social behaviour and emotional reaction, and who do not as a rule show enough insanity to be certifiable as insane. Referring to the opinion of the judge presiding

[1] H.M. Advocate v. Savage, [1923] S. C. (J). 49
[2] Kirkwood v. H.M. Advocate, [1939] S. C. (J.). 36
[3] H.M. Advocate v. Braithwaite, [1945] S. C. (J.). 55
[4] H.M. Advocate v. Carraher, [1946] S. C. (J.). 108

at Carraher's trial, he said: 'I also have great doubt whether it was evidence of anything approaching to mental disease, aberration or great peculiarity of mind. . . . in this instance much of the evidence given by the medical witnesses is, to my mind, descriptive rather of a typical criminal than of a person of the quality of one whom the law has hitherto regarded as being possessed of diminished responsibility. . . . I am of opinion that the plea of diminished responsibility, which, as was said in Kirkwood's case, is anomalous in our law, should not be extended or given wider scope than has hitherto been accorded to it in the decisions.'

In his evidence to the Royal Commission on Capital Punishment, Sir David Henderson felt that psychopathy should be included as a mental state which would justify the reduction of the verdict from murder to culpable homicide, but it is evident from these rulings that this has not been accepted in Scottish law. Drunkenness, as such, is equally unacceptable as an extenuating circumstance mitigating punishment when a murder has been committed after taking alcohol.

The Royal Commission on Capital Punishment examined the doctrine of diminished responsibility, admitting that the arguments in favour of its introduction into English law were strong. Nevertheless, for a number of reasons, they felt unable to accept these arguments. A considerable body of medical evidence opposed its introduction on the grounds that such a doctrine would throw great responsibility on the medical witness, that it would be too difficult a matter for an English jury to decide, and that it would be wisest to leave it to the executive to make proper inquiries after sentence had been passed should circumstances warrant such an inquiry.[1] On the matter of diminished responsibility the Royal Commission recommended that the sentence of death should not be carried out on any person certifiable as a mental defective; that when murder is committed by an epileptic there is a strong presumption that the underlying abnormality of the brain of the accused would have a bearing on the killing which would lead one to question whether the death sentence should be carried out; and that psychopathic personality, though not of itself justifying a defence of insanity, ought to be given due weight in deciding whether capital punishment should be inflicted.

According to Gibson and Klein[2] between the years 1957 and the end of 1960, 96 persons originally charged with murder were found guilty of manslaughter under section 2 of the Homicide Act. From 1952–1956, 362 persons were committed for trial for offences finally recorded as murder; 12 per cent were acquitted, 40 per cent were

[1] Royal Commission on Capital Punishment (1949–53), Cmd. 8932, para. 410
[2] Gibson, E. and Klein, S. (1961). *Murder*. London; H.M. Stationery Office

convicted and sentenced and 47 per cent were found to be insane. Between 1957–1960, 392 persons were committed for trial for offences finally recorded as murder or manslaughter by reason of diminished responsibility; 14 per cent were acquitted, 39 per cent were convicted and sentenced for murder, 24 per cent were convicted and sentenced for manslaughter by reason of diminished responsibility and 22 per cent were found to be insane. The total proportion of persons found to be suffering from mental abnormality was almost exactly the same after the Homicide Act as before, but the defence of diminished responsibility had to a considerable extent replaced the plea of insanity.

According to the Home Secretary, the total number of cases between March 24, 1957, the date on which the Homicide Act came into force, and the end of 1961, in which the charge of murder was reduced to manslaughter on the ground of diminished responsibility was 128.[1] It is evident from these figures that English juries and medical witnesses have less difficulty in coming to decisions on this subject than was feared. Nevertheless, a number of cases have come before the Court of Criminal Appeal with conflicting results. It is probably too early to expect absolute clarity about the working of the Homicide Act but from the judgments given so far it is possible to detect certain broad trends in its operation.

The wording of the Act implies the widest possible interpretation of 'abnormality of mind'. Certainly it includes mental subnormality, thereby embodying numerous recommendations in the past that deficient intelligence should be recognized as a factor which might cause persons to commit serious crimes for which they are not fully responsible. The general terms in which the Act is phrased also appear to allow the inclusion of cases suffering from frank psychosis which would, presumably, in the past have been dealt with within the framework of the M'Naghten Rules. In such cases one might have expected that the Crown could call for evidence of insanity to rebut the defence of diminished responsibility, but so far there appears to be no definite ruling on this point.[2] Both Tickell[3] and Rowley[4] suffered from schizophrenia yet were found guilty of manslaughter on the ground of diminished responsibility and sent to prison. Presumably such cases could be removed from prison to hospital if their mental state warranted treatment and, from the judge's remarks in both cases one might deduce that this was the intention. In which case one is left wondering why a hospital order was not made at the time as was done in a case recently tried at the Oxfordshire Assize.

[1] *The Times*, June 9, 1962   [2] [1961] Crim. L. R. 507
[3] R. *v.* Tickell (1958), *The Times*, Jan. 24
[4] R. *v.* Rowley (1960), *The Times*, July 19

In the case of Byrne,[1] Lord Parker, C.J. said: '"Abnormality of mind" . . . means a state of mind so different from that of ordinary human beings that the reasonable man would term it abnormal. It appears to us to be wide enough to cover the mind's activities in all its aspects, not only the perception of physical acts and matters and the ability to form a rational judgment whether an act is right or wrong, but also the ability to exercise will-power to control physical acts in accordance with that rational judgment.' Lord Parker went on to indicate that it is for the jury to consider all the evidence (not only medical evidence) in coming to a conclusion whether the accused suffers from abnormality of mind. 'They are not bound to accept the medical evidence if there is other material before them which, in their good judgment, conflicts with it and outweighs it.' From this pronouncement one can conclude that it is for the jury to assess how substantial was the degree of impairment of mental capacity, and that this difficult assessment is not one to be decided by the medical witness. Undoubtedly, the medical expert will be asked to express his opinion on the matter. Having done so, as was affirmed in the case of Jennion[2] it is left to the jury to decide medical issues and when there is a conflict of opinion on the degree of impairment of responsibility only the jury can decide which evidence carries the most weight.

In Rose v. R.[3] it was held that diminished responsibility is not to be equated with defect of reason under the M'Naghten Rules. From the judgment in this case it appears that mental abnormality can be invoked to account for a temporary loss of control which is very different from the meaning generally ascribed to legal insanity. This ruling appears to conflict with that given in the cases of Spriggs[4] and Walden[5] to which reference will be made later.

As was implied in the recommendations of the Royal Commission on Capital Punishment, epilepsy would be good grounds for a plea of manslaughter due to diminished responsibility when murder is the charge. In a number of cases this has been accepted. In the case of Bailey,[6] the appellant, an epileptic, had been found guilty of murder despite undisputed medical evidence supporting a plea of diminished responsibility. Lord Parker, C.J. held that in the face of uncontradicted medical evidence the jury must find in accordance with the evidence. The verdict was reduced to manslaughter but the sentence of life imprisonment remained unchanged. In this case Lord Parker's views

[1] R. v. Byrne, [1960] 3 All E. R. 1
[2] R. v. Jennion, [1962] 1 All E. R. 689
[3] Rose v. R., [1961] 1 All E. R. 859
[4] R. v. Spriggs, [1958] 1 All E. R. 300
[5] R. v. Walden, [1959] 3 All E. R. 203
[6] R. v. Bailey, [1961] Crim. L. R. 828

on perverse verdicts ignoring medical evidence are in marked contrast to those of Lord Goddard, C.J. in the case of Rivett,[1] a judgment which, by implication, was criticized by Mr. Justice Edmund Davies in the recent case of Jennion. Epilepsy as a cause of diminished responsibility was accepted in the case of Abbott charged with capital murder,[2] but again the medical evidence was not challenged.

Because of the wording of the Homicide Act few cases of mental defect exonerated under section 2 have been reported. Matheson,[3] a subnormal sexual psychopath, was originally convicted of capital murder, but the verdict of manslaughter on the grounds of diminished responsibility was substituted by the Court of Criminal Appeal, largely because the uncontroverted medical evidence as to the mental abnormality of the accused was ignored by the jury. Williams,[4] a boy aged 15 years, charged with murdering an 8-year-old child in a children's home, was found guilty of manslaughter by reason of retarded or arrested development of mind and was ordered to be detained for 10 years. No doubt many other cases have been dealt with without much difficulty largely because the wording of the act specifically mentions those suffering from arrested or retarded development of mind as being persons suffering from mental abnormality who might show impaired responsibility.

It is difficult to discover how far neurotic illness can be accepted as leading to substantial impairment of mental responsibility. Neustatter[5] is of the opinion that neurotic patients do qualify and a number of cases have been reported in which evidence of such illness has been presented and accepted by the court. In the case of Bastian[6] the accused, who was charged with the murder of his two sons, initially pleaded guilty to the charge but later changed the plea to one of 'not guilty'. It was alleged that he committed the murder in 'a state of frenzy'. The prosecution asked for a verdict of guilty but insane but the jury found him guilty of manslaughter. Neustatter, who was a medical witness in the trial, wrote to the *British Medical Journal*[7] stating that one month before the murder the accused was a patient in a mental hospital but the diagnosis seems to have been undecided. Nevertheless, Dr. Neustatter and Dr. Brisby, the Principal Medical Officer of Brixton Prison, were both in agreement that Bastian was suffering from a disease of the mind which would render him incapable of

---

[1] R. *v.* Rivett (1950), 34 Cr. App. Rep. 87
[2] R. *v.* Abbott (1962), *The Times*, June 30
[3] R. *v.* Matheson, [1958] 2 All E. R. 87
[4] R. *v.* Williams (1960), *The Times*, Oct. 20
[5] Neustatter, W. L. (1960), *Med.-Leg. J.* **28**, 92
[6] R. *v.* Bastian, [1958] 1 All E. R. 568
[7] Neustatter, W. L. (1958). *Brit. med. J.* **1**, 1063

knowing what he was doing at the time of the act. From such evidence as is available it seems that Bastian had been suffering from depression or hysteria, but the question of schizophrenia was not ruled out.

By contrast Harrison was sentenced to life imprisonment for the murder of his wife despite the evidence of hysterical personality which was regarded as an abnormality of mind not amounting to insanity.[1] Barber[2] was more fortunate, for the medical evidence of immaturity and mental instability was accepted in reducing the charge of murder to one of manslaughter for which he was sentenced to 3 years imprisonment.

Morris[3] was said to suffer from depression and a chronic anxiety state. He was found guilty of manslaughter by reason of diminished responsibility but was given a life sentence.

Lawrence,[4] who suffered from hysteria which was regarded by the doctors who gave evidence as a disease of the mind, was found guilty of manslaughter, a verdict also returned in another case of hysteria, that of McDonnell.[5]

From a study of these reported cases it is difficult to obtain any general guidance. Presumably where there is clear evidence of neurotic illness or personality disorder the defence can put up a case of diminished responsibility due to the mental state of the accused. There is nothing in the wording of the Homicide Act to exclude such illness and it is left to the jury to decide how acceptable the plea is to them. If found guilty of manslaughter by reason of diminished responsibility the sentence may vary from life imprisonment, as in the case of Morris, to 3 years probation as in the case of McDonnell.

As might have been expected the greatest difficulty in applying the Homicide Act has been encountered in the case of psychopaths. The present situation seems to be that aggressive psychopathy as such is a poor defence unless other factors such as epilepsy, mental defect or sexual abnormality are present in addition to the psychopathy. However, in a recent case,[6] it seemed to be implied that if the accused, an aggressive psychopath, had committed the murder in a sudden explosion of violence without premeditation he would show substantial impairment of responsibility. The Court of Criminal Appeal substituted a verdict of manslaughter for that of capital murder mainly because they felt there had been some misdirection of the jury on this point of premeditation.

The question of psychopathy has been considered in a number of

[1] R. v. Harrison (1957), *The Times*, Sept. 19
[2] R. v. Barber (1959), *The Times*, Apr. 19
[3] R. v. Morris, [1961] Crim. L. R. 481
[4] R. v. Lawrence (1958), *The Times*, May 9
[5] R. v. McDonnell (1962), *The Times*, Mar. 14
[6] R. v. McCrorey (1962), [1962] Crim. L. R. 703

instances by the Court of Criminal Appeal. In the case of Dunbar,[1] the accused was convicted of capital murder in furtherance of theft. The prisoner was a psychopath who had given notice of his intention to steal and, fearing that he might have been recognized, he killed a woman in the house by hitting her with a bottle. The appeal was allowed on a point of law in that the judge had failed to indicate the nature of the burden of proof resting on the defence who had pleaded diminished responsibility.

In the case of Spriggs[2] the accused was convicted of capital murder for shooting a barman who had turned him out of a public house. Following the murder the prisoner attempted suicide and at his trial evidence was offered that he had been discharged from the R.A.F. on account of personality disorder, psychiatric troubles and inadequacy. The EEG was abnormal, suggesting emotional instability. The appeal was based on the grounds that the trial judge should have directed the jury on matters of mental abnormality and diminished responsibility in the light of the medical evidence of psychopathy. It was felt that the summing-up had been unfair to the appellant's case. The appeal was dismissed by Lord Goddard, C.J. saying: 'It is not for judges, when Parliament has defined a particular state of things, as they have defined here what is to amount to diminished responsibility, to re-define or attempt to define the definition.' Jurists were quick to point out that Parliament had done nothing of the sort, and it was left to Mr. Justice Hilbery, in the case of Walden,[3] and Lord Parker, C.J., in the case of Byrne already mentioned, to make some attempt at explaining what is meant by mental abnormality.

Walden was convicted of capital murder for shooting two persons. At the trial evidence was given for the defence that the accused was a paranoid personality sufficient to constitute an abnormality of mind which would impair his responsibility. He shot a man talking to a girl to whom he, the accused, had proposed marriage, and then shot the girl. The Court of Criminal Appeal felt that there had been no misdirection and in the face of conflicting medical evidence the jury's verdict should be allowed to stand.

In a more recent case in which there was medical evidence of paranoid personality[4] the accused had killed his wife believing her to be unfaithful. It was suggested that this belief was a delusion but Lord Parker, C.J. criticized the medical evidence on the grounds that it had not been fully tested in the court. He said that it was not for doctors

[1] R. v. Dunbar, [1957] 2 All E. R. 737
[2] R. v. Spriggs, [1958] 1 All E. R. 300
[3] R. v. Walden, [1959] 3 All E. R. 203
[4] R. v. Ahmed Din, [1962] 2 All E. R. 124

to decide whether a man had or had not reasonable grounds for believing his wife to be unfaithful. The appeal against conviction of non-capital murder was refused.

Matheson[1] was convicted of capital murder in furtherance of theft. The accused was a confirmed homosexual of low intelligence who killed a boy in peculiarly revolting circumstances. The boy had been his homosexual partner and medical evidence, which was un-contradicted, indicated that because of his low intelligence Matheson was suffering from diminished responsibility. The jury ignored the medical evidence but the Court of Criminal Appeal felt that they were wrong in doing so and substituted a verdict of manslaughter.

As Williams pointed out[2] the conflicting decisions reached in the cases of Walden and Spriggs on one hand and in Matheson's case on the other appear to rest on the fact that whereas Walden and Spriggs, despite evidence of psychopathy, were men of normal intelligence, Matheson was sub-normal. It looks as if the courts feel that while psychopaths of normal intelligence should have proper control of their emotions, less should be demanded in this respect of those of subnormal intelligence. This of course, ignores the well-known medical fact that psychopathy has little to do with intelligence.

In the case of Byrne[3] the medical evidence of sexual psychopathy was insufficient to persuade the jury that he showed diminished responsibility on that account. Admittedly, the successful appeal rested largely on a point of law, yet it is possible that the unanimous medical opinion on the prisoner's mental abnormality played a part in securing the lesser verdict of manslaughter. From consideration of these cases one would conclude that a psychopath of normal intelligence who commits murder will be unlikely to avoid conviction on this charge unless there is other evidence of mental abnormality which includes sexual abnormality.

In the case of Di Duca[4] the appellant was convicted of capital murder in furtherance of theft. He pleaded that because he had been drinking beforehand his responsibility was thereby diminished. At trial the jury asked the judge whether, if a man's mind was affected by alcohol when he killed another, the verdict could be reduced to manslaughter. The judge gave them the usual answers (to be discussed in the next chapter) indicating that drink as such did not excuse a man of the consequences of his actions, but the appeal was based on the grounds that he did not direct the jury on the effect of drunkenness on diminished responsibility.

[1] R. v. Matheson, [1958] 2 All E. R. 87
[2] Williams, G. (1960). *Medicine, Science and the Law*, Vol. 1, p. 41
[3] R. v. Byrne, [1960] 3 All E. R. 1
[4] R. v. Di Duca (1959), 43 Cr. App. Rep. 167

On appeal the Court held that whether or not there was 'injury', caused by alcohol, within the meaning of the Homicide Act, there was no evidence to suggest that there was abnormality of the mind as a result: the appeal was dismissed.

From this ruling there is just a hint that if alcohol so affected a person's mind as to produce some abnormality of behaviour other than the criminal act, it might be possible to plead diminished responsibility; but in view of the ruling in Beard's case[1] this is extremely doubtful. Nevertheless, in the case of Di Duca, the Court of Appeal to some extent dodged the issue of whether drink can impair responsibility by arguing that as there was no evidence of impairment in this particular case the question did not arise.

In the case of Jennion[2] already mentioned, although it was accepted that she was a psychopathic personality there was a conflict of medical opinion as to whether this would substantially impair her responsibility. As the issue was left to the jury they decided that she was responsible and she was, accordingly, convicted of non-capital murder.

In a recent case before the Court of Criminal Appeal[3] the conviction was quashed mainly because of some uncertainty concerning the judge's summing-up. The appellant was an aggressive psychopath convicted of capital murder in furtherance of theft. Medical evidence for Crown and defence was satisfied that he was abnormal from inherent causes, a psychopath liable in moments of crisis to explode into violence. There was ample evidence of premeditation of the theft but it was suggested by the medical evidence that if the killing was premeditated there would be no case for diminished responsibility, but that if he killed in a crisis when taken by surprise there would be substantial impairment of his responsibility. It remains to be seen what effect this reasoning will have on future decisions in murders by aggressive psychopaths, but as the decision in Rose v. R.[4] indicated that, where mental abnormality is present to account for a temporary loss of control, the verdict can be one of manslaughter rather than murder, one might expect that sudden impulsive murders by psychopaths should be placed on the same footing.

The present situation in regard to the working of the Homicide Act can be summed up by saying that where there is clear evidence of mental abnormality, whether this be psychosis, epilepsy, subnormality or in some instances neurosis, a plea of diminished responsibility will be accepted. In the case of psychopathy whether this is of the aggressive

[1] Director of Public Prosecutions v. Beard, [1920] A. C. 479
[2] R. v. Jennion (1962), [1962] 1 All E. R. 689
[3] R. v. McCrorey, [1962] Crim. L. R. 703
[4] [1961] 1 All E. R. 859

CRIMINAL RESPONSIBILITY AND MENTAL ILLNESS

type or manifested by extreme touchiness and suspicion (the hallmarks of the paranoid personality) it seems unlikely that a plea of diminished responsibility will be allowed. However, should there be evidence of other mental abnormality along with the psychopathic disorder, there is a good chance that the verdict will be reduced to one of manslaughter.

The effect of drink on responsibility within the framework of the Act has yet to be tested in the Court of Criminal Appeal, but judging by other cases, before the 1957 Act came into force, it seems improbable that the fact that a man was drunk when he committed his murder will be to his avail.

Besides the question of the actual verdict reached in these cases a number of other problems have developed, not the least of which is the matter of sentence after the verdict of section 2 manslaughter has been returned.

As has already been shown by Gibson and Klein,[1] although there has been a substantial decline in the number of verdicts of 'guilty but insane' since 1957, the combined sum of such verdicts with those of section 2 manslaughter comes to the same as the total number of special verdicts before the Homicide Act. This implies that a number of persons who would have been given a Broadmoor sentence before 1957 are now being given prison sentences of varying duration. Of 96 section 2 manslaughter cases recorded between 1857 and 1960, 35 received life sentences, 32 were sentenced to between 5 and 10 years of imprisonment, 14 received sentences of less than 5 years, 2 were detained during Her Majesty's pleasure, and 13 were disposed of in other ways which presumably include hospital orders and probation.

It follows, therefore, that a number of persons who might otherwise have received an indefinite sentence to Broadmoor will be released after comparatively short periods of imprisonment. No doubt, before release, the mental state of the prisoner will be examined and some in any case, may well have been transferred to hospital following sentence. Nevertheless, there is a possibility that mentally ill persons who have committed homicide will be released without any treatment leading to a betterment of their mental state. It is possible to exaggerate this risk but cases are on record of persons being released from State mental hospitals and committing a second murder. One would feel happier about this situation if there was evidence to show that prisoners convicted of section 2 manslaughter would definitely receive treatment during their period of detention. Possibly the new psychopathic prison at Grendon Underwood will take charge of some of these patients who can have no certainty of psychiatric treatment in the ordinary long-stay prisons.

[1] Gibson, E. and Klein, S. (1961). *Murder*, p. 40. London; H.M. Stationery Office

It will have been noticed that cases diagnosed as suffering from psychosis have been dealt with under the Homicide Act. One would have thought that this not only would be against the interest of the prisoner but also contrary to public intention. There already exists a perfectly satisfactory mechanism for dealing with such persons against whom a special verdict could be returned leading to their transfer to one of the State hospitals. One alternative would be, if a verdict of section 2 manslaughter is returned, for the judge to make a hospital order under the Mental Health Act empowering the hospital to detain the patient either for a limited period or for an indefinite time subject to the powers of the Home Secretary.

According to Lady Wootton,[1] out of 43 section 2 manslaughter cases occurring since the inception of the Mental Health Act, 15 have been made the subject of hospital orders. It is likely that the use of these powers will increase but they are unlikely to be invoked too frequently for the disposal of psychopaths unless to one of the special hospitals as in the case of a boy aged 14 years suffering from a psychopathic disorder and found guilty of administering poison to a number of persons, including his father. In this particular case[2] the judge committed the boy to Broadmoor, placing a 15 year restriction on his discharge unless leave was granted by the Home Secretary.

Another alternative would be for the Crown to have power to ask for a verdict of 'guilty but insane' rather than one of manslaughter due to diminished responsibility when such a verdict seems more appropriate or in the public interest. So far there does not appear to be any definite ruling as to whether the prosecution have this right but in the case of Nott[3] leave was given to the prosecution to submit evidence that the accused was not insane but showed diminished responsibility under the Homicide Act. In this particular case the jury returned a verdict of 'guilty but insane'. Conversely, in the case of Bastian[4] it was decided that, where a man sets up a defence of diminished responsibility, it is open to the prosecution to show that he was insane. On the other hand, in the case of Dixon,[5] where diminished responsibility was not pleaded, the judge refused to allow the prosecution to call evidence of insanity saying that it was for the defence to do this on behalf of the accused.

Evidently there are conflicting opinions on these points for in the case of Bratty[6] Lord Justice Denning said: 'The old notion that only the

---

[1] Wootton, B. (1962). *Violence and the Mental Health Services*, p. 15. London; National Association of Mental Health
[2] *The Times*, July 6, 1962   [3] R. *v.* Nott (1958), 43 Cr. App. Rep. 8
[4] R. *v.* Bastian, [1958] 1 All E. R. 568
[5] R. *v.* Dixon, [1961] 3 All E. R. 460
[6] Bratty *v.* Attorney-General for Northern Ireland, [1961] 3 All E. R. 523

defence can raise a plea of insanity is now gone. The prosecution are entitled to raise it and it is their duty to do so rather than allow a dangerous person to be at large.' He went on to argue that the Trial of Lunatics Act, 1883, does not specify that the evidence for insanity should come only from the defence.

From the type of mental disorder justifying a plea of diminished responsibility arises the difficult problem of the psychopathic personality. It has been already indicated that Scottish law does not regard evidence of this disorder as adequate. As Lord Cooper said in the case of Braithwaite[1]: 'It will *not* suffice in law for the purpose of this defence of diminished responsibility merely to show that an accused person has a very short temper, or is unusually excitable and lacking in self-control.' Unfortunately these characteristics of behaviour are those so often seen in aggressive psychopathy; and until one can find some other evidence to support the diagnosis the mere fact that the prisoner is violent and explosive makes it very difficult to say whether or not this is the result of mental disorder or abnormal wickedness. The point has been considered on a number of occasions by Lady Wootton who concludes that, in fact, it is not possible to make this differentiation. With some justification she points to the vagueness of such concepts as 'mental instability', 'emotional immaturity' and other value judgments pinned on to psychiatric diagnoses. Such descriptions can only be drawn from observation of the behaviour of the individual concerned and although in a good many cases there is other evidence to justify the diagnosis of psychopathy this is not always the case.

The same point was made by Williams[2] when he wrote: 'The experts may say . . . that the accused was unable to control his emotions in the normal way. . . . But although this much may be a matter of objective fact there is no logical means by which a proposition as to moral responsibility may be deduced from a proposition as to objective fact. The deduction can be made only if it is agreed that lack of self-control is equivalent to conclusive evidence of diminished responsibility. . . . Thus, an approach in terms of self-control creates the possibility of finding diminished responsibility in every charge of crime.' Manifestly, this is precisely what the courts are not prepared to do, leaving the old problem of whether the accused suffered from an irresistible impulse or merely failed to exercise normal restraint in the unresolved state which has existed for many centuries.

So far, the courts have taken the view that acts of aggression are insufficient to justify the diagnosis of psychopathy and the plea of

[1] H. M. Advocate *v.* Braithwaite, [1945] S. C. (J.). 55
[2] Williams, G. (1960). *Medicine, Science and the Law*, Vol. 1, p. 41

diminished responsibility. When there is evidence of other disturbances of mental function such as subnormality, sexual psychopathy, epilepsy and so forth, then the additional evidence of psychopathy may be thought sufficient to reduce the verdict from one of murder to manslaughter. Furthermore, when the medical evidence on these points is unanimous it would appear that the Court of Criminal Appeal will uphold the diagnosis even though the jury at the time of trial felt justified in ignoring the opinions of psychiatrists and prison medical officers alike.

No doubt it can be said that the exclusion of the purely aggressive psychopath from the category of persons whose mental state warrants a plea of diminished responsibility makes for injustice: yet unless this is done it is hard to see how the courts can act otherwise unless given additional evidence to show that the aggressive act of which the prisoner is accused is but one manifestation of a more general disturbance of personality.

The question of whether or not the effect of drink or drugs on a psychopathic personality justifies the reduction of the verdict to manslaughter has yet to be decided. The problem will be given further consideration in the next chapter; but in one condition, that of pathological intoxication, a case could be made out for the proposition that, because of the abnormal personality, a violent act occurring during the course of this state would not be the act of a normal, responsible person.

In cases of homicide when diminished responsibility is pleaded it is necessary for the medical evidence to be as clear as possible. The courts require to be shown the existence of some definite category of mental disorder from which it can be inferred that, at the time of committing the offence, the prisoner's responsibility was substantially impaired. Fortunately, it is not for the medical witness to decide how substantial this impairment has to be to justify the lesser verdict. In the case, say, of a person of subnormal intelligence, so far as possible the degree of subnormality should be indicated, with any observations of the effect of such abnormality on the emotional control of the accused. It will be for the jury to decide whether or not the case has been made out for substantial impairment of responsibility and when there is clear evidence of epilepsy, subnormality or other mental disorders, it should not be too difficult to reach a proper decision.

When murder is associated with gross sexual psychopathy it is less easy to convince a jury that some peculiarly revolting detail connected with the crime is a feature of mental abnormality. To some extent, therefore, it is understandable that in the cases of Matheson and Byrne, the jury ignored the medical evidence of sexual psychopathy to return the verdict of murder. No doubt confusion over deviation from accepted sexual morality and sexual peculiarity due to mental disorder accounted in part for the verdicts. When the disturbance of sexual behaviour is so gross as to be beyond the comprehension of the ordinary person it will probably be easier to convince a court that such behaviour is due to mental illness and not to sheer moral perversity.

When aggressive acts are the main manifestations of psychopathy it will be difficult to convince the jury that these are not due to ordinary inconsiderateness, ill-temper and absence of self-control. Should there be other evidence of psychopathic behaviour such as a bad work record, previous convictions for lesser offences, repeated, motiveless acts of violence and disturbed interpersonal relationships it might just be possible to convince the jury that, coupled with this earlier behaviour, the final act which has brought the accused before the court is of the same calibre. In the case of Spriggs[1] such evidence did not help him although there can be little doubt that he was an aggressive psychopath whose abnormality had a direct bearing on his homicidal act.

When the signs of psychopathy are those of abnormal suspiciousness, sensitivity and explosive temper amounting to a diagnosis of paranoid personality, it will also be difficult to convince the court that this abnormal touchiness is due to a mental peculiarity which will impair the offender's self-control in certain situations. Where there is evidence of paranoid suspiciousness it is necessary to be cautious before concluding that the possibly delusional beliefs are without foundation. In the case of Ahmed Din[2] the Lord Chief Justice had some pertinent comments to make on this point saying that doctors did not approach the defence of diminished responsibility with a sufficient degree of definition. They tended to mix up opinions based on medical evidence and those based on facts outside their province. It is, of course, very difficult in all instances to be certain whether a delusion has some justification for its existence, but few psychiatrists would come to a firm conclusion on the matter without obtaining supplementary evidence of other symptoms of mental illness. Nevertheless, this particular case indicates how careful one must be to distinguish between opinion and fact in medical evidence. This is particularly difficult in the case of psychopathic disorder. As the courts encounter greater uncertainties in this class of mental illness than in any other it is arguable that medical evidence, unless very carefully phrased, may not be of any real assistance to the court.

[1] R. v. Spriggs, [1958] 1 All E. R. 300
[2] R. v. Ahmed Din, [1962] 2 All E. R. 124

8—Drunkenness, Automatism and Fitness to Plead

Drunkenness

The law relating to drunkenness and crime can be stated fairly simply. In general, mere drunkenness is no excuse for a crime committed while in an intoxicated state; but it may afford a partial answer to the charge if it can be shown that the degree of drunkenness is sufficient to make it impossible for the accused to have formed the necessary intent to commit the crime with which he is charged.

In the case of Beard[1] the legal problems of drunkenness and crime were fully reviewed by the Lord Chancellor, Lord Birkenhead. Prior to the nineteenth century it would appear that, if drunkenness did not actually aggravate the offence, it certainly did little to mitigate it. In Reniger v. Fogossa[2] it was stated that 'if a person that is drunk kills another, this shall be felony, and he shall be hanged for it, and yet he did it through ignorance, for when he was drunk he had no understanding nor memory; but inasmuch as that ignorance was occasioned by his own act and folly, and he might have avoided it, he shall not be privileged thereby'. Coke felt that drunkenness aggravated the crime but Hale thought that it was neither an aggravation nor an excuse but that the drunken man was to have the same judgment as if he were in his right senses at the time of his offence.[3] Hawkins[4] was of the same opinion as Hale, but Blackstone[5] appeared to agree with Coke that drunkenness was an aggravation rather than an excuse for a criminal offence. It is quite clear that these uncompromising opinions did not confuse the mental state caused by excess alcohol with other forms of mental illness, but it is doubtful whether acute or chronic psychosis caused by alcohol would have been differentiated from acute intoxication by these earlier jurists. However, in the light of more recent judgments, it is important that this distinction should be emphasized as it is quite clear that a psychosis induced by drink or drugs would be an adequate answer to a serious charge for an offence committed during the period of the psychosis. The accused would be found guilty but insane in exactly the same manner as would occur if he had been suffering from

[1] Director of Public Prosecutions v. Beard, [1920] A. C. 479
[2] (1550), 1 Plowd 1. 19
[3] Hale, M. *Pleas of the Crown*, Vol. 1, 32
[4] Hawkins. *Pleas of the Crown*, Bk. I, c. 1, s. 6
[5] Blackstone's Commentaries, Bk. 4

some other form of mental illness. For, as Lord Birkenhead observed, the law takes no note of the causes of insanity.

By the early part of the nineteenth century the rather rigid opinions of Hale and Blackstone showed some signs of modification. In 1819, at Worcester Assizes in R. *v.* Grindley, it was held that although voluntary drunkenness was no excuse, if a murder carried out in a drunken state was done in the heat of the moment and was not premeditated, this fact could be taken into account. Admittedly, this opinion was retracted later[1] but it is clear that some change had occurred in judicial attitudes to crime and drunkenness, for in the case of Cruse[2] it was held that, although drunkenness is no excuse for a crime, it was possible for a person to be so drunk as to be unable to form any intention at all.

By 1881 it was accepted that a temporary insanity such as delirium tremens would excuse a man if he had committed an offence during his delirious state.

In the case of Davies, the accused was charged with wounding with intent to murder[3] during an attack of delirium tremens. On this point, Mr. Justice Stephen remarked, 'drunkenness is one thing and the diseases to which drunkenness leads are different things; and if a man by drunkenness brings on a state of disease which causes such a degree of madness, even for a time, which would have relieved him from responsibility if it had been caused in any other way, then he would not be criminally responsible. In my opinion, in such a case the man is a madman, and is to be treated as such, although his madness is only temporary'. This ruling was re-affirmed by Lord Birkenhead in Beard's case.

In the case of Meade[4] the prisoner was charged with the murder of his wife. In a drunken state he had grossly ill-treated her so that she died from the injuries she received. In defence it was stated that the accused was so drunk at the time that he would not have been able to foresee the consequences of his acts or intend to do grievous bodily harm. However, the jury found that he had threatened to beat his wife and, consequently, had already formed the intent, drunk or sober, to injure her. Had he been able to show that he had no such intent in mind his drunken state would, in the opinion of Lord Justice Coleridge have reduced the charge from murder to one of manslaughter.

Meade's case was given further consideration during the appeal hearing in D.P.P. *v.* Beard.[5] The appellant had been found guilty of murder in furtherance of rape. In order to prevent the girl crying out

---

[1] R. *v.* Carroll (1835), 7 C. P. 145
[2] R. *v.* Cruse (1838), 8 C. P. 541
[3] R. *v.* Davies (1881), 14 Cox C. C. 563
[4] R. *v.* Meade, [1909] 1 K. B. 895
[5] [1920] A. C. 479

for help he placed a hand over her mouth and a thumb on her throat so that she suffocated. The defence rested on the drunken state of the accused at the time of his crime, alleging that because of drink he was unable to foresee the consequences of his act and that he had no intention of killing the girl. In his direction to the jury Mr. Justice Bailhache said that if the accused was so drunk as to be incapable of knowing what he was doing and that it was wrong the crime should be reduced to one of manslaughter.

Beard was convicted and sentenced to death but the Court of Criminal Appeal reversed the verdict on the grounds that the judge had been wrong in applying the M'Naghten test in a case of drunkenness. However, the House of Lords re-affirmed the original conviction holding that in this case the judgment in Meade's case did not apply. Had the accused been so drunk as to be incapable of forming the intent to commit rape then the charge could be reduced to one of manslaughter. In this instance this was patently not the case and it was only necessary to prove that the violent act causing death was done in furtherance of the felony of rape.

Contrasting Meade with Beard, Lord Birkenhead said that in the former case it had been necessary to prove that Meade had intended bodily harm to his wife and that his drunkenness did not rebut this intention. In Beard's case it was manifest that he had formed the intent to commit rape and that he was not so drunk as to be incapable of this violent act. Consequently, his state of drunkenness was irrelevant to the further violence resulting in the girl's death. The Lord Chancellor went on to criticize the original direction to the jury which confused drunkenness with insanity. It should be clear that there is an important difference in law between the mental state induced by acute alcoholic intoxication and insanity caused by prolonged abuse of alcohol. Whereas it was proper to apply the M'Naghten test in the latter class of case this test is irrelevant in ordinary drunkenness. 'The defence founded on insanity is one thing; the defence founded on drunkenness is another.'

The law in the matter can be summarized in the following way.

(1) Insanity induced by drink is an answer to the crime charged being on the same level as insanity through any other cause. Even if the psychosis is short-lived, as in the case of delirium tremens, the accused will be exonerated if he comes within the framework of the M'Naghten Rules.

(2) Evidence of drunkenness of such a degree as to render the accused incapable of forming the specific intent essential to constitute the crime should be taken into consideration with the other facts proved in order to determine whether or not he had that intent.

(3) Evidence of drunkenness falling short of a proved incapacity in the accused to form the intent necessary to constitute a crime, and merely establishing that his mind was affected by drink so that he more readily gave way to some violent passion, does not rebut the presumption that a man intends the natural consequences of his act.

It is evident from these rulings that acute alcoholic intoxication is not, in law, to be equated with acute insanity even though some authorities are of the opinion that, because of the known effects of alcohol, a person in a state of acute intoxication is just as much suffering from a short-lived mental illness as would be the case if he had experienced an attack of acute delirium.[1] This opinion will be discussed more fully in later pages but before doing so it will be necessary to consider one further recent case in which alcohol played a major part, as well as those types of mental disorder induced by alcohol, over and above acute intoxication.

In the case of the Attorney-General for Northern Ireland v. Gallagher,[2] the accused was convicted of murdering his wife. The facts in the case were not in dispute. The accused was described as an aggressive psychopath of dull intelligence who drank to excess. The marriage had been marred by repeated quarrels and acts of violence towards his wife by the accused. Four months before the killing, having been admitted to hospital following a particularly violent quarrel, he made a satisfactory improvement, so much so that he returned home on 3 months' trial. However, following a period of drinking he once more assaulted his wife and was readmitted to a mental hospital. On being given leave of absence for one day he went out and bought a knife with a 7-inch blade. He then bought a bottle of whisky and was shortly afterwards seen riding a bicycle towards his wife's house. Some hours later he staggered into a neighbour's house in an intoxicated state with blood on his hands saying that he had killed his wife. He gave himself up to the police who found his wife to be dead from terrible injuries inflicted with a knife and a hammer. The bottle of whisky was almost empty. At the police station Gallagher said that he had made up his mind to kill his wife some 2 or 3 weeks previously. He now had no regrets for having done so.

At trial the defence rested on two propositions, the first being that he was insane at the time of the killing and so should be found guilty but insane under the M'Naghten Rules or, secondly, that by reason of drink he was incapable of forming the necessary intent to murder

---

[1] Mercier, C. (1911). *Crime and Insanity.* London; Williams. And Davis, O. C. M. and Wilshire, F. A. (1935). *Mentality and the Criminal Law.* Bristol; Wright

[2] Attorney-General for Northern Ireland v. Gallagher, [1961] 3 All E. R. 299

his wife. The plea of diminished responsibility under the Homicide Act, 1957, was not available in Northern Ireland.

Gallagher was convicted of murder, for it was clear from his own statement and his purchase of the knife that he had formed the intent to kill his wife, and despite the fact that he was under treatment in a mental hospital it was not shown that he was suffering from a disease of the mind within the M'Naghten test. However, on appeal it was held that the judge had misdirected the jury by asking them to apply the M'Naghten test to the state of mind of the accused at the time before he took alcohol and not at the time of the killing. Had Gallagher been suffering from a disease of the mind before he became intoxicated the question of his drunkenness would have been comparatively irrelevant. However, it was one of the contentions of the defence that because of his psychopathic condition he would show an abnormal reaction to drink which would render him liable to a violent explosion of rage over which he would have no control. It was not claimed that the drink would have induced a state of insanity so it was necessary for the jury to consider his mental state before he took drink. If he was not insane at that time he was guilty of murder as there was abundant evidence to show that he had formed the intent to kill his wife, so that it could be presumed that his drinking merely took the brake off such limited control present when he was sober.

However, because the M'Naghten Rules specifically refer to the state of mind of the accused at the time of committing the act, the Court of Criminal Appeal of Northern Ireland quashed the verdict of murder. They felt unable to substitute a verdict of manslaughter or a special verdict and Gallagher was acquitted despite the fact that he had admitted to killing his wife.

Application was made to appeal to the House of Lords and a certificate of appeal was granted in which the Lords were asked to consider whether a person in a psychopathic condition which is quiescent, may become insane within the meaning of the M'Naghten Rules as the result of the voluntary consumption of intoxicating liquor, if the effect of the liquor is to bring about an explosive outburst in the course of a mental disease, although the mental disease was not itself caused by intoxicating liquor. Put a little more simply, what was being asked was whether the well-known effect of alcohol on persons of Gallagher's temperament and limited intelligence can be regarded as insanity or disease of the mind sufficient to bring the accused within the framework of the M'Naghten Rules.

It should be said straight away, with all respect, that the certificate of appeal rested on a gross misunderstanding of the nature of psychopathy. As has already been explained, psychopathy is a disturbance of personality and character. Consequently it is not possible to say that such a disorder waxes and wanes, is sometimes active and at other times in remission. We do not say that an irascible man is in a state of remission merely because he is not in a raging temper at the time of seeing him. Given a fair knowledge of his character we can predict that certain situations will produce displays of anger, and the fact that he is not angry all the time gives us no cause to believe that should these situations recur, all will be calm and sweet reasonableness.

In the case of Gallagher there was medical evidence, accepted by the Courts, that he was an aggressive psychopath given to outbursts of violence which were more likely to be triggered off when he had been drinking. Nobody with any experience of psychopathic behaviour is likely to expect that a short period in hospital will make any serious difference to an aggressive psychopath's behaviour. Indeed, so far as Gallagher was concerned a month in hospital had such little effect that he had to be readmitted following another display of violence towards his wife. There is no evidence to show that he had recovered from his psychopathic disorder at the time of killing his wife, and it would be quite incorrect to say that his psychopathy was quiescent.

However, on appeal, it was held that the original verdict was the correct one. Lord Reid felt that the only point raised by the appeal was whether the 'explosive outburst' amounted to insanity within the M'Naghten Rules, and he as well as Lord Goddard felt that there was no evidence of insanity sufficient to justify the special verdict. Lord Goddard accepted that Gallagher was an aggressive psychopath which is not the same as legal insanity. He also accepted that his tendency to aggression would be made worse by alcohol leading to loss of self-control. He felt that to regard a self-imposed intoxication as insanity would be contrary to the ruling in Beard's case and in any case there was no evidence to show whether Gallagher had consumed his whisky before or after killing his wife. The general opinion of the Court seems best summarized in the words of Lord Denning. 'If a man, whilst sane and sober, forms an intention to kill and makes preparation for it, knowing it is a wrong thing to do, and then gets himself drunk so as to give himself Dutch courage to do the killing, and whilst drunk carries out his intention, he cannot rely on this self-induced drunkenness as a defence to a charge of murder, nor even as reducing it to man-slaughter. . . . So, also, when he is a psychopath, he cannot by drinking rely on his self-induced defect of reason as a defence of insanity. . . . A psychopath who goes out intending to kill, knowing it is wrong, and does kill, cannot escape the consequences by making himself drunk before doing it.'

It seems generally to be agreed that had Gallagher's case been tried in England he would have been found guilty of manslaughter due to diminished responsibility.[1] However, in the light of Lord Denning's remarks, which make it quite clear that drunkenness would not exonerate a psychopath from the consequences of a crime which he had intended to commit before taking alcohol, it seems at least questionable whether section 2 of the Homicide Act would have been of any avail in this case.

As mentioned in the case of Di Duca[2] the question of the effect of drink and diminished responsibility has yet to be tested in the English courts.

In the light of the judgment in McCrorey[3] it does seem possible that a psychopath who killed as a result of an explosive outburst induced by drink would have a charge of murder reduced to one of manslaughter by reason of diminished responsibility, but only if the killing was not premeditated.

In the case of Gallagher this was emphatically not so even though there was every evidence to show that drink did render him liable to outbursts of violence. What is quite certain is that the mental state of the psychopath who has taken drink is not to be equated with disease of the mind within the framework of the M'Naghten Rules. How far such a ruling would apply in a clear case of pathological intoxication is uncertain, but as psychopathic personality is the most usual basis for this disorder it seems improbable that a display of violence which so often accompanies this condition would be treated in any different fashion from that generally accorded to more ordinary forms of intoxication.

For obvious reasons, leaving aside the legal ruling in Beard's case, it would be quite impractical to equate drunkenness with disease of the mind and insanity. No doubt a case could be made out for the thesis that a drunken person is suffering from a short-lived psychosis, but if this were to be accepted it would result in a number of persons charged with serious crime while in an intoxicated state being sent to Broadmoor, a conclusion which hardly squares with common sense. In such circumstances there is something to be said for the verdict 'drunk but dangerous' proposed by Williams.[4] Unfortunately, however effective such a verdict might be in restraining the occasional excessive drinker from repetition of his offence it would have little influence on the behaviour of the genuine addict.

Evidence of drunkenness in charges less than murder or manslaughter can, presumably, be taken into account in sentencing policy so that, if

[1] Goodhart, A. L. (1961). *The Listener*, Dec. 28
[2] R. *v.* Di Duca (1959), 43 Cr. App. Rep. 167
[3] R. *v.* McCrorey, [1962] Crim. L. R. 703
[4] Williams, G. (1961). *The Criminal Law*, 2nd ed. Sect. 183. London; Stevens

necessary, appropriate medical treatment can be given to prevent a recurrence of the offence. However, when the sentence is fixed by statute the question of drunkenness only becomes relevant if it will reduce a charge of murder to the lesser one of manslaughter. Any treatment which may seem appropriate can then only be an adjunct to punishment without giving much inducement to the offender to mend his ways. The gravity of the offence may be sufficient to convince a man that alcohol is a danger, but in view of the likelihood that many such persons will be psychopaths one could not rely upon this factor in securing total abstention in the future.

It is quite clear that a psychosis induced by alcohol is a disease of the mind within the framework of the M'Naghten Rules. Even if the illness is short-lived, as in delirium tremens, a serious crime committed during this state will be excused, provided it can be shown that the offender was unaware of the nature and quality of his act and did not know that it was wrong. Similar considerations apply to such alcoholic psychoses as alcoholic hallucinosis, Korsakow states, and dementia, provided the factors necessary to negative *mens rea* are present.

Williams is of the opinion that hypoglycaemic episodes and epilepsy induced by alcohol as well as chronic alcoholism, would lead to a return of the special verdict should a person commit a serious crime during a disturbance of consciousness resulting from these conditions.[1] If that is so it will mean that a person who has had a short-lived psychotic episode from which he has now recovered will be sent to one of the State hospitals for an indefinite period. It is certainly arguable that a chronic alcoholic requires a prolonged period of treatment, particularly if his drinking habits have resulted in his committing a serious crime. On the other hand, such persons may derive greater benefit from treatment in an ordinary mental hospital provided reasonable circumstances of security can be observed. Similar considerations apply to persons who kill during an attack of delirium tremens, although it is worth pointing out that once the illness has developed fully, the degree of incoordination of movement and purpose might make a determined assault improbable. It is during the pre-delirious phase, when consciousness is clouded sufficiently to bring about intense fear reactions, that violent acts are most likely to occur.

Mania à potu, or pathological drunkenness, has been defined by Jellinek[2] as a state of blind rage with or without confusion and amnesia, following the ingestion usually of small quantities of alcohol. It is generally agreed that in the great majority of instances the condition

[1] Williams, G. (1961). *The Criminal Law*, Sect. 179. London; Stevens
[2] Jellinek, E. M. (1962). *Alcohol Addiction and Alcoholism*, p. 91. London; Cumberlege

occurs in psychopathic personalities and is rare after head injuries or in hypoglycaemic or epileptic states induced by alcohol. Macdonald evidently is doubtful about the existence of pathological intoxication as an entity for he quoted with approval a statement from the *Quarterly Journal of Studies on Alcohol* in which it is held that the association of amnesia, violence and alcohol does not justify the diagnosis of the dubious hypothetical syndrome of pathological intoxication.[1] However, Roth[2] described a case of a shy, inadequate psychopath who became violent and dangerous after a few drinks, and the author can recall a man, recently released from prison for violent behaviour who, having taken a pint of beer, went on to assault a ticket collector at a London terminus. When seen in hospital a few hours later he had recovered but had no recollection of the episode. There was sufficient evidence to suggest that he had not taken more to drink than was admitted. The assault itself was completely pointless and the patient could not account for his action in any way. It could be assumed that he had experienced some change in conscious awareness which had left him without any knowledge of his actions during the episode. Had he done some serious injury during the attack presumably he would have been found guilty but insane and sent to one of the special hospitals.

The position of the alcohol addict and the chronic alcoholic requires some clarification for whatever may be said about the occasional heavy drinker who commits a crime while intoxicated, he is in a very different position in relation to his drinking when compared with the genuine addict. Following Beard's case it is evident that intoxication, whether by drink or drugs, is not to be equated with a disease of the mind. On the other hand, as Dr. Hobson argued in a recent discussion, the addict, as opposed to the ordinary drinker, is in a very different category.[3] The addict and chronic alcoholic are both suffering from illnesses which could reasonably be classed as diseases of the mind. Such persons are wholly unable to control their drinking habits, so much so that it would be proper to hold that they are not in any ordinary sense fully responsible for their actions. It seems reasonable to maintain that such persons are suffering from disease or injury by their intemperance so much so that, should they kill in an intoxicated state, they could ask that the charge be reduced to one of manslaughter by reason of diminished responsibility. Needless to say, had they formed the intent to kill before they took liquor such a plea would be dismissed despite the evidence of addiction beforehand.

Three final points must be mentioned in connection with crimes

[1] Macdonald, J. M. (1958). *Psychiatry and the Criminal*, p. 136. Springfield, Ill.; Thomas

[2] Roth, M., personal communication

[3] Hobson, J. A. (1962). *Med.-leg. J.* **30**, 85

committed while under the influence of drink or drugs. It is said that a person who commits a serious crime due to a genuine mistake or ignorance caused by drink can ask for the factor of his drunkenness to be taken into account, even though the drunkenness does not excuse the mistake. He may, for example, believe that he is to be assaulted by a bystander and carry out a dangerous assault in self-defence. If the facts can be proved he would have a partial answer to the charge.[1]

It should be emphasized that although the foregoing pages have referred constantly to alcohol as a cause of intoxication they apply equally to other forms of intoxication or psychosis induced by drugs other than alcohol. Because narcotic addiction is a comparatively rare disorder in Great Britain it is natural to relate the legal aspects of intoxication to the more widely used drug—alcohol. A wide variety of narcotic and stimulant drugs can and do lead to transient psychoses during which violent acts may occur. However, as Maurer and Vogal pointed out,[2] the majority of narcotics, being sedatives, are unlikely to lead to aggressive crime. Because of the psychopathic nature of so many addicts it is probable that any aggressive behaviour induced by drugs is merely a release of latent violent tendencies. In such circumstances they will be judged in the same way as a psychopath subject to violent outbursts brought about by drink, so that much will depend on other evidence before it can be decided how responsible they were for their actions during the period of intoxication.

Finally, nothing has been said about drink and the Road Traffic Acts largely because it is an absolute offence to drive a vehicle while under the influence of drink or drugs. In such circumstances, whether the drink was ingested without the offender's knowledge, and whether or not he is an addict or liable to disturbances of consciousness as a result of drinking is irrelevant to the charge. Once it has been proven that he was, in fact, under the influence of drink or drugs any antecedent circumstances appear to have little bearing on the offence. In view of the present controversy on drink and driving nothing further will be said on this topic lest greater confusion should prevail.

To summarize, it can be said that if a person develops a psychotic illness as a result of abuse of drink or drugs, he will be found guilty but insane if he commits a crime during his illness, provided it can be shown that at the time of the offence he was insane within the framework of the M'Naghten Rules. If he was so drunk at the time as to be incapable of forming the necessary intent to commit a crime this factor will be taken into account in reaching a final verdict. Should he kill in

---

[1] Williams, G. (1961). *The Criminal Law*, Sect. 183. London; Stevens
[2] Maurer, D. W. and Vogel, V. H. (1954). *Narcotics and Narcotic Addiction*, p. 209. Springfield, Ill.; Thomas

such a state it is likely that the verdict will be one of manslaughter. On the other hand, mere drunkenness insufficient to negative intent but adequate to remove the normal moral restraints will be of no avail to the offender. Should he kill in such a state he will be found guilty of murder.

The position of the psychopath is still somewhat uncertain for although, medically, there is evidence to show that some such persons have an abnormal reaction to alcohol it does not seem that the courts regard this reaction as a disease of the mind or abnormality of mind induced by disease or injury which would justify a plea of diminished responsibility. However, as has been suggested, if a psychopath kills in a state of violent frenzy induced by alcohol it could be argued that in such a state, provided his crime was not premeditated, he would show diminished responsibility sufficient to reduce the verdict to one of manslaughter. When alcoholic excess causes some impairment of consciousness during which a violent crime is committed it seems improbable that unless the degree of disturbance is sufficiently severe to negative intent, evidence of such impairment will be of much help to the accused. It is even more certain, as will be discussed in the next section, that such a disturbance of consciousness caused by alcohol, with or without amnesia, would not amount to a state of automatism.

Automatism

In the recent case of Bratty[1] automatism was defined as connoting the state of a person who, though capable of action, is not conscious of what he is doing. It is to be equated with unconscious, involuntary action, and it is a defence because the mind does not go along with what is being done. In Watmore v. Jenkins[2] Mr. Justice Winn said that automatism was a modern catchphrase which the courts had not accepted as meaning more than an involuntary movement of the body or limbs of a person. It is to be presumed that this somewhat inadequate definition, which would include ordinary reflex action within its terms, implies that there must be some attendant disturbance of conscious awareness. Undoubtedly automatic states exist and medically they may be defined as conditions in which the patient may perform simple or complex actions in a more or less skilled or uncoordinated fashion without having full awareness of what he is doing. He may have a confused memory of his act or the amnesia may be total for the duration of the episode. The memory cannot be recovered by psychiatric techniques. This definition seems to cover most forms of automatic behaviour observed in psychiatry but it should be noted that amnesia

---

[1] Bratty v. Attorney-General for Northern Ireland, [1961] 3 All E. R. 523
[2] Watmore v. Jenkins, [1962] 2 All E. R. 868

for an act is not to be equated with automatism. The claim that the accused experienced a 'blackout' for the whole of the criminal act is a common one and, unless supported by adequate evidence, it is of no value to the defence.

Clinically, automatism has been described in a wide variety of conditions. These include epileptic and post-epileptic states, clouded states of consciousness associated with organic brain disease, concussional states following head injuries and, less commonly, in some types of schizophrenia and acute emotional disturbances. Metabolic disorders such as anoxia and hypoglycaemia as well as drug-induced impairment of consciousness can be manifested by automatic behaviour. Finally, as is well known, automatic acts can occur during sleepwalking and hypnagogic states. It should be made clear at once that not all these conditions are to be equated with the legal concept of automatism, and in the case of Padgett[1] the judge withdrew the plea of automatism from the jury although the defence had claimed that he had killed while in a condition of partial anoxia due to a chronic lung disease—pneumoconiosis. In this case he was found guilty but insane.

The law appears to differentiate between sane and insane automatism. A person suffering from a disease of the mind so as not to know the nature and quality of his act or that it is wrong, who kills when his conscious awareness is disturbed, will be found guilty but insane within the terms of the M'Naghten Rules and sent to Broadmoor. However, if the automatic behaviour leading to killing or wounding is not due to mental disease then the accused cannot be found guilty of an act which he could not have intended, and so will be acquitted. Consequently, this somewhat odd result can lead to the acquittal of a potentially dangerous patient who might, unless he receives proper treatment, repeat his act should the automatic state recur. This situation has been commented on by Cross[2] who argued that in such cases it should be possible for the court to detain the accused until it is satisfied that everything possible has been done to prevent such a recurrence. The test of whether or not an episode of automatism is to be judged as sane or insane seems to rest on the likelihood of its repetition. It would be difficult for anyone to guarantee that a person who kills in a state of somnambulism will not repeat his act, and it may well be that Lord Denning had this difficulty in mind when he argued that any mental disorder which has manifested itself in violence and might recur is to be regarded as a disease of the mind. The principal result of such a rigorous ruling would be the committal of a small

[1] R. v. Padgett (1962), The Times, May 18
[2] Cross, R. (1961), The Listener, Dec., p. 967: and (1962), 78 L. Q. R. 236

number of sane sleep-walkers to Broadmoor, but if the courts could use a more flexible sentencing policy in such cases it would be possible to avoid this undesirable result with benefit to the patient and to the safety of the public.

It is not proposed to consider in detail all those types of mental illness which might be attended by automatic behaviour. Something has been said already about epileptic and post-epileptic automatism, and where there is clear evidence of such a condition attendant upon a criminal act the defendant will be judged guilty but insane.

In the leading case on automatism[1] there was some suggestion that the accused suffered from psychomotor epilepsy. The importance of the case appeared to lie in the various judicial pronouncements made concerning the evidence required for automatism to be accepted by the courts as well as the proper burden of proof to be laid on the defence and prosecution in such cases.

Bratty killed a girl whom he had taken for a ride in his car. He alleged that at the time of the killing a blackness came over him, he did not know what he was doing and did not realize anything. There was some evidence of previous episodes of 'blackness', odd behaviour, backwardness, headaches and 'religious leanings'. It was suggested that he might be subject to attacks of psychomotor epilepsy. At trial the defence asked the jury either to acquit the accused on a plea of automatism, to find him guilty of manslaughter, or to find him guilty but insane by reason of disease of the mind which would have rendered him incapable of knowing what he was doing and that it was wrong. At trial the judge withdrew the plea of automatism from the jury on the grounds that there was no evidence to support it. The jury did not find him to be suffering from a disease of the mind and he was convicted of murder. On appeal the judge's direction on the matter of automatism was upheld and the matter went to the House of Lords where the appeal was rejected. Lord Denning made a careful distinction between non-insane automatism and insanity arguing that if the defence is insanity due to disease of the mind it cannot be one of automatism. Hence, if a person kills while in a clouded state of consciousness due to disease of the mind which is persistent or recurrent the verdict must be one of guilty but insane. He went on to contrast the cases of Charlson[2] with that of Kemp[3] to which reference will be made later.

The plea of automatism is likely to be raised only by the defence, and in order to do so they must provide reasonable evidence for this

[1] Bratty v. Attorney-General for Northern Ireland, [1961] 3 All E. R. 523
[2] R. v. Charlson, [1955] 1 All E. R. 859
[3] R. v. Kemp, [1957] 1 Q. B. 399

condition before the prosecution can rebut it. It is not enough for the accused to say that he had a 'blackout'; there must be some satisfactory medical evidence to support the assertion, although it should always be remembered that the particular episode which has brought the prisoner before the courts might, in fact, be his first attack of epileptic automatism. In Bratty's case the medical evidence of previous disturbances of consciousness was weak and, understandably, the jury felt justified in rejecting such evidence when they found the prisoner to be sane and responsible.

The question of automatism in association with organic brain disease has been considered in the cases of Charlson and Kemp. In the former case the defendant was accused of causing grievous bodily harm to his son aged 10 years. He called the boy over to the window to look at a rat swimming in the river, hit him on the head and threw him out of the window. There was not the slightest motive for this act of which Charlson had little recollection beyond stating that he knew he had done something dreadful to his son. The medical evidence was somewhat unsatisfactory but indicated the possibility of a cerebral tumour which could lead to disturbance of consciousness and impulsive violent behaviour. On this basis the defence of automatism was accepted and Charlson was acquitted. The decision has since then been criticized by Lord Denning in Bratty's case, arguing that a cerebral tumour was as much a disease of the mind as schizophrenia. He compared unfavourably the decision in Charlson's case with that reached in R. v. Kemp. In the latter case the defendant was accused of wounding his wife with intent to murder her. There was no motive for his assault and every evidence to show that he was of good character and devoted to his wife. He suffered from cerebral arteriosclerosis and the attack is said to have occurred during a temporary lapse of consciousness due to this disease. The defence argued that he suffered from a disease of the brain which was different from a disease of the mind, asking that he should be acquitted on the ground of automatism. The Crown refuted this argument saying that he did suffer from a disease of the mind sufficient to warrant a verdict of guilty but insane. In his direction to the jury Mr. Justice Devlin said that there was no generally agreed definition of insanity. In this case everyone was agreed that the accused showed a defect of reason going on to say that as the courts were not concerned with the aetiology of mental disease it did not matter whether a person who showed a defect of reason suffered from an organic or functional mental illness. In effect he directed the jury to ignore the medical arguments in the case asking them to consider whether or not Kemp suffered from a disease of the mind sufficient to bring him within the M'Naghten Rules. He was found to be guilty but insane. There can be little doubt that this was the correct decision which appears to have been followed in the case of Padgett.[1]

If organic and functional psychoses and epilepsy do not support a plea of automatism what evidence is required to obtain an acquittal on this ground? Since Lord Denning's remarks in Bratty's case it is clear that the onus of proof or disproof rests on the prosecution in these cases. On the other hand, a bare assertion on the part of the accused that he was in a state of automatism when he committed the act with which he is charged will not suffice. If, on a balance of probability, he can show that he was in such a state it will be necessary for the prosecution to show beyond any reasonable doubt that this was not so before the plea can be rejected. Evidence of existing neurosis and of previous episodes of automatic behaviour supported by sound medical testimony will doubtless be of great value to the accused in substantiating his plea of automatism.

Where this condition is due to some metabolic upset such as spontaneous or insulin-induced hypoglycaemia or anoxia, the ability to reproduce this automatic state experimentally would also carry weight as factual evidence.

The nature of the offence carried out while in the alleged automatic state needs to be taken into account. Sudden, spontaneous, unmotivated violence is more likely to be the product of automatism than more carefully contrived or premeditated crimes. In the case of Harrison-Owen[2] the accused claimed that he committed burglary while in a state of automatism. His conviction was quashed because the trial judge had allowed evidence of previous convictions to be called to rebut the defence of automatism, but Lord Goddard, C.J. considered the defence to be a pack of absurdities. In a somewhat similar case[3] a man was convicted of larceny and shopbreaking. He claimed that he was a diabetic and that, because of an overdose of insulin, he was in a state of mind which rendered him incapable of knowing what he was doing. On appeal this conviction was also quashed on a point of misdirection concerning the burden of proof in such cases, but there seems little reason to regard the plea of automatism as a particularly well-founded one.

In the case of Sell[4] the accused was convicted on three charges of embezzlement, two of falsification of accounts and one of obtaining money by false pretences. He claimed that being epileptic he was in a state of automatism when he committed these offences and on appeal

[1] R. v. Padgett (1962), The Times, May 18
[2] R. v. Harrison-Owen, [1951] 2 All E. R. 726
[3] R. v. Bentley, [1960] Crim. L. R. 777
[4] R. v. Sell, [1962] Crim. L. R. 463

he was acquitted of the first five charges, again on the grounds of mis-direction concerning the onus of proof. Because of the manifest absurdity of a defence of automatism to a charge of obtaining money by false pretences this last conviction was allowed to stand.

When a defence of automatism is offered to rebut a charge of motive-less and unpremeditated violence it is probable that a more sympathetic hearing will be given by the court. In the somewhat special circum-stances of murder committed during sleep-walking, however, it must be very hard to substantiate the case. Hopwood and Snell[1] recount one such case which they regarded as genuine. The accused had killed his wife while asleep and there was good evidence of previous somnambul-ism and that other members of his family were similarly affected. On the night before his crime he had taken alcohol although it was stated that he was not intoxicated when he came home. He woke later to find himself battering his wife's head with a shovel. So great was the shock that he fainted and, on recovering and finding his wife to be dead, he attempted suicide. The crime was motiveless and he had no recollection of getting out of bed to get the shovel. As he was sent to Broadmoor it is to be presumed that he was found guilty but insane and that automatism was not raised on his behalf.

In the more recent case of the American airman,[2] the accused, who had taken a girl home, woke to find that he had strangled her. Again, as in the previous case, he had been drinking during the evening beforehand. He had a total amnesia for the killing but recalled that on discovering what he had done he took the girl's body into another room, dressed her, and then went back to sleep. In his summing-up Mr. Justice Glyn-Jones asked the jury to consider whether it was possible to go through the experience of strangling the girl and yet not awaken. The jury acquitted him on the grounds that he was suffering from automatism at the time.

Podolsky recounts a number of cases of somnambulistic homicide, including one of a man who gave himself a number of mortal stab wounds while asleep.[3] Unfortunately, the medical facts are insufficient to allow any definite conclusions to be reached in these cases. It has to be admitted that the basis of sleep-walking is but poorly understood for, although common enough in children, it is not particularly frequent in adults. Whereas it can be accepted that it is possible for the sleep-walker to perform complex acts with a high degree of co-ordination while asleep it is difficult to believe that he would be able to remain asleep should he be subjected to any form of restraint or struggle or

[1] Hopwood, J. S. and Snell, H. K. (1933). *J. ment. Sci.* **79,** 27
[2] R. *v.* Boshears (1961), *The Times*, Feb. 18
[3] Podolsky, E. (1961). *Med. Sci. Law* **1,** 260

exposed to loud noises such as gunshots. Most persons would examine a plea of somnambulism in such circumstances with some scepticism but there seems to be little doubt that somnambulistic murder can occur and the case recounted by Hopwood and Snell seems to be as well documented as any other in medico-legal literature.

Something must be said concerning the defence of automatism to changes arising out of the Road Traffic Acts. In Hill v. Baxter[1] the defendant, charged with dangerous driving, claimed that he had 'blacked out' at the time of the accident. Such medical evidence as was available did nothing to support this plea and the driver had no previous disturbances of consciousness. In this case, therefore, the unsupported claim to have been in an automatic state at the time of the accident was of no avail, for Lord Goddard, C.J. said that the onus of proof was on the driver to show that he had, in fact, lost consciousness. The other appeal Judges agreed that there must be *prima facie* evidence to support the claim of automatism but reserved their opinion as to where the onus of proof lay.

In the case of Sibbles[2] the defendant was accused of causing the death of a woman while driving under the influence of alcohol. He had had some beer, was stopped by a policeman and charged with an offence. However, he was permitted to drive his car home and it was during this part of his drive that the accident occurred. It was said in his defence that he suffered from hypertension and that the emotional shock of being charged had led to a disturbance in conscious awareness leading to the accident. He claimed to be in a state of automatism at the time of the accident. Because offences under the Road Traffic Act are classed as absolute offences which do not require *mens rea* for their commission Sibbles was convicted. Again there was little evidence to support the plea of automatism beyond the defendant's own assertion. In the circumstances he should have appreciated his disturbed state of mind and refused to drive the car after being stopped by the police.

The question of automatism and dangerous driving was further considered in the case of Watmore v. Jenkins.[3] The defendant, a diabetic recovering from an attack of infective hepatitis, had been obliged to give himself higher doses of insulin to counteract the effect of a raised blood cortisone content caused by his infection. He drove his car for some 5 miles in an erratic and dangerous manner, overshot the turning to his home and finally collided with a stationary car. He was found to be in a dazed condition due to hypoglycaemia induced by the higher insulin dosage and claimed to have no memory for the last

---

[1] Hill v. Baxter, [1958] 1 All E. R. 193
[2] R. v. Sibbles, [1959] Crim. L. R. 660
[3] [1962] 2 All E. R. 868

5 miles of his drive. The justices acquitted him of the charges of dangerous driving and driving under the influence of drugs—insulin—but the Divisional Court did not accept the plea of automatism although they upheld the original acquittal of the charge of driving under the influence of drugs. The Court felt that as he had managed to drive that distance in some fashion he must have had some degree of control of the car which would be incompatible with a state of automatism.

It was said that because of the defendant's recent liver infection the liver would not discharge glycogen in response to the raised insulin level, and that he would not experience the normal sweating reaction which occurs when the blood-sugar is low. In point of fact it is surely more correct to say that the sweating is due to the release of adrenaline in response to a low blood-sugar and not to the conversion of glycogen to glucose by the liver. What seems more probable is that, because of the low glycogen content of the liver following his hepatitis, the period of warning would be so brief that any sweating would pass unnoticed. There seems to be little doubt that the immediate consequences would be a disturbance of consciousness and loss of self-awareness which would effectively prevent the driver from knowing that he was driving dangerously even though he managed to control the car to some extent. Had he been aware of his defect no doubt he would have stopped the car rather than continue his journey. With all respect to the learned judges it does seem that, despite the fact that he managed to stay on the road for 5 miles, he had no conscious awareness of his actions, and was in precisely the same state as a sleep-walker who is able to carry out complex movements and journeys without mishap, despite his total unawareness of his actions.

If automatism is to be equated with a sudden loss of consciousness, such as might occur following a brain haemorrhage, then all those classes of automatism which occur in clouded states will no longer be accepted by the courts as true states of automatism. The fact is that conditions of partial anoxia and hypoglycaemia are characterized by exactly that type of behaviour described by the defendant in this case in which one might have thought that the plea of automatism was fully substantiated. Certainly the prosecution do not appear to have disproved the claim and in the light of the ruling in Bratty's case one might have thought that the evidence of automatism was strong enough to be accepted.

Fitness to Plead

The question of fitness to plead to a charge comes up from time to time and was raised acutely in the recent case of Podola[1] in which it

[1] R. v. Podola, [1959] 3 All E. R. 418

was claimed that because the accused man had a total amnesia for the crime with which he was charged, he was unable to instruct his counsel or to plead to the charge. The case raised legal problems of considerable interest as well as medical controversy centering on the differences between feigned and genuine amnesia. Some of these matters will be discussed in later pages.

East wrote[1]: 'A prisoner is unfit to plead to an indictment when he suffers from such disease of the mind as prevents him from challenging a juror, from understanding the nature of the proceedings in court, from distinguishing between a plea of guilty and not guilty, from examining witnesses or instructing counsel on his behalf, or otherwise making a proper defence or from following the evidence intelligently.' According to the Royal Commission on Capital Punishment[2] the question of fitness to plead can be raised by the defence, the prosecution or the presiding judge. It is more usual for the defence to bring the matter to the attention of the court in the light of any medical evidence offered to the court by the prison medical officer. Should his evidence of the prisoner's insanity be unchallenged it will be usual for the judge to direct the jury to find him insane on arraignment. In accordance with the provisions of the Criminal Lunatics Act, 1800, he will then be detained until Her Majesty's pleasure be known.

The question of whether or not a prisoner is fit or unfit to answer the charge and stand trial is based on evidence of mental illness, severe subnormality, deaf-mutism and, more recently, when the accused claims to have no memory of the events for which he is to be tried. Clear medical evidence of insanity in the ordinary sense—it does not need to fulfil the conditions of the M'Naghten Rules—as well as evidence of serious mental defect will probably not be challenged. However, procedure has varied over the centuries and there does not appear to be any final agreement on how these cases are to be taken. Opinions also differ as to who bears the onus of proof in these cases but there seems to be some measure of agreement that it rests with whoever raises the issue. Presumably, if it is raised by the judge it will be for the prosecution to show whether, in fact, the prisoner is unfit to plead.

Occasionally the prisoner may refuse to agree that he is insane and insist on pleading guilty. This occurred in the case of Vent[3] in which the accused pleaded guilty, although his counsel said he was unfit to plead. The prison medical officer said that he was fit and the trial proceeded. If the judge thinks that the prisoner is unfit to plead he can ask the jury to try the issue. Should they disagree another jury can be

[1] East, W. N. (1927). *Forensic Psychiatry*, p. 32. London; Churchill
[2] Royal Commission on Capital Punishment (1949–53). Cmd. 8932, para. 220
[3] R. *v.* Vent (1935), 25 Cr. App. Rep. 55

empanelled to settle the matter. These problems have been discussed by Prevezer[1] who quoted Halsbury[2] as saying that it is for the Crown to prove that the prisoner is fit to plead and not for the defence to prove his unfitness.

Prevezer goes on to suggest that the matter should be proved by whoever raises the issue. In Podola's case, however, it was ruled that it was for the defence to prove the issue of unfitness on a balance of probability, a decision which appears to contradict law as stated in Halsbury.[3] In so far as it was ruled in Woolmington's case[4] that except for the issue of insanity within the meaning of the M'Naghten Rules it was for the prosecution to prove the prisoner's guilt and not for the defence to prove his innocence one might have thought that the same rule would have been followed in Podola's case despite the obvious difficulties inherent in obtaining such proof. Clearly this is a complex legal dispute which troubles the minds of jurists more than those of laymen, and no doubt a firm ruling on the point will be given on a later occasion.

If the prisoner is manifestly suffering from a mental illness at the time of arraignment it is likely that, given adequate evidence from the prison medical officer, the court will decide that he is insane on arraignment and unfit to plead. However, in the case of Rivett, despite the unchallenged medical evidence of insanity, the jury, to whom the issue was put, over-ruled the medical evidence which declared him unfit to plead.

Presumably the Court of Criminal Appeal felt bound by an earlier decision[5] that they could not consider appeals against a finding that the accused was fit to plead. However, in Podola's case, the Court of Criminal Appeal did consider this point and because, in Rivett's case, the medical evidence was unchallenged, one might suppose that had his case been heard today the jury's verdict, which ignored the medical evidence on this point, would have been reversed on appeal. It should be emphasized that unfitness to plead is based on ordinary medical views on insanity. In general, if the prisoner is certifiably insane he would be regarded as unfit to plead. In theory, should he recover from his illness, it would be possible to bring him back to stand trial. This has very rarely happened. From time to time a prisoner is found to be mute on arraignment and it then becomes necessary to discover the cause of his mutism, and whether or not he is fit to plead. In the case of Pritchard[6] the prisoner was accused of bestiality. A jury was empanelled

---

[1] Prevezer, S., [1958] Crim. L. R. 144
[2] Halsbury's *Laws of England*, 3rd ed. Vol. 10, p. 403. London; Butterworths
[3] Dean, M., [1960] Crim. L. R. 79
[4] Woolmington v. Director of Public Prosecutions, [1935] A. C. 462
[5] R. v. Jefferson (1908), 24 T. L. R. 877
[6] R. v. Pritchard (1836), 7, C. & P. 303

to decide whether he was mute from malice or by visitation of God or, to use more everyday terms, whether he was malingering or whether his mutism was due to some functional or organic mental disorder. The jury found that he was mute by visitation and were then asked to decide whether he could plead to the indictment. After concluding that he was fit they were then asked whether he was unfit to stand trial by reason of insanity. On finding that he was unfit to stand trial by reason of severe mental defect he was detained under the Criminal Lunatics Act, 1800.

Mutism is not a particularly common psychiatric symptom but is seen in severe depressive states, catatonic schizophrenia, hysteria and severe mental defect. It can also occur as a manifestation of dysphasia in a variety of progressive organic brain disorders, and in the majority of these cases the diagnosis is rarely in doubt. Congenital and acquired deaf-mutism may occur as one feature of severe subnormality or the intelligence may be sufficiently high to allow the patient to learn speech with suitable training. The history of the case will usually establish the diagnosis. In general it is unusual for a severely subnormal patient to be totally mute. He may be able to convey his wishes by grunts and other noises but be totally unable to respond to questions because of his lack of understanding. Although total mutism can occur as an hysterical symptom it is more usual for the patient to lose his normal voice but still be able to converse in whispers. In such cases he would be able to plead and understand the proceedings of his trial.

If the prisoner remains mute on arraignment and it is thought that he is malingering, once the issue has been decided, the judge will enter a formal plea of 'not guilty' on his behalf and the trial can proceed. This seems to be a common-sense procedure which might well be adopted in all such cases unless there is such clear evidence of severe mental disease that the patient is unfit to stand trial.

In the case of Roberts[1] the accused, a deaf-mute from birth, was charged with murder. He was found to be mute by visitation of God and counsel for the Crown argued that the finding presumed a degree of mental defect which would render him unfit to stand trial. The defence denied that Roberts was an idiot, as was alleged, and Mr. Justice Devlin ruled that the general issue of the charge of murder should be tried so as to give the defence a chance to plead not guilty and, if possible, exonerate the accused man. In the case of Benyon[2] the defendant was not mute but the Crown asked that the question of fitness to plead should be considered before going on to the trial of the charge of murder. The defence, relying on the ruling in Roberts' case, asked

[1] R. v. Roberts, [1954] 2 Q. B. 329
[2] R. v. Benyon, [1957] 2 Q. B. 111

that he should be allowed to plead to the indictment, but after consideration Mr. Justice Byrne ruled that the preliminary issue should be taken first. In this he was following not only the precedent in Pritchard's case but also the ruling in R. *v.* Dyson[1] in which the defendant stood mute. After a formal plea of 'not guilty' had been entered on his behalf the jury were required to find whether he was sane or not so as to stand trial. It was found that because of mental defect he was not fit for trial.

In the case of Sharp[2] the defendant stood mute and the judge ruled that it was for the prosecution to prove that he was mute from malice. The jury found him to be mute by visitation of God but declared that he was able to plead by giving suitable signs, and that he would be able to follow the proceedings in an intelligent fashion. The question of whether or not the symptom of mutism in any given case is genuine or feigned will rest largely on medical testimony, and where there is clear evidence of an organic or functional psychosis or of severe subnormality, no particular difficulty will occur. Whether the symptom is due to hysteria or malingering is less easy to decide, but, in a sense, the issue is not important. In either case the defendant should be able by signs to indicate what he is pleading; and if he fails to do so it is possible for a plea of not guilty to be entered by the judge on his behalf. The question of insanity so as to be unfit for trial does not arise as neither hysteria nor malingering can be equated with legal insanity. It would be unlikely for a person to develop simultaneously, hysterical mutism, deafness, and incapacity to write, and should all these symptoms occur at one and the same time it would be reasonable to suspect that in the absence of any other more serious disorder the defendant was malingering.

The question of whether or not amnesia is to be regarded as genuine or false has received some consideration in medico-legal circles since the case of Podola.[3] The claim to have no memory of the time when the alleged crime is committed is by no means an uncommon one and Hopwood and Snell[4] studied 100 cases committed to Broadmoor who had claimed amnesia when charged with a crime. They felt in 78 cases the claim was genuine, that 14 were malingerers and that the diagnosis was uncertain in the remaining 8 cases. There was a high incidence of associated mental disorders, past and present, and a particularly high incidence of alcoholism. Only 3 of the cases were total abstainers whereas 38 were definite alcoholics. As in the case of mutism, difficulties only occur in differentiating an hysterical from a feigned amnesia.

---

[1] (1831), 7 C. & P. 305
[2] R. *v.* Sharp (1957), 41 Cr. App. Rep. 197
[3] R. *v.* Podola, [1959] 3 All E. R. 418
[4] Hopwood, J. S. and Snell, H. K. (1933). *J. ment. Sci.* **79**, 27

When there is clear evidence of organic brain disease sufficient to justify the plea it is usually possible to reach a conclusion on the matter with relative ease.

It has been argued with some reason that it is not particularly important and, in many cases, impossible to make a differentiation between hysteria and malingering. The case was put by Hays[1] that as both states can coincide it is quite impossible to distinguish conscious deception from an hysterical amnesia which appears to subserve the same end—forgetfulness of an alleged crime with which the defendant is charged. In Podola's case, however, it was argued that because of the alleged amnesia for all events prior to a lumbar puncture carried out after his arrest, he was unfit to stand trial on the grounds that, having no knowledge of the facts with which he was charged, he could neither instruct his counsel nor follow the proceedings properly. If the amnesia was false this claim would clearly be of no avail. It could be argued that had the court followed the procedure in the Scottish case of Russell v. H.M. Advocate[2] a great deal of conflicting medical evidence which brought little credit to anyone would have been avoided. Russell, accused of fraud over a period of 7 years, claimed to have no memory of the events with which she was charged. Lord Cooper ruled that the onus of proof is always on the accused to justify a plea in bar of trial and the trial proceeded after a plea of not guilty had been entered by the defendant.

Hopwood and Snell said that whereas in feigned amnesia the beginning and end of the episode is often sudden, in genuine amnesia the beginning and end are usually blurred. Furthermore, in the genuine case the loss of memory prior to the committal of an alleged crime is of much shorter duration than that of the subsequent period before normal consciousness resumes control. On both these tests Podola would be shown to be malingering, a conclusion which was reached by Dr. Brisby.[3] In a discussion on Podola's case he said: 'Loss of memory for the whole previous life is extremely rare except in brain damage, dementia or hysteria of the grossest type . . . and would render the man manifestly unfit to plead.' Whether hysteria would render the accused person unfit to plead is a disputable point although it would readily be agreed that when amnesia is but one symptom of a severe organic or functional psychosis the attendant symptoms of mental illness would make it unlikely that the defendant could plead or stand trial. As East pointed out,[4] Hess's assertion during

---

[1] Hays, P. (1961). *Med.-leg. J.* **29**, 27
[2] Russell v. H.M. Advocate (1946), S. C. (J) 37
[3] Brisby, F. (1960). *Med.-leg. J.* **28**, 117
[4] East W. N. (1949). *Society and the Criminal*. London; H.M. Stationery Office

the Nuremburg trial in 1946 that he was unfit to plead because of his amnesia did not prevent his trial proceeding. Should a motorist suffer amnesia for an accident due to a head injury such amnesia would not prevent his being tried for manslaughter should he have killed someone in the accident. Again, Hale's opinion[1] that a person *non sana memoria* is unable to plead and stand trial does not help the accused who pleads amnesia, for in the opinion of Lord Parker, C.J.[2] the words used by Hale do not refer to recollection as such but to the general mental state of the prisoner.

The conclusion to be drawn from an examination of these cases and opinions is that amnesia, whatever the cause, is no bar to trial unless it is but one symptom of a more serious psychosis or dementia. Whether the amnesia is hysterical or feigned is immaterial, for provided the jury have been properly instructed on the possible effects of the amnesia on the prisoner's defence, the trial could proceed in the normal way. There is nothing in amnesia to prevent the accused person pleading 'not guilty' but it is up to the prosecution to show that he has, in fact, committed the crime with which he is charged and not for the defence to prove his innocence.

[1] Hale, M. *Pleas of the Crown*, Vol. 1, p. 34
[2] R. *v.* Podola, [1959] 3 All E. R. 418

9—Procedure, Comment and Conclusions

Reference has been made on a number of occasions in previous chapters to the various legal rulings invoked when it comes to dealing with the points raised by mental illness in criminal proceedings. Some methods and precedents seem to be more binding than others, and with a small number the final decision concerning the proper method of dealing with the offender has yet to be made. Some of these procedures will be summarized under the heading of fitness to plead and to stand trial, the plea of insanity and diminished responsibility at trial, and statutory medical inquiries after conviction. Before doing so, one point is worth emphasizing: the opinions of medical witnesses must be based upon the clinical findings in the case. If a definite diagnosis can be made, whether of psychosis, neurosis or psychopathy, the facts supporting the diagnosis should be presented; and if an opinion on whether the prisoner's responsibility was substantially impaired by mental disorder, or whether he is insane due to disease of the mind within the framework of the M'Naghten Rules is asked for, it is proper to give the opinion.

It must always be remembered, however, that in the last analysis it is for the jury, and the jury alone, to decide the issue, and that the medical expert is there to assist the court and not to attempt to make decisions which are the prerogative of the court. This fact was emphasized in the case of Rivett[1] and although unchallenged medical evidence ignored by the jury may well lead to a reversal of a decision by the Court of Criminal Appeal it has been made clear on two occasions recently[2] that medical issues are for the jury to decide and that it is their duty to probe the facts on which medical opinions are expressed.

According to the Royal Commission on Capital Punishment,[3] unfitness to plead means insanity in the ordinary medical sense. The medical facts of the case are likely to be presented to the court by the prison medical officer and it would appear that the issue of fitness or otherwise can be raised by the defence, the prosecution or by the presiding judge. The Royal Commission did not feel that a finding of

---

[1] R. v. Rivett (1950), 34 Cr. App. Rep. 87
[2] R. v. Jennion, [1962] 1 All E. R. 689; and R. v. Ahmed Din, [1962] 2 All E. R. 124; (1962), Brit. med. J. 2, 1084
[3] Royal Commission on Capital Punishment (1949–53), Cmd. 8392, para. 220

being insane on arraignment led to any miscarriages of justice, but it could be argued that such a finding might preclude an innocent but insane man from establishing his innocence. Furthermore, although a man may be suffering from a psychosis, it does not follow in all cases that he is unfit to plead and stand his trial. The decision would have to rest on the facts of the case which would be presented to the jury for their consideration.

The question of who bears the onus of proof to show that the accused is unfit to plead or stand trial was debated in the case of Podola[1] and it was held by the Court of Criminal Appeal that it is up to the accused, if he raises the issue, to show on a balance the probabilities that he is, in fact, unfit to plead. They upheld the decision of Mr. Justice Edmund Davies who ruled that the defence should prove the facts of loss of memory and fitness to stand trial. The ruling has been criticized by jurists on the grounds that it conflicts with the decision reached in the case of Woolmington[2] which held that it was for the prosecution to prove the facts of the case and not for the defence to establish the innocence of the accused. The only exception to this ruling is where the accused pleads insanity at the time of committing the offence. He has to establish that this was the case as a matter of probability.[3] As has already been shown, earlier rulings conflict with that reached in Podola's case, not only in that it has been held in the past that it is for the defence to raise the issue of fitness to plead,[4] but that it is for the Crown to prove fitness rather than for the defence to prove unfitness.[5]

In the special circumstances of muteness and fitness to plead it was held in the case of Sharp[5] that it was up to the prosecution to prove that the defendant was mute from malice[6] so that one might have thought that in the comparable circumstances of deciding between a feigned and genuine amnesia it would be up to the prosecution to prove that the defendant was malingering.

The fact that it is very difficult to differentiate between the two conditions seems to be no reason why the defence should have to carry the onus of proof in such cases if the courts feel it is sufficiently important to make the differentiation. From strictly practical considerations one would not have thought that amnesia *per se* was a good reason for asserting that the accused could not plead or stand trial. No doubt the inability to instruct counsel is something of a disadvantage,

---

[1] R. v. Podola, [1959] 3 All E. R. 418
[2] Woolmington v. Director of Public Prosecutions, [1935] A. C. 462
[3] Sodemann v. R., [1936] All E. R. 1133; and R. v. Carr-Briant, [1943] 2 All E. R. 156
[4] R. v. Roberts, [1954] 2 Q. B. 329
[5] R. v. Sharp (1957), 41 Cr. App. Rep. 197
[6] Halsbury's *Laws of England*, 3rd ed., Vol. 10, p. 402

but provided the jury is aware of the special difficulties it still remains for the prosecution to prove their case against the accused.

On the more general issue of fitness to plead for reasons other than amnesia or mutism it would seem best to leave it to the defence to raise the matter if they feel this to be desirable. Admittedly, Lord Denning in Bratty's case[1] said that the Trial of Lunatics Act, 1883, did not specify that evidence for insanity should come only from the defence; but if the Crown can ask for the issue of fitness to plead to be taken before the trial a finding of unfitness would effectively preclude the accused man from establishing his innocence. It seems, therefore, more reasonable to leave the matter in the hands of the defence, a ruling which would not affect the right of the Crown to raise the issue of insanity during the actual trial when diminished responsibility is pleaded.

At trial the question of insanity, diminished responsibility or automatism may be raised. In general, it will be for the defence to bring up these pleas as it has been ruled that both insanity at the time of committing the alleged offence and diminished responsibility[2] have to be proved by the defence as a matter of probability. When automatism is pleaded it has to be shown that the cause alleged for an unconscious or involuntary act is not the same as a defect of reason from disease of the mind within the meaning of the M'Naghten Rules, for, should this not be shown, there is no room for a defence of automatism which differs from insanity even though unconscious automatic acts occur as symptoms of a psychosis. Furthermore, when automatism is pleaded there must be proper evidence to support the plea which cannot rest solely on the defendant's unsupported testimony. Both these points were made in the case of Bratty[3] but so far as the question of evidence for automatism is concerned it should always be borne in mind that the loss of consciousness leading to a criminal offence might be the first attack experienced by the accused. In such a case it will be very difficult to supply good medical evidence to support the plea even though it was ruled by the House of Lords in Bratty's case that when automatism not due to insanity is pleaded it is not for the defence to prove automatism but rather for the prosecution to disprove it. However, they must be given some evidence to disprove although in the case of the American airman who killed while in a state of somnambulism[4] there appeared to be no supporting evidence beyond the fact of the case and the accused's own statement. Presumably, a wholly

[1] Bratty v. Attorney-General for Northern Ireland, [1961] 3 All E. R. 523
[2] Homicide Act, [1957] Section 2 (2)
[3] Bratty v. Attorney-General for Northern Ireland, [1961] 3 All E. R. 523
[4] R. v. Boshears (1961), The Times, Feb. 18

unmotivated and pointless offence would carry considerable weight in support of a plea of automatism even though at first sight the plea may appear somewhat unsubstantial.

Although it has usually been the task of the defence to raise the question of insanity and diminished responsibility, differing opinions have been expressed on whether it is open to the prosecution to prove insanity when diminished responsibility is pleaded, or diminished responsibility when insanity is put forward as a defence. On a number of occasions where one or other defence has been offered the prosecution has sought to obtain verdicts of insanity or manslaughter by reason of diminished responsibility. In the case of Kemp[1] the defence asked for an acquittal by reason of automatism, but the prosecution obtained a verdict of guilty but insane. The defence in the case of Bastian[2] asked for a verdict of manslaughter because of diminished responsibility while the Crown sought to prove that he was insane; in this case the manslaughter verdict was given. In the case of Nott[3] the defence was insanity while the prosecution asked for the diminished responsibility verdict. In this case the defendant was found to be guilty but insane.

On these issues, Lord Denning in Bratty's case said: 'The old notion that only the defence can raise a defence of insanity is now gone. The prosecution are entitled to raise it and it is their duty to do so rather than allow a dangerous person to be at large.' This sensible ruling is forced by the different sentencing policies which the two verdicts entail. If the defendant is found to be guilty but insane he will be committed to one of the State hospitals for an indefinite period and will not be released unless all concerned are satisfied that he has fully recovered from his illness. If he should be found guilty of manslaughter by reason of diminished responsibility he will be given a fixed sentence with the possibility of release after a fairly short period, whether or not his mental state has improved sufficiently to ensure that there will be no risk of his repeating his offence.

As has already been shown the number of those found guilty but insane before the passage of the Homicide Act, 1957, is about equal to the combined totals of those found guilty but insane and guilty of section 2 manslaughter since the Act came into force.

The conclusion to be drawn from these figures is that a number of persons who would have been detained for an undefined period in hospital will now obtain their release after a fixed and limited sentence in prison. One would like to be assured that before this takes place

[1] R. v. Kemp, [1957] 1 Q. B. 399
[2] R. v. Bastian, [1958] 1 All E. R. 568
[3] R. v. Nott (1959), 43 Cr. App. Rep. 8

they will be submitted to a thorough medical examination to take note of their mental condition. Without such assurance there seems to be every reason for the prosecution to ask for a verdict of insanity, should the mental state of the defendant warrant such a verdict, rather than the lesser one of manslaughter because of diminished responsibility. On the other hand, there seems to be little point in allowing the prosecution to ask for a verdict of diminished responsibility when the defence is one of insanity. If there is sufficient mental abnormality to warrant the latter verdict it is surely better that the accused should receive proper medical treatment under conditions of maximum security rather than that he should be allowed to go to prison where his mental state might be overlooked. No doubt, if after being received in prison following a section 2 manslaughter verdict, it was found that he was certifiably insane, arrangements would be made for the transfer of the prisoner to hospital under section 72 of the Mental Health Act, 1959. It does not appear obligatory that such patients should go to one of the special hospitals although in a case of homicide it is improbable that an ordinary mental hospital would be able to provide the conditions of security required. Presumably the conditions governing the discharge of such patients, once their sentences have expired, would depend on the discretion of the Home Secretary acting on medical recommendations under section 74 of the Mental Health Act.

Lord Denning's opinion that it is right and proper for the prosecution to raise the question of insanity runs counter to previous decisions on the point and goes even further than the recommendation of the Royal Commission on Capital Punishment[1] that this right should be given to the judge as well as to the defence. In the cases of Oliver-Smith[2] and Casey[3] the Court of Criminal Appeal ruled that it is for the defence alone to bring up the matter of insanity, although it is right that any evidence to this effect communicated to the prosecution by the Prison Medical Officer should be made available to the defence. Nevertheless, the passage of the Homicide Act, 1957, which admits the plea of diminished responsibility into English law makes the right of the prosecution to bring up the question of the prisoner's mental state both more imperative and more justifiable. That the judiciary are alive to the risk of too early a release of a person convicted of manslaughter by reason of diminished responsibility is shown in the recent case of Heron.[4] The accused was sentenced to life imprisonment and the judge stated that although this did not mean that he would remain

---

[1] Royal Commission on Capital Punishment (1949–53). Cmd. 8932, para. 454
[2] R. v. Smith (1910), 6 Cr. App. Rep. 19
[3] R. v. Casey (1947), 32 Cr. App. Rep. 91
[4] R. v. Heron (1962), *The Times*, Sept. 18

in prison for the rest of his life it did imply that he would not be released until a thorough investigation of his mental state had made it clear that it would be safe for him to be at liberty again.

Enough has been said about the M'Naghten Rules to indicate that in the light of modern psychiatric knowledge the tests which they established are wholly obsolete. The author would agree with the recommendation of the Royal Commission on Capital Punishment, made with three dissentients, that it would be best to abrogate the M'Naghten Rules and leave the jury to determine whether at the time of the act the accused was suffering from disease of the mind or mental deficiency to such a degree that he ought not to be held responsible. To some extent the working of the Homicide Act, 1957, has already supplanted the M'Naghten test in that a number of persons who might have been found guilty but insane before 1957 are now found guilty of manslaughter under section 2 of the Act. It seems fairly evident that what is required now is not necessarily the abrogation of the M'Naghten Rules by statute, but a more flexible sentencing policy which would allow the courts to dispose of the accused man in a manner most appropriate to the offence and his mental state. A woman who kills her children during a depressive illness is more in need of mental hospital care under section 60 of the Mental Health Act than of an indefinite Broadmoor sentence which is automatic should she be found guilty but insane under the M'Naghten test. On the other hand, to send to prison a schizophrenic patient who killed his mother, as in the case of Tickell,[1] yet was found guilty of manslaughter by reason of diminished responsibility, is surely an unwise procedure, which is neither in the interest of the accused man nor of society. It could be argued that these cases could be taken under the Homicide Act, 1957, and that once the issue of diminished responsibility has been proved it would be for the judge to order the future disposal of the case in the light of the medical evidence.

When there is clear evidence of a psychosis or other chronic mental condition unlikely to improve, the need for long-term detention in a hospital with maximum security conditions is obvious. Committal to Broadmoor of a person suffering from a short-lived psychosis from which he may have recovered by the time of the trial is certainly not in the interests of the patient and probably not required for the protection of society. Whether or not the M'Naghten Rules are finally abolished may not be of any great importance now that the plea of diminished responsibility is admissible. What is of greater consequence is to ensure that those who need long-term detention and treatment, whether found guilty but insane or guilty of section 2 manslaughter,

[1] R. v. Tickell (1958), The Times, Jan. 24

should have it; while those whose condition does not require such a protracted period of detention should be treated in an ordinary mental hospital to be released on recovery on the understanding that they should be followed-up and supervised as out-patients for some years after the episode which brought them before the courts. In such circumstances it would still be possible for the courts to require their re-admission should there be the slightest evidence of relapse.

It is very right that society should be protected from the psychotic murderer; it is also vital that such persons should be detected at the earliest possible moment so that treatment can be given to avert the first homicidal act and to prevent any repetition in the future. Some such persons undoubtedly should never again be allowed free in society. One merely hopes that some of those sentenced to detention in prison following a conviction for section 2 manslaughter will not be included in this category. No doubt an increasing number of persons found guilty of manslaughter because of diminished responsibility will be made subject to a hospital order rather than to detention in prison. According to Lady Wootton,[1] since the coming into force of the Mental Health Act, in 43 cases manslaughter because of diminished responsibility was successfully pleaded; 15 of these cases were sent to hospital rather than prison, so it is evident that the judges are alive to the implications of diminished responsibility as a feature of mental illness which requires treatment. Precisely where the line is drawn between treatment and punishment is a problem actively being debated. Because of the high incidence of mental abnormality in persons who commit homicide it is at least a tenable proposition that all such cases should receive psychiatric treatment whether they go direct to hospital or to prison. What is equally important is the need for close psychiatric observation before and after trial, and it would seem that in general this facility is available.

The question of psychiatric examination and reports to the court on the findings in cases of alleged murder was discussed by the Royal Commission on Capital Punishment[2] who recommended that procedure in England should be similar to that practised in Scotland. They felt that every prisoner charged with murder should be specially examined by two doctors as to his state of mind, of whom one at least should be a psychiatrist of standing who is not a member of the prison medical service, and the other usually an experienced member of that service.

---

[1] Wootton, B. (1962). *Violence and the Mental Health Service*, p. 15. London; National Association for Mental Health
[2] Royal Commission on Capital Punishment (1949–53). Cmd. 8932, paras. 414–441

Such a procedure would not in any way deprive the right of either defence or prosecution to call for independent reports should these seem to be required. On the other hand, a psychiatric report available impartially to the court would, to some extent, obviate the need for further examinations; and it would do much to lessen the frequency of occasions on which each side calls for evidence from psychiatrists or neurologists who conflict irreconcilably. Such evidence can be of no assistance to the court, so much so that one has some sympathy with the judge in the case of Terry[1] who, rather than attempt to sort out the medical conflict as to whether the accused suffered from schizophrenia or not, merely handed the transcript of the medical evidence to the jury with the implied advice that they should try to sort it out themselves. No doubt this was an unfortunate procedure, but when medical evidence as to fact and opinion is totally at variance the most likely result will be disregard of all medical evidence in the case to the possible detriment of the accused man. A sound opinion based on the careful examination of the defendant by impartial witnesses would do much to avoid such an *impasse* although there is always the risk that in such cases any dissenting opinion from a witness called independently will receive less credence than the testimony provided by the court medical witnesses.

No firm guidance can be given on the type of evidence to be offered to the court in these cases. Every opportunity for a thorough examination of the prisoner should be taken lest in court the medical witness is ignored on the grounds that he cannot know sufficient about the accused having seen so little of him. When circumstances call for ancillary tests such as psychological testing, electroencephalographic examination and any other special physical or biochemical tests, it is right that these should be requested and performed. They may well be the best supporting evidence for the opinion that a given person was suffering from a mental disorder at the time he committed the alleged offence.

Once all the available evidence on the medical state of the prisoner has been collected and sifted it is still essential to bear in mind the difference between medical facts and medical interpretations. In the case of Ahmed Din[2] the medical witnesses went beyond the facts in asserting that as the defendant was suffering from paranoia he had no reasonable grounds for believing that his wife, whom he killed, had been unfaithful to him. Quite obviously the question of the wife's fidelity was an inference based on the medical diagnosis of paranoia but most psychiatrists have experienced cases where what, at first

[1] R. v. Terry, [1961] 2 All E. R. 569
[2] R. v. Ahmed Din, [1962] 2 see Brit. med. J. 2, 1084

sight, is a delusional belief turns out to have been an expression of the truth. Because a person is suffering from a psychosis it does not follow that every opinion he voices, however fanciful it may seem, is a delusion. Hence, the need to take great care lest the medical expert finds himself giving opinions about matters on which he is in no better position to judge than the members of the jury.

English law takes no note of the causes of mental illness and although a clear account of aetiology and diagnosis may be of great value it is still necessary to relate these facts to the requirements of the M'Naghten Rules. In the United States of America, judging by a recent paper, 'dynamic' accounts of aetiology and development of a mental illness seem to be received more favourably than would be the case in an English court.[1] Whatever one's views about the unconscious roots of behaviour it is probably wisest to keep them for case discussions with one's colleagues rather than air them in court. A vigorous cross-examination may well cause them to appear somewhat ill-founded and they are unlikely to be of much assistance to the accused. As Lady Wootton commented on psycho-analytic interpretations of criminal behaviour: 'So long as the opinions of every medical man are subject in the courts to lay criticism and in the last resort to lay adjudication, it seems unlikely that one section of the medical profession, and that by no means the most orthodox, will, in the foreseeable future, win the right to speak with unquestioned authority.'[2]

Any medical witness who gives psychiatric evidence in the court will be subject to cross-examination. Provided he has a firm grasp on the facts and is able to separate fact from opinion he should be able to stand up to the most searching cross-examination, even when such questioning appears to be directly hostile to himself. If he has taken every care to examine the patient as fully as possible and does not feel personally involved when his opinions are questioned by laymen he should have little difficulty in the witness box. For obvious reasons he cannot possibly give firm answers to all the questions he will be asked. In such instances it is right that he should give his opinion yet not be afraid to agree that it is but an opinion and not a piece of factual information. If such information is by its very nature unavailable then let him not be unwilling to admit ignorance; he is in no worse plight, in most instances, than anyone else in court—judge and counsel included. What is to be avoided at all costs is a façade of knowledge which cloaks a lack of information. He is unlikely to

---

[1] Salzman, L. (1962). 'Psychodynamics of a Case of Murder.' *Comprehensive Psychiatry*, Vol. 3, p. 152
[2] Wootton, B. (1959). *Social Science and Social Pathology*, p. 236. London; Allen and Unwin

deceive his opponents even if he deceives himself; and to be publicly unmasked will not add to his stature, least of all in his own eyes.

One of the very real difficulties which has to be faced is the need to give evidence concerning the mental state of the accused at the time of the alleged crime rather than at a later date. The examining psychiatrist may not have seen the defendant until some days or weeks have passed following his arrest. At the very best, therefore, his views concerning the prisoner's degree of responsibility and self-control at the time of the alleged offence will be matters of inference derived from his mental state at the time of examination and the history obtained from relatives and medical sources prior to the episode which has brought the accused man before the court. Should he find evidence of frank psychosis, epilepsy, or other illnesses accepted as diseases or disorders of mind, he can justifiably infer that such illness played a part in the action with which he is now being charged. Even so, he will be required to show that the accused, whatever his mental illness may be, either fulfils the requirements of the M'Naghten Rules or that his illness has caused a substantial impairment of his responsibility.

Did he know the nature and quality of his act, and did he know that it was wrong? Enough has been said about these terms in an earlier chapter to indicate in what circumstances it would be reasonable to infer that the defendant did not know these facts. Macdonald[1] listed a number of questions which the expert witness should be able to answer. Not all of them are relevant to English practice but undoubtedly the medical witness should be sufficiently knowledgeable about the M'Naghten Rules to be able to say whether in his opinion the accused is insane through disease of the mind to such a degree as to be covered by them.

If diminished responsibility is being pleaded he may be asked to state whether or not the accused's responsibility was substantially impaired at the time of the alleged offence. In a sense, this is an unanswerable question which can only be answered as a matter of inference and probability. Much would depend on the clinical diagnosis in the case as well as on a history, if available, of similar loss of control in the past which has not led to such tragic consequences. The problem is likely to be most acute in the case of the unstable, aggressive psychopath who by drink and provocation has killed in a moment of explosive fury over which he has no control. Somewhat similar problems are likely to arise in cases of epilepsy and subnormality and only all possible available information will enable the court to decide, on a balance of probability, what were the true circumstances at the time of the killing. Should, despite the evidence of mental disorder, the verdict of the

---

[1] Macdonald, J. M. (1958). *Psychiatry and the Criminal*, pp. 39–40. Springfield, Ill.; Thomas

court go against the defendant, finding him guilty of murder or capital murder, there remain provisions for his further examination and, if necessary, his removal to hospital.

Under the terms of the Criminal Lunatics Act, 1884, it was possible for the Secretary of State to order a statutory enquiry into the mental state of prisoners under sentence of death. Section 2 (4) of the Act stated: 'In the case of a prisoner under sentence of death, if it appears to a Secretary of State, either by means of a certificate signed by two members of the visiting committee of the prison in which such prisoner is confined, or by any other means, that there is reason to believe such prisoner to be insane, the Secretary of State shall appoint two or more legally qualified medical practitioners, and the said medical practitioners shall forthwith examine such prisoner and inquire as to his insanity, and after such examination and inquiry such practitioners shall make a report in writing to the Secretary of State as to the sanity of the prisoner, and they, or the majority of them, may certify in writing that he is insane.' No rules governed the procedure for the finding of insanity in these cases which were judged by the ordinary clinical standards which would warrant certification and committal to hospital of any person suffering from such a degree of mental illness as to be regarded as insane.

The degree of insanity in condemned prisoners did not have to fulfil any legal requirements such as the M'Naghten Rules and it is clear that a person found guilty of murder and sentenced to death, despite a defence of insanity which did not fulfil the M'Naghten test, could still be reprieved and sent to hospital. As the Royal Commission on Capital Punishment pointed out,[1] the issues of insanity at the time of trial and the issue of insanity after conviction were totally different problems. The statutory inquiry did not in any way affect the finding of the court that the prisoner was guilty of the act with which he was charged. It did mean that, had he been sentenced to death, he would have been reprieved and sent to hospital. In theory it was possible, should he recover, for him to be returned to prison for execution but such a procedure was so repugnant to normal feelings as to preclude its happening.

Despite the fact that some witnesses expressed strong criticism of the procedure invoked in statutory medical inquiries[2] it is a fact that in a number of cases in which the Judges of the Court of Criminal Appeal were unwilling to upset a verdict of murder and capital sentence, they indicated that note will be taken of the appellant's mental state in due course; an observation which suggested that in some respects,

[1] Royal Commission on Capital Punishment (1949–53), Cmd. 8932, para. 366
[2] Royal Commission on Capital Punishment (1949–53), Cmd. 8932, para. 365

the power of the Home Secretary in this matter was a useful safeguard against the execution of insane persons.[1] The Royal Commission was satisfied that some kind of medical inquiry was held on all persons about whose mental condition at the time of, or subsequent to, the crime, doubts had been raised. This was particularly the case where a person had pleaded insanity as a defence but had had his plea rejected. Such inquiries had no statutory basis, but if they found the prisoner to be insane or suffering from some degree of mental abnormality they could call the attention of the Home Secretary to their findings and express any opinions they might care to offer. Again, such inquiries were not bound by the criteria of legal responsibility laid down in M'Naghten's case but were guided by the ordinary clinical tests of mental disorder.

The Criminal Lunatics Act, 1884, was repealed by the Mental Health Act, 1959, but under section 72 (1) of this Act authority is given for the transfer of prisoners found to be mentally ill. The section states: 'If in the case of a person serving a sentence of imprisonment the Secretary of State is satisfied, by reports from at least two medical practitioners (complying with the provisions of this section)—(a) that the said person is suffering from mental illness, psychopathic disorder, subnormality or severe subnormality; and (b) that the mental disorder is of a nature and degree which warrants the detention of the patient in a hospital for medical treatment; the Secretary of State may, if he is of opinion having regard to the public interest and all the circumstances that it is expedient so to do, by warrant direct that that person be removed to and detained in such hospital (not being a mental nursing home) as may be specified in the direction.'

Under section 72 (4) it is laid down that at least one of the medical practitioners submitting the report shall have been approved under section 22 of the Act by a local authority as having special experience in the diagnosis or treatment of mental disorders. No special reference is made to prisoners under sentence of death in this section but presumably such persons are covered by subsection (6) (a) which, for the purposes of this section, includes 'a person detained in pursuance of any sentence . . . made by a court in criminal proceedings'.

No special conditions are laid down governing the criteria for the diagnosis of insanity in such cases, which is obtained solely by the ordinary clinical investigations required for the diagnosis of mental disorder. The fact that a person may be found to be insane after conviction in no way affects the finding of the court that he was guilty of the act charged, although such a finding when insanity has been offered as a defence implies that the symptoms described did not fulfil

[1] R. v. True (1922). 16 Cr. App. Rep. 164; R. v. Flavell (1926), 19 Cr. App. Rep. 141; R. v. Codère (1916), 12 Cr. App. Rep. 21

the requirements of the M'Naghten Rules. It is, in a sense, anomalous that although a man may not be ill enough to escape conviction or to have the verdict reversed by the Court of Criminal Appeal he should be found so disordered by ordinary medical standards after conviction as to justify his immediate transfer to hospital. It is rare for a person to be sane at trial but to become mentally ill afterwards, so it is likely that any signs of mental disorder found by medical examination after conviction will have been present throughout the period of remand and trial and, in all probability, had a direct bearing upon the offence for which the prisoner was convicted.

In so far as it is desirable that justice should be done publicly it would be helpful if the Court of Criminal Appeal had the right in such cases to re-examine the medical evidence, call for any further opinion should this seem necessary and enter a verdict of guilty but insane if this seemed more correct in the light of their own findings. No doubt this sounds a simple enough procedure, but it is one which would, in all probability, conflict with many precedents as well as the time-honoured principle that the decision of the jury is final unless it can be shown to rest on some misdirection or misinterpretation of the law. Only when the medical evidence of insanity has been unchallenged yet, despite this, the jury has still returned a verdict of guilty, will the Court of Criminal Appeal at present reverse the verdict on the grounds that any verdict must conform with the evidence. Such reversals appear to be commoner when there has been a question of diminished responsibility rather than insanity.[1] Even so, according to the ruling of Lord Parker, C.J. in the case of Byrne[2] the jury are not bound to accept the medical evidence if there is other material before the court which, in their good judgment, conflicts with it and outweighs it. Undoubtedly, when the medical evidence conflicts, as in the case of Jennion,[3] it is for the jury to decide the issue one way or the other, but when medical evidence is unanimous as to the legal insanity or substantial impairment of responsibility on the part of the defendant it is difficult to see what other facts could permit a jury to set aside such medical evidence. If facts related by expert witnesses are unchallenged it is surely unreasonable that they should be ignored. If they are, there seems little point in asking for expert evidence in these cases even though it will be agreed that the quality of such evidence varies from case to case.

The foregoing pages can be summarized by recapitulating the various stages at which psychiatric advice may be called for in criminal cases.

[1] R. *v.* Matheson, [1958] 2 All E. R. 87; and R. *v.* Bailey, [1961] Crim. L. R. 829; but compare with R. *v.* True (1922), 16 Cr. App. Rep. 164; and R. *v.* Rivett (1950), 34 Cr. App. Rep. 87
[2] R. *v.* Byrne, [1960] 3 All E. R. 1
[3] R. *v.* Jennion, [1962] 1 All E. R. 689

In most serious charges the defendant's medical state will be inquired into either by the prison medical officer or, where it seems appropriate, by an independent psychiatrist called by the defence. If there seem to be sufficient grounds to claim that the defendant is unfit to plead, medical testimony to that effect will be required and, again, this will be forthcoming from the prison medical officer or from medical evidence called by the defence. In the case of mutism on arraignment it may be necessary for a doctor to discuss the cause of the symptom, although evidence of deaf mutism from birth will probably be available from other sources. If amnesia is pleaded as a reason for acquittal or unfitness to plead it will have to be shown whether the amnesia is true or feigned, although, for the reasons given, there appears to be little prospect that amnesia will be accepted by the court as a good reason for stopping the trial. Once the trial has started psychiatric evidence as to insanity or diminished responsibility of the prisoner at the time of the act with which he is charged may be called. Finally, if the accused man is convicted and sentenced a medical inquiry as to his state of mind might lead to his transfer to hospital rather than permit sentence of death to be carried out, should that have been the sentence of the court.

Perhaps one somewhat controversial point might be permitted. It has been said, with good reason, that there are few occasions when an accused man pleads insanity or diminished responsibility unless there is a likelihood that he will receive a capital sentence should he be convicted. The prospect of an indefinite period in Broadmoor Hospital rather than a limited prison sentence is only to be preferred when the alternative is death. No doubt there will be many occasions when it is vital that the state of mind of the defendant should be inquired into to ensure that an insane person receives proper treatment rather than that he should be sent to prison with the possibility of a repetition of a serious offence on discharge. There will, in consequence, always be a place for proper and careful psychiatric examination of certain classes of offenders so that the courts may be guided in coming to a right conclusion about the disposal of the defendant. Yet it could be said that only when the charge is a capital one does the sanity or insanity of the defendant become of such crucial importance as to make it seem as if all that matters is the outcome of a conflict of medical opinion which, possibly, would not arise so acutely did not the outcome of the conflict include the possibility of death for the accused man. One wonders, in consequence whether the struggle, the tension, the seeking of facts and opinions which at the best can only be expressed in a somewhat tentative fashion, are worth the time and energy devoted to the problem. In charges less than capital murder one feels that it is possible to come to a reasonable conclusion about the prisoner's mental condition in a reasonably calm and professional manner. It is very important that such conclusions should be reached and it is desirable that they should be made for good scientific and objective reasons uninfluenced by any emotional bias attributable to the medical witness.

It would be very difficult indeed for anyone to preserve complete detachment from the outcome of a trial in which medical evidence is sought as to the mental state of a man on a capital charge, and it could be argued that such involvement is not in the interests of justice, or necessarily, sound of reasoning. Between the coming into force of the Homicide Act, in March 1957, and the end of 1960, 19 persons were executed for capital murder. One might be permitted to ask whether the retention of capital punishment to be used in such few instances can any longer be justified. One could certainly conclude that much of the medico-legal controversy which in the past has developed over such cases would cease, leaving the courts and the medical witnesses to get on with their work with the minimum of conflicting opinion. Some conflict will always arise in cases where degrees of responsibility are under consideration; it is likely to be less bitter and irreconcilable when a man's life does not depend upon the outcome.

Indices

CASES CITED

Reniger *v.* Fogossa (1550), 1 Plowd. 1 109
Rivett (1950), 34 Cr. App. Rep. 87 . . . 24, 41, 99, 133, 145
Roberts, [1954] 2 Q. B. 329 . . . . . . 129, 134
Rose *v.* R., [1961] 1 All E. R. 859 . . . . . 98, 103
Rowley (1960), *The Times*, July 19 97
Russell *v.* H.M. Advocate, [1946] S. C. (J.) 37 131

Savage, [1923] S. C. (J.) 49 95
Sell, [1962] Crim. L. R. 463 123
Sharp (1957), 41 Cr. App. Rep. 197 . . . . 130, 134
Sibbles, [1959] Crim. L. R. 660 125
Smith (1910), 5 Cr. App. Rep. 123 29
Smith (1910), 6 Cr. App. Rep. 19 137
Sodemann *v.* R., [1936] 2 All E. R. 1133 . . . 25, 26, 134
Spriggs, [1958] 1 All E. R. 300 . . . . . 98, 101
Straffen, [1952] 2 All E. R. 657 . . . . . 30, 66

Terry, [1961] 2 All E. R. 569 140
Thomas (1911), 7 Cr. App. Rep. 36 26
Tickell (1958), *The Times*, Jan. 24 . . . . . 97, 138
Townley (1863), 3 F. & F. 839 . . . . . 24, 32
Treadaway (1877), cited in *The Insane and the Law* (1895) . . 28
True (1922), 16 Cr. App. Rep. 164 . . . . 46, 144, 145

Vaughan (1844), 1 Cox C. C. 80 33
Vent (1935), 25 Cr. App. Rep. 55 127

Walden, [1959] 3 All E. R. 203 . . . . . 98, 101
Waring *v.* Waring (1848), 6 Moo. P. C. C. 341 . . . 36, 40
Watmore *v.* Jenkins, [1962] 2 All E. R. 868 . . . 119, 125
Webb *v.* Webb (1962), *The Times*, May 21 40
White (1795), cited in Collinson on Lunacy (1812). . . . 15
Williams (1893), cited in *The Insane and the Law* (1895) . . 29
Williams (1960), *The Times*, Oct. 20 99
Windle, [1952] 2 All E. R. 1 . . . . . . 27, 33
Woolmington, [1935] A. C. 462 . . . . 25, 128, 134

Name Index

eco GUIDES

A Teen Guide to

Being Eco in Your Community

Cath Senker

Raintree

Raintree is an imprint of Capstone Global Library Limited, a company incorporated in England and Wales having its registered office at 7 Pilgrim Street, London, EC4V 6LB – Registered company number: 6695582

To contact Raintree:
Phone: 0845 6044371
Fax: + 44 (0) 1865 312263
Email: myorders@raintreepublishers.co.uk
Outside the UK please telephone +44 1865 312262.

Text © Capstone Global Library Limited 2013
First published in hardback in 2013
The moral rights of the proprietor have been asserted.

Edited by Andrew Farrow, Adam Miller, and
  Vaarunika Dharmapala
Designed by Richard Parker
Original illustrations © Capstone Global Library
  Ltd 2013
Illustrated by HL Studios
Picture research by Tracy Cummins
Originated by Capstone Global Library Ltd
Printed and bound in China by CTPS

ISBN 978 1 406 24983 5
16 15 14 13 12
10 9 8 7 6 5 4 3 2 1

British Library Cataloguing in Publication Data
Senker, Cath.
A teen guide to being eco in your community. -- (Eco guides)
363.7'0525-dc23
A full catalogue record for this book is available from the British Library.

Acknowledgements
We would like to thank the following for permission to reproduce photographs: Alamy pp. 9 (© David J. Green – electrical), 11 top (© Construction Photography), 20 (© Anthony Pleva), 22, 23 (© Jeff Greenberg), 25 (© Peter Titmuss); Capstone Library pp. 43, 45, 47 (Karon Dubke); Corbis pp. 21 (© Reuters), 34 (© Tim Pannell); Getty Images pp. 5 (Echo), 6 (Mark D Callanan), 10 (Photo Researchers), 13 (AARON MAASHO/AFP), 15 (KidStock), 31 (Andrew Holt), 41 (Jupiterimages); LA Photo Party p. 33 (Brian Miller); Lothrop Science, Spanish, Technology Magnet Omaha Public Schools p. 36 (Pamela Galus); Shutterstock pp.4 (Dmitriy Shironosov), 8 (Kuramyndra), 11 (bottom) (manfredxy), 14 (Nikola Spasenoski), 29 (left) (Zoran Vukmanov Simokov), 29 (right) (gillmar), 30 (rangizzz), 32 (AVAVA), 35 (Andre Blais), 38 (jabiru), 39 (Leftleg), 40 (monticello), 48 (Claus Mikosch), 49 (Inc); Superstock pp. 7 (© imagebroker.net), 12 (© Belinda Images), 26, 37 (© Ambient Images Inc.).

Cover photograph of a couple working in a garden reproduced with permission of Corbis (© Mika). Cover logo of eco sticker reproduced with permission of Shutterstock (Olivier Le Moal).

Every effort has been made to contact copyright holders of material reproduced in this book. Any omissions will be rectified in subsequent printings if notice is given to the publisher.

All the Internet addresses (URLs) given in this book were valid at the time of going to press. However, due to the dynamic nature of the Internet, some addresses may have changed, or sites may have changed or ceased to exist since publication. While the author and publisher regret any inconvenience this may cause readers, no responsibility for any such changes can be accepted by either the author or the publisher.

Contents

Some words are shown in bold, **like this**. You can find out what they mean by looking in the glossary.

Important!

Please check with an adult before doing the projects in this book.

How can I be eco?

We all know that human activities have a huge impact on our environment, from using up the world's resources to affecting **climate change**. We realize it makes sense to reduce that impact as much as we can. Although the problems may seem vast, every one of us can make a difference. It's easy to get started – there are many quick, simple, and cheap things we can all do.

This book considers how you can be eco in your community. So, who *are* your community? They are the people around you – your neighbours and people in local shops, places of worship, and schools. Sports and outdoor activity clubs, Scouts, and music or dance organizations are also communities.

We benefit from being part of one or many communities just as we thrive from having friends and family around us. If any of the communities you belong to are not already involved in eco actions, they might be interested in adopting some eco ideas. As well as helping the environment, it may save them money!

The girls at this dance club could consider making the lighting more eco friendly.

Meeting neighbours

Zocalo is a small community scheme in Brighton. Once a year, people are encouraged to get to know their neighbours by putting a couple of chairs on the pavement outside their house. People wander up and down the street, sharing food and drink. At simple events like these, the seeds of community projects can be planted. At one Zocalo event, a group of neighbours decided to set up a communal compost heap.

The range of issues to tackle may seem bewildering – from saving energy and water, reducing waste, and environmentally friendly food, to encouraging nature and **biodiversity**. So, why not consider where you could most easily make changes, and start from there? This book has realistic projects you can do right now, with a little help from others in your community. Millions of people all over the world are doing these things. So, what are you waiting for?

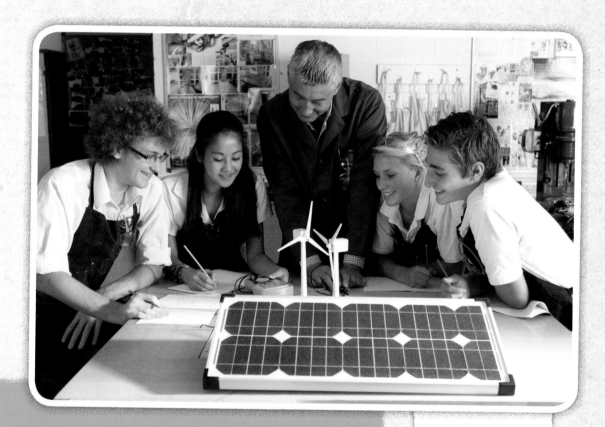

The sky's the limit: wind turbines

Local eco groups may be able to build up to ambitious projects. Wausau East High School in Wisconsin, USA, has installed its own **wind turbine** to produce energy. The wind turbine provides about 5 per cent of the school's power needs, saving about £9,100 a year on electricity bills.

This teacher and pupils are discussing how wind power works.

What's in it for me?

By promoting and protecting nature, you can make the places where you live, study, and socialize more pleasant. You could help your family save money by reducing energy bills. If you can help reduce costs significantly, your parent or carer might reward you!

Why be eco at school?

Your school is a ready-made community so it's an easy place to start being eco. It can be good for your education, too. Working in the fresh air on outdoor gardening and nature projects makes a welcome change from sitting in a classroom. Seeing the results of your work provides great motivation to continue. Imagine spotting the first winged visitors to your nature area or harvesting your home-grown vegetables!

People all around the world enjoy nature. Here, residents of Jalisco, Mexico are celebrating the arrival of spring.

New friends, new skills

If you become more involved in your school and local community, you'll make friends with people of different ages and backgrounds as well as gain useful skills. The ability to co-operate with a variety of people and to organize activities will look good on your CV when you apply for college, university, or jobs.

This vegetable patch grows in an urban garden in Detroit, Michigan, USA. You don't have to live in the country to go green!

"By taking the concept of **sustainable** living beyond the narrow, individualistic [focused on individuals] approach, we can learn to see our interconnectedness to our environment and its inhabitants. By getting involved in our communities, by talking to our neighbors, by supporting local groups, and by re-imagining where we live, we can green not only our own lifestyles, but our streets, neighborhoods, towns, cities and, ultimately, our societies. Who knows, we may even make friends doing it."

Sami Grover, writer and environmental activist, North Carolina, USA

Eco jobs

If you enjoy being eco in your community, you may decide to pursue a career in environmental work. Here are a few possible occupations:

- Environmental **conservation** involves managing parks and countryside recreation areas, waste management, and the protection of wild birds.
- Forestry includes the management of trees, forests, and woodlands.
- Within businesses, environmental officers are responsible for improving **energy efficiency** and waste management.
- **Non-governmental organizations** need people to undertake practical conservation, educate the public, and campaign on specific issues.
- Newspapers and television programmes need writers and researchers who are knowledgable about the environment.

YOUR COMMUNITY: Energy, water, and waste

Reducing energy and water use and reducing the waste we produce may sound like huge tasks, but there are several simple eco actions you can easily adopt at home or your sports clubhouse, school, community centre, or place of worship. They will soon become habits. When many individuals work together, you can make a real difference.

Save energy, save money

Take the challenge and adopt these simple ideas for saving energy:

- Accept that it's cold in winter! Do you really need to keep your home as hot as a sauna so you can go round in a T-shirt? Embrace winter by wearing a warm, cosy jumper.
- You tend to feel cold when you are sitting still. Instead of turning up the heating when you're watching TV or using the computer, consider snuggling up with a soft blanket around you.
- Don't stand by! It's effortless to switch off appliances when you stop using them so you don't leave them guzzling energy on standby. See if you can borrow an energy monitor (see panel on page 9) to check how much energy your household is using. Then see if you could reduce it.

Snuggling up in a blanket to read can be a real pleasure.

Energy monitors

Energy monitors allow you to check how much electricity your appliances are using. The simplest ones can be connected to an appliance. There are also small wireless monitors with a transmitter (device that sends electronic signals) to connect around the cable of your electricity meter. Some energy monitors can store data, which you upload to a computer. All provide useful information about the running costs of your appliances. Try checking how much energy you are currently using at bedtime. In fact, almost every appliance except the fridge can be turned off!

Keep cool, avoid waste

When it's hot in summer, it's tempting to crank up the air conditioning or switch on fans to keep cool. But there are ways to reduce the heat without using up large amounts of energy. For example, did you know that direct sunlight on a window can produce as much heat as a radiator? To cut out heat, close blinds and curtains during the hottest part of the day. Open the windows in the cool of the morning and the evening to lower the temperature. Electrical appliances and lights produce heat as well as light, so it's sensible to turn them off when not in use.

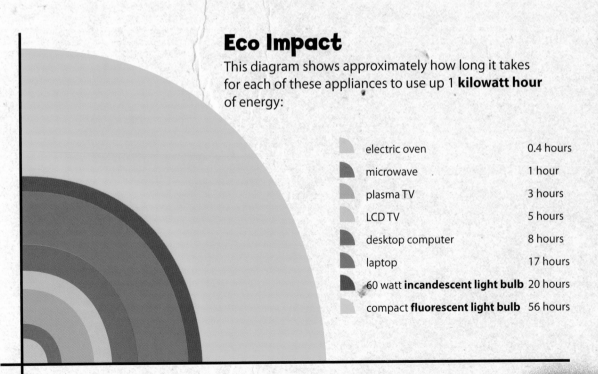

Eco Impact

This diagram shows approximately how long it takes for each of these appliances to use up 1 **kilowatt hour** of energy:

electric oven	0.4 hours
microwave	1 hour
plasma TV	3 hours
LCD TV	5 hours
desktop computer	8 hours
laptop	17 hours
60 watt **incandescent light bulb**	20 hours
compact **fluorescent light bulb**	56 hours

Eco groups can help!

If you're part of a group of like-minded people, they'll support you to change your habits and stick to greener ways. For help finding a group, try www.ecoteams.org.uk.

Eco scouts

In the United States, the Scouting Movement is going eco. In 2011, they introduced eco-friendly Scout jerseys. The jerseys are made from Repreve, a recyclable wool produced using water bottles made of PET (a type of plastic). Normal sportswear is made from synthetic fabrics which use crude oil. Every 450 grams (1 pound) of Repreve used saves 1.9 litres (0.5 gallons) of oil.

Some eco groups use technology to help people work out how to save energy. In the United Kingdom, the Three Villages Eco Group carries out **thermal imaging** to show people where heat is escaping from their homes. To minimize heat loss from the doors and windows, the residents can put in **draught proofing** and line their curtains.

In this thermogram of a home in winter, the red areas show where heat is escaping.

Be clean and green

The way we wash has a major impact on our water usage. Don't worry – you can be squeaky clean and eco friendly, too! If you usually have a bath, how about having a refreshing five-minute shower instead?

Bear in mind that some power showers use even more water than the average bath, and that having a long shower may have the same effect as having a bath!

To ensure you can have a great shower while still using water responsibly, why not talk to your family about buying a water-saving shower head? This small device reduces the flow of water but you can still enjoy a powerful shower. It's quite cheap to buy and soon saves money on your hot water bill. It will also reduce the amount of water that has to be extracted from rivers and the ground.

You can fit a water **flow restrictor** (shown left) to every tap in your house to reduce the amount of water you use.

Save water

- Check the dishwasher or washing machine is full before you run it. Are you using the most efficient energy and water settings?
- Try using a sinkful of water to wash up a large pile of dishes twice a day rather than washing up every time you have a snack or drink.
- While you're waiting for the water to run hot when you're doing the washing up, you could fill up a bowl with cooler water for rinsing.
- If you boil just the water you need in the kettle, you'll save energy and your drink will be ready quickly.
- When you're washing your hands or face, pop in the plug and run just the water you need.
- You could pour left-over glasses of water on your plants.

How to tackle waste

It's not hard to reduce, reuse, and recycle and still have everything you need! Some people like to add a fourth "R" – refuse to purchase. Before you buy something, think carefully about whether you really need it. For example, you might want access to a product but you don't really need to own it. You can read the latest magazines and newspapers in a library for free. It's also free to borrow library books, and cheap to hire CDs and DVDs. For the purchases you do need, invest in a durable shopping bag so you can avoid coming home clutching plastic bags.

When you shop, try to find items made from recycled material.

Swap or sell

Reusing goods is simple, too. See if you can join a Freecycle group in your area. People give away goods they no longer need rather than throwing them in the bin. (Check with a parent before you join and always go with a trusted adult to collect items.) Or why not hold a car boot sale and sell those old toys, games, and clothes? You will learn some bargaining skills and hopefully make some money.

Buying second-hand products is another great idea. How about investing in some retro clothing? An interesting, original item from a charity shop will help you stand out from the crowd.

Recycling

You probably already recycle paper, card, and plastic. Did you know that you can also recycle household items such as batteries, CDs, DVDs, and light bulbs? Check your local council website to find out where to take them. Of course, it's no use recycling unless people buy the new goods produced, so look out for interesting products made from recycled materials.

Eco Impact

Tyres are tough, resistant to chemicals, and do not melt. They are made from nylon fabrics and metal, covered with hard rubber. Once they have worn down, car users have to replace them. In the United Kingdom, about 25 million tyres are thrown away each year. One company, Remarkable, shreds used tyres into tiny pieces and turns them into a smooth, flexible sheet. This sheet is made into pencil cases, mouse mats, and notepads.

This woman runs a successful business in Ethiopia, making shoes from recycled tyres and fabrics.

Being green - summing up

- Save energy by wearing cosy clothing at home.
- Turn off appliances when not in use.
- Have quick showers to stay clean and fresh.
- Use just the water you need.
- Keep reducing, reusing, and recycling.

Nature and biodiversity

How can you make your neighbourhood nature-friendly? Perhaps there's a nature club in your area that you could join. Otherwise, why not gather some friends and neighbours together to encourage wildlife to your local area?

You can plant herbs and wild flowers to attract beneficial (helpful) insects such as butterflies, bees, and ladybirds. Bees and butterflies **pollinate** plants, while ladybirds feed on aphids (small insects that damage plants). Make sure the varieties you choose are suitable for your local climate. These are all quite easy to grow:

Herbs: Basil, Borage, Dill, Fennel, Lavender, Parsley, Thyme, Sage

Flowers: Cornflower, Clematis, Hydrangea, Mexican Hat, Zinnia

Eco Impact

One-third of the human diet can be traced to bee pollination. Bees pollinate crops, so they can be fertilized and reproduce. Bee populations have dwindled, but it's easy to create a bee-friendly environment. In Stirling, Scotland, the On the Verge project asks schools and community groups to plant wild flowers and **nectar-rich** plants in the spring to help the bee population recover.

As these bees fly among the buttercups and daisies, they will pollinate both types of flower. Encouraging bees does not mean you will get stung, as long as you are careful.

These volunteers are planting a tree. Once it's in the soil, they will add **mulch** and water it.

Attracting the right visitors

There's nothing worse than planting herbs and flowers only to find they have been munched by insects. Luckily, there are several ways to encourage beneficial insects and deter harmful ones naturally, without harming wildlife or the environment. A popular method is companion planting – combining plants that help each other by deterring pests. For example, plant chives, garlic, or coriander to repel aphids. Dill attracts beneficial insects such as hoverflies and wasps that eat aphids. Find out more at www.bbc.co.uk/gardening/basics/techniques/organic_companionplanting1.shtml.

The benefits of trees

Trees play an important role in our environment. In urban areas, they attract wildlife, and provide greenery and shade in summer. In places that are prone to flooding, they retain water and reduce the run-off of water. The School Tree Nursery Programme helps school children to plant trees to improve their local habitat. The children help to raise the saplings within the school grounds, and once they are big enough, they plant them out in the community. In Lewes, East Sussex, for instance, trees have been planted on the **floodplain** to try to reduce the harmful effects of future flooding by local rivers.

Attracting birds

You could make a small nest box with a hole to attract tit species and sparrows. It's wise to find out the kinds of birds that nest locally so you make the right kind of home for them. For information, try www.bto.org/nnbw/which.htm.

Why make a nest box?

Many bird species depend on holes in trees and buildings to make their nest. These sites disappear when woods and gardens are tidied, and people repair old houses. Nest boxes can help make up for the loss.

Putting up your nest box

Attach your box at the end of winter, using galvanized (rust-proof) or stainless-steel nails. Check that it will be sheltered from the **prevailing wind**, rain, and strong sunlight. The front of the nest should be angled slightly downwards to prevent rain from dripping into it. Either put the box 1–3 metres (3–10 feet) above the ground on a tree, on a wall, or on the side of a shed. Check that predators such as cats or squirrels cannot easily reach the nest. Also check that it is not near bird feeders so visiting birds won't disturb the nesting birds. For more information, go to www.bto.org/nnbw/essentials.htm.

Make a nest box for birds

You will need:

Plank of wood 15 cm x 117 cm (6 x 46 in) and at least 1.5 cm (0.6 in) thick. (It's sensible to allow a little extra in case something goes wrong.)
Saw
Drill
Pencil
Galvanized or stainless-steel nails
Waterproof material such as car tyre inner tube or Butyl rubber to make the hinge

Please ask an adult to supervise this project.

Method:

1. Saw the parts to the sizes shown in the diagram.

2. Drill small holes in the base piece to drain out rainwater.

3. Drill a hole in the front piece. It should be:

   2.5 cm (1 in) or larger for a Blue, Coal, or Marsh tit

   2.8 cm (1.1 in) or larger for a Great tit or Tree sparrow

   3.2 mm (1.3 in) for a House sparrow

4. Drill a hole in the back piece to attach the nest box.

5. Mark in pencil where the sides, roof, and base will fit on to the back piece.

6. Cut a groove in the back piece where the roof will slot in. Make sure the roof fits snugly.

7. Nail the sides to the back piece, then nail on the base.

8. Nail the front to the sides and base.

9. Make a hinge to attach the roof. First, cut the rubber to the width of the box. Then nail the rubber along the back of the box and to the roof. Finally, attach the box to a tree.

Source: National Nest Box Week, www.bto.org/nnbw/index.htm

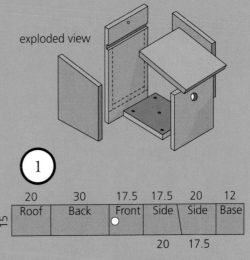

exploded view

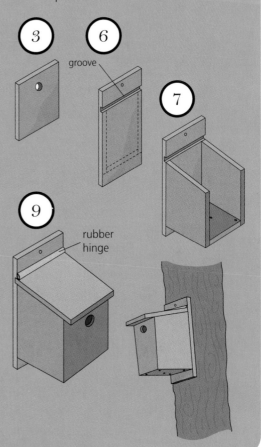

(1)

20	30	17.5	17.5	20	12
Roof	Back	Front	Side	Side	Base

15

20 17.5

plank size 15cm x 117cm

(3) (6)

groove

(7)

(9)

rubber hinge

Attracting wildlife

A small pond is a wonderful way to attract wildlife. Before you start, there are some points to consider. Can you position your pond away from overhanging trees and in partial shade? You'll need to think about the shape of your pond. It should have shallow areas to allow creatures to get in and out easily, and birds to bathe. It's important to get the right balance of plants, too.

Build a small pond

You will need:

Spade
Pond liner, bought from a garden centre or online (try to buy one that is recycled or made from rubber). Use this formula to work out how much you need: (length + [depth x 2]) + (width + [depth x 2]). For example, if your pond is 2.5 m (8 ft) long by 1.5 m (5 ft) wide, and 1 m (3 ft) deep, you'll need: 2.5 + 2 + 1.5 + 2 m = 8 m (8 + 6 + 5 + 6 ft = 25 ft) of pond liner.
Soft sand
A few rocks
Long grass seed (optional)
Plants

Please ask an adult to supervise this project.

Method:

1. Measure out the area of the pond.

2. Dig the hole. Start with a hole at least 80 cm deep (2 ft 7 in) at one end. The other end should come up at a slope of 20°.

3. Remove sharp stones or roots. Leave a step on which to later place shallow water plants.

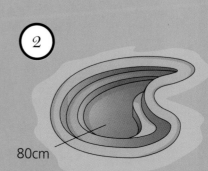

2

80cm

Aquatic plants

Use four types of plants to keep your pond healthy:

- *Oxygenators* keep the water clear. Try water milfoil or willow moss.
- *Floating plants* provide shelter. Try water hyacinth or water lettuce.
- *Marginal plants* provide protection from predators. Try marsh marigolds or water forget-me-nots.
- *Deep-water aquatics* should be planted 30 cm (1 ft) deep or more. Their leaves provide shade and shelter. Try water hawthorn.

Being green – summing up

- Plant herbs and wild flowers to encourage beneficial insects.
- Plant trees to help improve the environment.
- Make a nest box to shelter birds.
- Build a pond to attract wildlife.

4. Add a layer of sand to the pond.

5. Place the pond liner in the hole, allowing for an overlap of 30–50 cm (12–20 in).

6. Place a few rocks around the shallow end. Mammals will be able to lean off them to drink the water.

7. If you'd like to attract frogs, plant some long grass seed around the deep end to provide shelter from predators and shade from the Sun.

8. If possible, fill the pond with rainwater. Otherwise, use tap water, but leave it for two weeks before adding plants to allow any chemicals to evaporate.

9. Add some aquatic (water-living) plants.

10. Cover the edge of the liner, to protect it, for example with turf or slate.

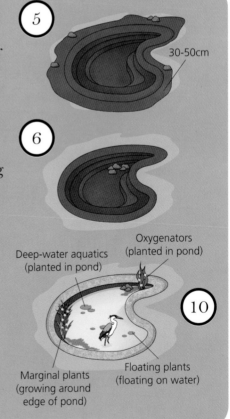

5

30-50cm

6

10

Oxygenators (planted in pond)

Deep-water aquatics (planted in pond)

Marginal plants (growing around edge of pond)

Floating plants (floating on water)

A healthy neighbourhood

Is your local area a mess? It's not hard to improve it a little. Simple tasks such as making posters to persuade people to use rubbish bins or to clean up dog mess can help your neighbours to clean up their act. It's also worth reminding people that it's illegal to drop litter and that they can be fined for doing so. You could even get together with friends to organize a litter pick (see page 23), plant some herbs, or encourage more walking and cycling.

Does this sound unrealistic? Well, it has been shown that people make the choice whether to litter, so putting up notices to focus attention on the issue can make a real difference. Keep Australia Beautiful ran a competition to create a 30-second advert with an anti-littering message aimed at under-25s. Robbie Reid was one of the young people who took up the challenge. He produced an anti-litter advert with a cute animated crab called Kevin, who advised viewers to "stash trash" in the bin. Robbie won an award of AUD$1,000 (£650)!

Much of this rubbish could have been recycled. You can see paper, card, a can, and plastic bottles. The plastic bags could have been reused.

Littering: the facts

Keep America Beautiful carried out a survey of littering and discovered that:

- Nearly one in five people (17 per cent) dropped litter in a public place, while most (83 per cent) disposed of it properly.
- People are more likely to litter if the area is already littered. In contrast, if there are recycling and rubbish bins handy, people tend to use them.
- Littering is an individual choice. People who believe littering is wrong use the bins. Individuals can encourage others not to litter and help to change habits.

A herb patch

Once you've tackled the rubbish ... how about community food growing? Is there a patch of unused ground in your area? If you are part of a community eco group, you could seek permission from your local council to plant some herbs for everyone to use. Or perhaps a local place of worship has a space where you could grow plants in pots. It is easy to do, and your cooking will be tastier with fresh herbs.

Rooftop gardens

Tokyo, Japan, is a densely populated city. Few people have gardens. In recent years, however, people have developed an interest in growing their own food. As space is an issue, these gardeners are ingenious, creating vegetable plots in front of railway stations and making rooftop gardens. Businesses have become involved, too. For example, in 2011 East Japan Railway opened a rental garden on the rooftop of the Lumine Ogikubo Building. People can rent plots to grow fruit and vegetables, as well as use the garden to relax and socialize.

Litter

Is there an area near you that is ruined by litter? Why not organize a litter pick? You could start with a small clean-up, for example, on your school fields. Perhaps you could ask pupils, parents, and teachers to sponsor you to raise the money you'll need for equipment.

These volunteers in Little Haiti (above) and Baynanza Biscayne Bay (page 23), both in Miami, Florida, USA, are taking part in a community day to clean up their neighbourhoods.

Stay safe!

It's important to find an adult to supervise your event in case you find dangerous materials. Make sure everyone in your group knows that if they spot syringes, they should not touch them. Syringes can cause injury or infection. After the litter pick, contact your local council and tell them where you found the materials.

Organize a community litter pick

Here's how to plan your litter pick:

1. Find some friends to form an organizing group, and an adult to support you.

2. You may need to get permission to work in your chosen area. Ask an adult to help you to check about **public liability insurance**.

3. Pick a day and time for the event. Two hours should be enough.

4. Publicize the event. You could tell the local media.

5. With an adult, carry out a **risk assessment** of the area. There may be hazards, such as broken glass, or syringes.

6. Find equipment. You can ask everyone to bring strong gloves and bin bags. You'll also need litter grabbers, and luminous jackets if possible. It's helpful to have some bags and containers to store sharp objects, and tape to seal them. Make sure you have a first aid kit. You may be able to get some equipment for free from Keep Britain Tidy (www. keepbritaintidy.org).

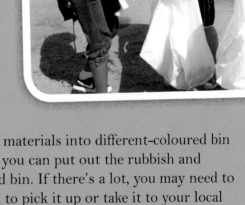

7. Work out how to dispose of the litter afterwards. For example, you could separate recyclable and non-recyclable materials into different-coloured bin bags. If there's not too much, you can put out the rubbish and recycling with your household bin. If there's a lot, you may need to arrange for your local council to pick it up or take it to your local waste and recycling centre.

8. Celebrate your work! It's worth taking "before" and "after" photos and sending them to the media. If you've done well, you're bound to get plenty of support for your next litter pick.

Source: LitterAction, www.litteraction.org.uk

Get on your bike!

We all know that vehicles use up precious **fossil fuels** and create air pollution. But how easy is it to change how you travel? Maybe you could start with a small change in your habits, such as replacing one journey a week in a vehicle by cycling or walking.

Cycling and walking

Pros
- Cycling and walking are good for your health.
- Cycling is cheap and walking costs nothing.
- The more people walk or cycle, the less traffic there is on the roads.
- Many towns and cities have bike lanes, often making it faster to use a bike than a car.
- On a bike, you can zip through traffic and park in many places.
- If you enjoy nature, you are more likely to spot interesting plants and animals than you would in a car.
- Cycling is a popular and sociable sport.
- Your bike needs regular maintenance to keep it in good working order but it is quite simple once you know how.

Cons
- Cycling or walking may not be practical for long distances.
- Road traffic can make it dangerous to cycle.
- Traffic fumes can make it unpleasant to walk or cycle.
- Many people feel unsafe walking or cycling in the dark.
- Not every climate is suitable for year-round cycling or walking. For safety, cyclists need to invest in good wet-weather gear and high-visibility clothing such as a bib or vest with reflective strips.

Eco Impact

In the United States in 2008, just 0.5 per cent of journeys to work were made by bike, while under 3 per cent were made on foot. However, there was an increase in cycling to work of 43 per cent between 2000 and 2008. This shows that habits can change over time.

Cycle safety

So, how can cycling be encouraged? Some simple changes can make a difference. It's helpful to have bike racks or other safe storage areas for bicycles at school, sports clubs, and other places in the community. Spreading knowledge about bike maintenance and safety is useful, too.

If you get involved in promoting cycling or any other eco project in your community, see if you can hold an event to promote your work, and get more people involved.

Transport survey

Ask your friends about the transport they use, how often they use it, and the distances they travel. Work out the average distance people walk or cycle, and how often. Ask what it would take to persuade them to walk or cycle more and further. Which key factors would help? Repeat the survey to see if you are having an impact on the behaviour of your friends.

Cycling is an easy, gentle exercise. It helps to improve your fitness which can reduce your risk of health problems in later life.

Being green - summing up

- Organize a litter pick to tidy up your local area.
- Put up posters to deter littering.
- Create a community garden.
- Replace some journeys with cycling or walking.

YOUR SCHOOL: Saving energy and water

Why would you want to be eco-friendly at school? Firstly, you spend a lot of time there, so you'll benefit if the school environment improves. Secondly, a school is a large community, so eco-friendly measures can make a real difference. Thirdly, eco projects allow you to become more involved in the running of your school.

Eco-Schools

Has your school joined the worldwide Eco-Schools Network? It enables you to share ideas and ask for advice. For example, Slovakian schoolchildren visited Berlin and Hamburg schools in 2009 and learnt methods for taking responsibility for eco projects.

Eco-Schools Scotland has a forum on its website. One pupil posted a question about how to get others involved in their eco committee. Other pupils suggested handing out fliers, putting up posters, and promoting projects in assembly at the start of term – when people are fresh from their holidays.

This community group are being given a demonstration on how to properly plant a tree.

Start small

Don't worry if your school isn't in the Eco-Schools Network. To kick off some activity, how about finding out if your friends might like to become involved? Then, see if you can find at least one teacher to support your environmental projects. You could set up an eco club or become an eco class. Maybe you can get your school caretaker on board, or the parents through the Parent Teacher Association.

It might be easiest to start by focusing on one theme. For example, at Eco-School Elie Faure de Lormont, France, the pupils focused on waste in the first year, food in the second year, and then biodiversity in the third year.

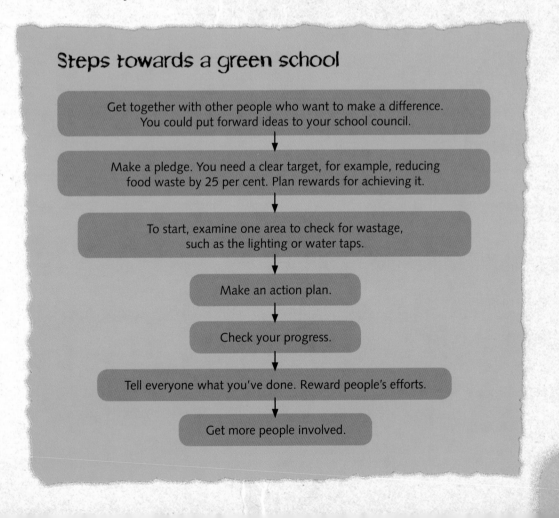

Steps towards a green school

Get together with other people who want to make a difference. You could put forward ideas to your school council.

↓

Make a pledge. You need a clear target, for example, reducing food waste by 25 per cent. Plan rewards for achieving it.

↓

To start, examine one area to check for wastage, such as the lighting or water taps.

↓

Make an action plan.

↓

Check your progress.

↓

Tell everyone what you've done. Reward people's efforts.

↓

Get more people involved.

Easy energy saving

Saving energy is a great idea – but how do you know where you need to cut back? It's worth carrying out an energy review to see how much energy you are using at the moment. This document includes a model you can use: www.ecoschoolsscotland.org/documents/PrimarySecondaryEnvironmentalReview2011.pdf.

The simplest way to cut energy use in schools is to look at lighting. Firstly, you could do a survey of lights left on in empty rooms. Also look at lighting levels. You need different levels of lighting for different tasks, for example, corridors require far less than classrooms or science labs. Some areas may have too much or too little light. You could carry out a similar survey for radiators. Are they being left on in unused rooms? Are some areas too hot or too cold?

Energy action plan

Next, work on your action plan. Start with easy actions, such as putting up notices reminding people to turn off lights when they are not needed. Studies have shown that natural light in classrooms is good for your health and helps you to learn better. So, if it's a bright day, you can switch off the lights. Another simple step is to change the light bulbs for energy-efficient ones. Have a chat with the school caretaker about this. You could also check whether the lights and heating are turned off during weekends and school holidays.

Energy-efficient light bulbs

Cheap energy-efficient light bulbs may seem like a bargain. However, they may not be as efficient as the top brands and won't save you money in the long run. Here's where a bit of maths comes in handy. You can buy a light bulb for £3.60 that has a rated life of 850 hours. The alternative is a bulb that produces the same light for 18,000 hours but costs £40. Energy use is the same for each bulb. Which bulb is a better buy? Check your answer on page 55.

Remember to be patient with the people you are trying to persuade. Explain the benefits of your proposals clearly and allow them time to make a decision. Here's an example you could mention: Sleepy Hollow Middle School in Sleepy Hollow, New York, USA, came up with a cheap, simple way to cut energy. They connected all their computers to a power strip. This made it effortless to switch them all off at the mains at the end of the day.

How long do different light sources last?

light source	efficiency (lumens/watt)	average life (hours)
standard incandescent	5–20	750–1,000
tungsten-halogen	15–25	2,000–4,000
compact fluorescent (5–26 watts)	20–55	10,000
compact fluorescent (27–40 watts)	50–80	15,000–20,000

Compact fluorescent bulbs can replace traditional incandescent bulbs in many light fixtures. Halogen lamps are a type of incandescent lighting but they are more efficient. They are commonly used in floor and desk lamps and for flood lighting.

compact fluorescent

standard incandescent

Progress check

Once you have some energy-saving measures in place, it's sensible to carry out regular reviews to check if usage is being reduced. This involves doing the surveys again. Hopefully, energy use will have decreased. If not, don't despair! Perhaps the message isn't getting across – why not do more publicity for your campaign? If you have managed to reduce usage, celebrate your achievements – then move on to your next campaign!

Ways to cut water waste

Another important area to tackle is water waste. You can adopt the same approach as for energy usage: carry out a review, develop an action plan, do a follow-up review to check progress, and assess if further action is required. Here's a sample water review that you can use: www.ecoschoolsscotland.org/documents/PrimarySecondaryEnvironmentalReview2011.pdf.

Water review

Areas to cover:

- School buildings: find out about water use in all the buildings and calculate the amount of water used per person per day.
- Water-using devices: discover how much water is used, for example, in the toilets, sinks, water fountains, showers, and science labs.
- School grounds: water used for watering the fields or gardens.

Materials you'll need:

- Figures for how much water the school used over the past 12 months or, if possible, the school's water bill
- Stopwatch for calculating the **flow rate** of taps, showers, and water fountains
- **Flow meter bags** or bucket
- Camera for recording observations and presenting results

Checking water flow

Reducing water flow from taps can save water and cut the cost of heating water. The flow rate need not be more than 9 litres (16 pints) per minute. If it's more, you can fix flow restrictors (see page 11) to the taps so the water doesn't come out so fast. To check flow rate:

1. Run water into a flow meter bag or bucket for 15 seconds.
2. Measure the water. Multiply by four to get the flow rate per minute.
3. If it's more than 9 litres per minute, recommend that your school buys flow restrictors.

This Ethiopian girl is transporting water in a heavy container. Many people around the world do not have the luxury of just turning on a tap in their home or school.

Water action!

Once you have carried out a review, brainstorm ideas for an action plan. Many actions cost nothing, or very little. You could make posters to encourage people not to waste water while washing their hands. At SOS Children's Village in Imzouren, Morocco, the children performed a play to inform others about the importance of saving water. You could ask the canteen staff to avoid using trays when possible, to reduce washing up. You'll probably need to talk to the maintenance staff, too. Perhaps there are leaking taps to mend, or they could cut down on using pressure washers to clean public areas.

Being green - summing up

- Become an Eco-School or start an eco club.
- Review water and energy use.
- Develop an action plan to cut usage.
- Check progress and carry out follow-up actions as needed.
- Celebrate what you've achieved!

Cutting waste: simple tips

What are the three Rs at school? Reduce, reuse, recycle! Most school waste is paper, packaging, and food waste. There are simple ways to reduce these kinds of waste and lighten the rubbish bags.

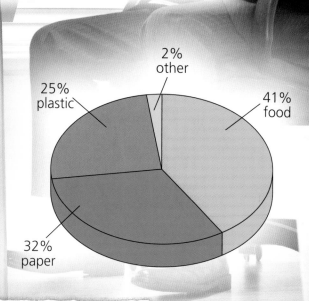

2% other

25% plastic

41% food

32% paper

At Black Mountain School in Scottsdale, Arizona, USA, pupils checked the principal's waste on one day (see pie chart). They then produced a plan to help her recycle more paper and plastic.

Reduce waste

If you have to print out work at school, print double-sided so you use half as much paper. What about litter? One Scottish pupil from an eco group was finding it hard to persuade others to reduce, reuse, and recycle litter. She asked for advice on the Eco-Schools forum. Another pupil replied that at his school pupils receive praise and rewards, such as a special postcard, if they follow the litter policy.

Another worthwhile project is to reduce the use of materials you don't need at all. At Nichols School, New York, USA, the pupils began a movement called Plasti-gone. They aim to persuade schools and businesses not to use single-use plastic products. For example, their "stop sucking" campaign encourages people to stop using drinking straws, which are a waste of resources.

From left to right: Paige Dedrick, Donata Lorenzo, and Caroline Fenn, the girls who started the Plasti-gone movement.

Wipe Out Waste

Around Australia, schools are taking part in the Wipe Out Waste programme. At Unley School, South Australia, pupil Emma Porter started the Environment Group, which set up a card and paper recycling scheme. To help the canteen staff to recycle cardboard, the group bought a trolley so they could transport the cardboard to the collection point. Paper that has been used on only one side is used to make notepads. Unley School also recycles as much plastic as possible.

Reuse

Now you might like to think creatively about how to reuse materials. As always, it's good to start with a survey. Find out how paper is reused. Many goods come in plastic pots – what happens to them once they are empty?

Your eco group could suggest some simple ideas for reusing items. Teachers and pupils can keep paper that has been used on one side for rough work. Plastic pots can serve as containers for pens and pencils. Seedlings can be planted in old drinks cans. When paper cannot be written on any more, try using it for art projects, from papier mâché models to masks. The students at Lyrup Primary School, South Australia, make their waste paper into bricks and sell them to local people for fuel! Here's how they do it: www.wow.sa.gov.au/uploads/pdfdocs/lyrupfinal.pdf.

Your art department should be able to reuse all kinds of material. Here, papier mâché has been used to make a giant model of the planet Saturn.

Not every school can start a major project such as paper-brick making. So, how can individual pupils reuse materials? A good way is to use lunch boxes and refill water bottles instead of using plastic bags and bottles (see pages 38–39 for ideas).

Recycle

At the International School of Paris, France, they switched from using bleached white paper to using recycled paper throughout the school. They could recycle the paper again afterwards. This kind of recycling is better for the environment than using a single-use product and chucking it straight in the recycling bin.

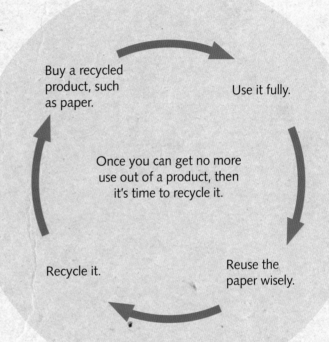

Buy a recycled product, such as paper.

Use it fully.

Once you can get no more use out of a product, then it's time to recycle it.

Recycle it.

Reuse the paper wisely.

Drinks in plastic bottles are refrigerated in shops, which uses a large amount of energy. Then resources are used for recycling the bottle – if the user remembers to recycle it! See pages 40–41 for greener alternatives.

Successful school recycling

At Lothrop Science and Technology Magnet School, North Omaha, Nebraska, USA, the pupils take the lead. Older pupils run the recycling programme, passing on their knowledge to younger children.

The project began during a science lesson. The pupils put on masks and thick gloves and emptied the rubbish bins – a disgusting but instructive task! They separated the recyclable materials, and realized many of the materials did not need to go in the bin.

The pupils devised a survey to see how the distance between recycling and rubbish bins affects recycling rates. (People are more likely to recycle if there's a recycling bin to hand.) They discovered that if a recycling monitor stands by the recycling bins at lunchtime, this encourages others to use them.

Now, three pupils each week are on paper patrol. They have 15 minutes to collect recycling from classrooms around the school. In the canteen, pupils sort out the recyclable plastic and collect food waste for composting. They have succeeded in reducing canteen waste from 20 to just 2 bags a day. The school also collects batteries, electronics, and glasses for recycling.

This is a primary school, so if they can do all of this, older students certainly can!

These Lothrop School pupils are putting their used containers into recycling bins.

Keep up the good work

Once you have a recycling scheme up and running, you'll want to ensure it keeps going. What incentives can you use? At Mount Gambier High School, South Australia, students who help to recycle can get AUD$1 (66p) vouchers to use in the canteen, with "triple pay" if they help out after school. Students who have worked particularly hard for the recycling programme can even win a cinema pass.

Boys at Downton Value School in Los Angeles are collecting food for the compost bin after lunch. The school also grows vegetables in their garden and in a greenhouse.

"Most classrooms and office areas have a box for cardboard [recycling]. Twice a term (more often in the office areas) and at the end of the year, we empty the boxes into the big white SITA dumpster."

Timothy Z, Portside Christian School, South Australia

Being green - summing up

- Cut waste by reducing, reusing, and recycling.
- Focus on reducing use of paper and plastic products.
- Reuse paper for rough work or art projects.
- Take charge of recycling and encourage others.

Eco-friendly food

What fast and simple changes can you make so your food and drink are more eco-friendly, cheaper, and better for you? Firstly, assess yourself! Are you wasteful or waste-aware?

Check the **disposable** items below. How does your packed lunch fare?
- sandwich in a card or plastic box
- salad in a plastic box
- pre-packed pie
- crisps, bars, or cakes in plastic packaging
- pot of yoghurt
- carton or bottle of drink
- plastic cutlery
- plastic bags

If you have a high score of disposable items in your lunch, consider the ideas below. Or if you're having pasta or rice for supper, why not make a little extra to keep for lunch the next day?

1. Pick a carbohydrate (bread, pasta, couscous, rice).
2. Choose fresh vegetables in season or tinned vegetables.
3. Add protein (prepared meat, tinned fish, cheese, cooked pulses).
4. Pack or chop fruit into natural yoghurt (from a large carton).
5. Put your meal and yoghurt into food containers.
6. Pour juice or water into a drinks bottle (strong plastic or metal).

All the plastic food containers in this healthy packed lunch can be reused again and again.

Try shopping at the weekend for packed-lunch items for the week. You can buy large sizes of goods, such as cartons of juice, which are cheaper and use less packaging than individual cartons. It will take only minutes to prepare your lunch each day. You'll save time queuing up in the canteen, save money, and have more time for lunchtime activities.

Fresh fruit needs no preparation – just pop it in your lunch box.

Eco snacks

Of course, it can be hard to be organized enough to prepare food every day. An eco tuck shop can help. At Ithaca Creek State Primary School, Australia, the tuck shop staff prepare sandwiches and salads with fresh ingredients – some of the produce comes from the school garden. They minimize food waste by only making meals or sandwiches when they are ordered. Any leftover food goes in the **wormery** along with fruit and vegetable peelings. The liquid from the wormery fertilizes the garden, and the whole cycle begins again!

Processed organic foods

Ready-made **organic** meals and snacks are convenient, but are they better for the environment?

- Pros: the ingredients are products of **organic farming**, which does not use chemical **fertilizers** that can harm wildlife.
- Cons: processing food requires a large amount of energy. Once produced, processed foods are packaged, transported, and often chilled in a refrigerator – just like non-organic foods.

Think about your drink

There's nothing wrong with buying a drink every now and again when you're out and about. However, although some bottled drinks are healthy, many contain a large amount of sugar and additives, and they are not cheap. Also, packaging, transporting, and refrigerating the beverages come at a cost to the environment.

So, how can you cut down on costs and waste but stay hydrated and healthy? If you live in an economically developed country such as the United Kingdom, your home will have a fresh water supply – and it's probably cleaner and safer than bottled water. In some areas, the water is safe but does not taste good. You could talk to your family about buying a water filter to make tap water taste better.

Eco Impact

A US report in 2010 showed that:

- 50 per cent of bottled water is actually tap water in a plastic bottle.
- 75 per cent of the bottles are thrown away, not recycled.
- The plastic in some bottles leaches (leaks) a substance called phthalate into the water. Some studies have linked this chemical with hormonal problems in people.
- Bottled water goes through fewer safety tests than tap water.
- Bottled water costs 100 times as much as tap water! Bottled water typically costs just over $1 for 3.8 litres (nearly 7 pints) and much more when you buy smaller bottles. Water from the tap costs about 1c per 3.8 litres.

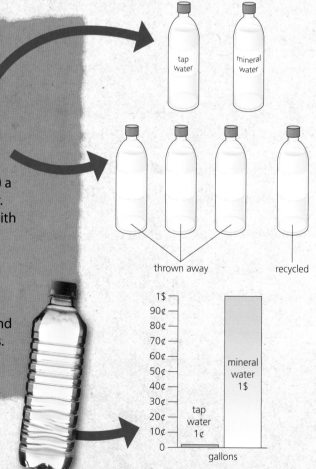

Be smart with smoothies

Do you like fruit smoothies or yoghurt drinks? You could save cash and packaging by filling up a drink bottle from a large bottle at home instead of buying small bottles. Even better, why not make your own smoothie with a blender? Fresh soft fruit in season is tasty or you can use tinned fruit. Bananas are great whizzed with natural yoghurt. It's easy and cheap to make your own smoothies.

Smoothie

You will need:

A few pieces of fruit, ideally two or three types, either fresh, tinned, or a mixture

About 250 ml (8.8 fl oz) of fruit juice, either fresh or from concentrate

A few ice cubes or some cold water

Method:

1. Wash and chop any fresh fruit into small pieces.

2. Put all the ingredients in a blender and whizz for about 30 seconds, until the mixture is smooth.

3. Add more juice or water if the smoothie is too thick.

4. If you have any left over, pour it into an ice lolly mould and freeze to make a healthy, eco-friendly summer treat.

Growing food

This is a cheap and easy way to grow food at school – even if there are no flower beds! Cylinder gardening uses containers that can be placed almost anywhere. You don't need any gardening experience and the preparation is simple. Why not give it a go?

Make a cylinder garden

You will need:

At least one 23-litre (5-gallon) bucket of the type used to transport food
  (you could ask a local café to supply clean buckets)
Potting soil
Vegetable seeds
Fertilizer

Method:

1. Work out where to place your cylinder garden. You can position it on top of soil or on a man-made surface, such as concrete. Try to find an area that will receive at least six to eight hours of sunlight and is close to a source of water.

2. Research vegetables that will grow during the season you're in. If you're gardening at school, look for varieties that you can harvest within a school term – 30 to 90 days. Search for compact varieties that can grow in a small space. The vegetables mentioned on page 47 are suitable for cylinder gardening, as are beans, carrots, parsley, peas, or tomatoes.

3. Cut off the bottom of the bucket and discard it. Then cut the rest of the bucket in half. You may need to ask an adult to help you. Now you have two cylinders. (NB If you are placing the bucket on concrete, it's better not to cut it but to ask an adult to drill drainage holes in the bottom.)

4. Put the cylinders in position.

5. Fill them with potting soil and mix in some fertilizer.

6. Plant your seeds, following the instructions on the packet for spacing, and water gently.

7. Monitor the seedlings as they grow, watering to keep moist and adding fertilizer regularly. **Thin out** the seedlings if they are squashed together.

Source: KidsGardening, www.kidsgardening.org

Food miles

Growing your own vegetables reduces **food miles**. The principle behind food miles is that the further away your food is produced, the worse for the environment. However, bear in mind that beans produced locally using oil-based fertilizers and ploughed by diesel tractors could be worse than beans grown by less energy-intensive methods abroad. Storing local food for a long time to be eaten out of season can also use up a lot of energy.

Being green - summing up
- Make eco-friendly packed meals and snacks.
- Stay hydrated by drinking tap water and home-made smoothies.
- Grow your own food in a cylinder garden.

Nature and biodiversity

Why would you bother encouraging nature and biodiversity at school? Well, you spend a lot of time at school so it's worth making your school grounds more attractive. Most students find nature and outdoor education programmes engaging and enjoyable. Also, a school nature project can be large enough to make a difference to local wildlife.

Small creatures such as bees, beetles, spiders, and snails form an essential part of the food chain. Solitary bees are essential for pollinating flowers; spiders eat insect pests; snails provide food for birds and other animals, such as hedgehogs. Looking after these small creatures is important, but few modern gardens have natural areas where they can shelter. So, how about making a bug hotel in the autumn to keep the insects and snails snug during winter?

Make a bug hotel

You will need:

1 square metre (10 square feet) of plastic mesh or chicken wire
Plastic-covered garden wire, twine, or garden string
Several dead plant stems or twigs
Pile of fallen autumn leaves
Flat piece of wood or plastic (big enough to cover the top end of the mesh when it has been made into a tube)
Two or three large rocks
A few tent pegs

Did you know?
- We need insects to produce honey, chocolate, coffee, and silk.
- Insects are a vital food source for birds and animals.
- 90 per cent of wild flowers could be threatened with extinction (being wiped out) if there were no insects to pollinate them.

Method:

1. Decide where to put your bug hotel. A quiet corner in the shade is best.

2. Curl the plastic mesh or chicken wire into a tube. Tie it in place using four twists of garden wire.

3. Poke some dead plant stems or twigs through the sides of the cylinder at the bottom. They should overlap to form a mesh, which will stop the leaves from falling out of the bottom if you move the bug hotel. They will also stop the leaves from touching the ground and becoming damp.

4. Now loosely fill the cylinder with dead leaves.

5. Use the piece of wood to make a lid. Place rocks on top to keep it secure.

6. If your bug hotel is in a windy position, you can pin the cylinder to the ground using tent pegs.

Source: Buglife, www.buglife.org.uk

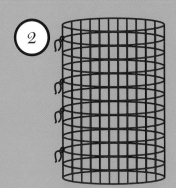

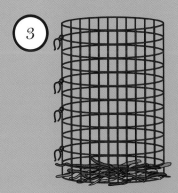

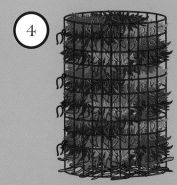

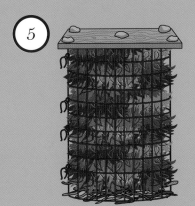

45

Make the most of your space

This raised bed is perfect for growing a variety of vegetables as well as wild flowers to attract wildlife. It's handy if you have a concrete patio or a small garden.

Build a no-dig raised garden bed

You will need:

Four planks of recycled wood to make a rectangle for the bed. Any length from 1 m (3 ft) upwards is fine. The depth should be at least 15 cm (6 in).
4 brackets, and galvanized screws to secure them
Several old cardboard boxes, more than enough to cover the base of the bed
Several old newspapers
A wheelbarrow or large tub for wetting the newspaper
Lucerne (alfalfa) hay
Manure
Straw
Some potting compost

Method:

1. Decide where to place the bed – either on bare earth or grass. Lay out the planks of wood.

2. Place brackets over the corners where the planks meet and screw them in. You may need an adult to help.

3. Lay the cardboard on the base of the bed, making sure it overlaps.

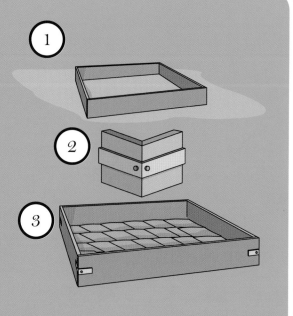

4. Put the newspaper in a wheelbarrow or large plastic tub and pour some water over it.

5. Spread the wet newspaper over the cardboard, making sure the layers overlap by one-third of their size. Make sure the entire surface is covered to cut out the light. The cardboard and paper will rot down into the soil.

6. Add a layer of lucerne hay. This will feed the soil as it breaks down.

7. Add a thin layer of manure.

8. Lastly, add a layer of straw. This adds **nutrients** and acts as a mulch, keeping plants warm in winter and holding in moisture in summer.

9. Make small holes in the top layer of straw to make space for your plants. Add a handful of potting compost in each hole before putting in the plants.

Source: No Dig Vegetable Garden, www.no-dig-vegetablegarden.com

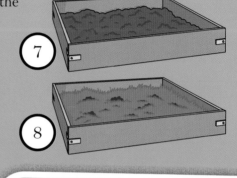

Easy-to-grow veggies

You can plant these vegetables directly in your raised bed:

- Lettuce: try "cut and come again" varieties. Once the lettuces are big, just cut off what you need and leave them to continue growing.
- Radishes: these don't need much care. You may need to thin them out if the seedlings sprout too close together.
- Spinach: the easiest to grow is spinach beet. You can pick off leaves, and the plant will keep growing.
- Chard: similar to spinach, and attractive with colourful red stems.
- Onions: it's simplest to plant onion sets, which are tiny onions.
- Potatoes: easy to grow but need plenty of water.

Bringing it together: Kent Meridian High School

Kent Meridian High School in Kent, Washington, USA, is a Bronze level eco-school and part of the Cool School Challenge, an environmental programme.

For the Cool School Challenge, Environmental Science teacher Dianne Thompson and her pupils carried out an energy review. Pupil Asha Salim reports: "The students and Mrs Thompson's environmental science class go into the other classes and have a one-on-one discussion with the teachers about how much energy they're using and what they can do to reduce it." The pupils then offer tips to the teachers on how to cut down their energy use. In a few months' time, they go back and see how much energy those teachers have saved.

The students also tackle water waste. First they undertake a water assessment, going around the school looking for leaking taps. They produce a report for the caretaker and then the head. The last time they did this, they discovered six leaking taps that needed repairing.

This urban garden has been created by cleverly stacking wooden beds to make the best use of the available space and light.

Strawberries make a great addition to an edible garden.

Recycling is an essential element of the programme. Edros Palisoc describes recycling at Kent Meridian. "We recycle in the whole school … At lunch we have students who monitor the kids who have lunch to tell them which items are recyclable."

The school has a garden that attracts all kinds of wildlife, including songbirds, hummingbirds, and butterflies. There is a pond which contains fish. There is also an edible garden. As Deven Moss explains, "The edible garden is … being used for the cooking class. They can use the food there instead of having to find produce elsewhere to use." No **pesticides** are used to grow the crops.

This case study shows how many people in the school working together have succeeded in reducing energy use and water waste, increasing recycling, and encouraging wildlife. They are eco stars!

Being green – summing up

- Take part in school nature programmes.
- Make a bug hotel to attract insects.
- Build a raised bed to grow vegetables and wild flowers.
- Many schools around the world have gone green. Maybe your school can, too!

Quiz

Are you an eco star or an energy guzzler? Do this quiz to find out! See page 55 for the results.

1. **When you're at home in the winter, do you . . .**
   a) crank up the heating so it's as hot as a sauna?
   b) keep the heating on all the time to keep the house warm?
   c) put the heating on for a few hours a day, and wear a cosy jumper or snuggle up with a warm blanket if you're cold?

2. **In your house, do you switch off lights and gadgets as soon as you've finished using them?**
   a) No, I leave them on in case someone else wants to use them.
   b) I turn off the lights but leave gadgets on standby so it's less effort to turn them on again later.
   c) Yes, I turn everything off – it's a waste of energy otherwise.

3. **Do you use the shower or bath?**
   a) There's nothing like a long, hot soak in a deep bath!
   b) I use the shower but I like a long, luxurious one.
   c) I have a quick, refreshing shower to save time and energy.

4. **How do you use water when you brush your teeth?**
   a) I run the tap while I'm brushing – it saves effort!
   b) I run the tap to wash my toothbrush and rinse my mouth.
   c) I fill a cup with water to rinse my mouth and the toothbrush.

5. **Are you an eco shopper?**
   a) Shopaholic more like! I have no willpower to resist the latest gadgets and accessories.
   b) I try to buy just the items I really need.
   c) I love rummaging in charity shops and rarely buy new goods.

6. How much do you recycle?

a) I don't bother. It's not going to change the world, is it?

b) I recycle paper, card, tins, and bottles.

c) Almost everything – I'm a total expert. I even know where to take old DVDs and batteries for recycling.

7. Do you have green fingers?

a) What, hang around in a muddy plot in the wind and rain? You've got to be joking.

b) I've tried growing some plants at home but they usually die.

c) Yes! I know how to look after plants and can raise easy-to-grow vegetables and herbs.

8. If you buy food or snacks when you're out, what do you do with the packaging?

a) I chuck it in the bin if there's one right there, otherwise on the ground.

b) I look for a bin or a recycling container.

c) I keep the packaging to wash and recycle once I get home.

9. How do you mostly travel around?

a) I like being driven around. I hate getting cold and wet when the weather's bad.

b) I sometimes get a lift in the car but I use the bus, walk, or cycle to some places.

c) I rarely go anywhere by car. I walk, cycle, or use public transport.

10. If you need to take a packed meal . . .

a) I buy everything pre-packaged to save time.

b) I make a sandwich or some pasta and take a carton of juice and a yoghurt or snack bar for convenience.

c) I make a sandwich or take some tasty cooked food from the fridge and some fresh fruit.

Glossary

biodiversity variety of plants and animals in a particular habitat or the world

climate change rising temperatures worldwide, caused by the increase of greenhouse gases in the atmosphere that trap the Sun's heat

compact fluorescent light bulb energy-saving light bulb. It is more efficient than an incandescent light bulb and lasts much longer.

conservation protecting wild habitats and their plants and animals

disposable made to be thrown away after being used once

draught proofing blocking up unwanted gaps that let in cold air, in order to save energy

energy-efficient using as little energy as possible for a task

fertilizer product added to soil or water to provide extra nutrients to help plants to grow

floodplain area of flat land alongside a river that regularly becomes flooded

flow meter bag bag with markings to measure the volume of water flowing in from a tap or shower

flow rate amount of liquid that flows in a given time, for example, 5 litres per minute

flow restrictor gadget designed to limit the amount of liquid that flows out of a tap or shower

food miles distance that foods travel from the point of origin to your table

fossil fuel energy source such as coal, gas, and oil, which was formed over millions of years from the remains of animals or plants

incandescent light bulb type of light bulb commonly used in homes. It is not energy efficient and is gradually being phased out.

kilowatt hour measurement of electricity use over an hour. A kilowatt hour is when you use 1,000 watts of energy in an hour, for example, using a 1,000-watt oven for one hour.

landfill area of land where large amounts of waste material are buried under the earth

lumens measurement of the amount of visible light a bulb gives out

mulch organic matter, such as leaves, straw, or bark chippings that is placed around the base of plants to improve the quality of the soil

nectar-rich rich in nectar, a sweet liquid produced by flowers and collected by bees for making honey

non-governmental organization non-profit organization that is not part of the government and works to help people

nutrient chemical that nourishes living things

organic produced without using man-made chemicals

organic farming method of farming that minimizes the use of harmful chemical fertilizers and pesticides. Organic farming is also known as all-natural farming.

pesticide chemical used to kill insects or other organisms that are harmful to crops

pollinate to put pollen into a plant so that it produces seeds

prevailing wind wind from the direction that is most common in a particular place or season

public liability insurance insurance to cover a group or event in case they have to pay out money to members of the public because of an injury or damage to their property

risk assessment careful examination of what could cause harm to people

sustainable way of doing something that does not use up too many natural resources or pollute the environment

thermal imaging measuring the surface temperature, for example of a house, so people can work out where heat is being lost

thin out remove weaker seedlings to allow space for the stronger ones to grow well

watt unit of power that measures the rate of using electricity

wind turbine huge fan that turns the moving energy of the wind into useful energy

wormery compost bin containing worms that are particularly effective at breaking down food waste, including cooked food

Find out more

Further reading

47 Things You Can Do for the Environment, Lexi Petronis, Karen Macklin, Jill Buck (Connections Book Publishing Ltd, 2012)

Generation Green: The Ultimate Teen Guide to Living an Eco-Friendly Life, Linda and Tosh Sivertsen (Simon Pulse, 2008)

Living Green: The Ultimate Teen Guide (It Happened to Me), Kathlyn Gay (Scarecrow Press, 2012)

The Eco-Student's Guide to Being Green at School, J. Angelique Johnson (Picture Window Books, 2010)

The Green Teen: The Eco-Friendly Teen's Guide to Saving the Planet, Jenn Savedge (New Society Publishers, 2009)

The Young Activist's Guide to Building a Green Movement and Changing the World, Sharon J. Smith (Ten Speed Press, 2011)

Websites

www.direct.gov.uk/en/environmentandgreenerliving/
greenercommunityandwork/dg_064439
Find out how to be greener in your community.

www.eco-schools.org
This is the website for the international Eco-Schools campaign.

www.keepbritaintidy.org/ecoschools
www.ecoschoolsscotland.org
www.eco-schoolswales.org
These are the Eco-Schools websites for England, Scotland, and Wales.

www.energysavingtrust.org.uk/In-your-home/Water
See the Energy Saving Trust's advice for saving water.

globalstewards.org
This website has a list of ways to reduce, reuse, and recycle.

www.keepbritaintidy.org
Details about the national campaign against litter.

www.wow.sa.gov.au
This Australian site focuses on school campaigns to cut waste.

DVDs

Food, Inc., director Robert Kenner (Dogwoof, 2010)

The Age of Stupid, director Franny Armstrong (Dogwoof, 2009)

The Truth about Climate Change, presenter David Attenborough (Eureka Entertainment, 2008)

More topics to research

Once you've read this book, you might like to research Eco-Schools in your area – perhaps you could link up with them and share ideas? It could be exciting to make contact with a school in another country, too. You may also want to find out what your local council is doing to protect the environment. Perhaps your eco group could come up with suggestions for how to promote eco policies to young people?

Answers to panel question (page 28):
You would need to buy about 21 bulbs that last 850 hours to get 18,000 hours of service (21 x 850 = 17,850 hours). Those 21 bulbs will cost you £75.60. So the £40 bulb is a better buy.

Answers to quiz (pages 50–51):
Mostly As:
Sounds like you're an energy guzzler but at least you're aware of it. Pick just a couple of ideas from this book and start being a little more eco-friendly.

Mostly Bs:
You're clearly making an effort. Look for a few ideas in this book to do more.

Mostly Cs:
You're an eco star! Keep up the good work and spread the message to others.

Index